paid by John Roddin.

FIELD GUIDE
TO THE
PICTISH SYMBOL STONES

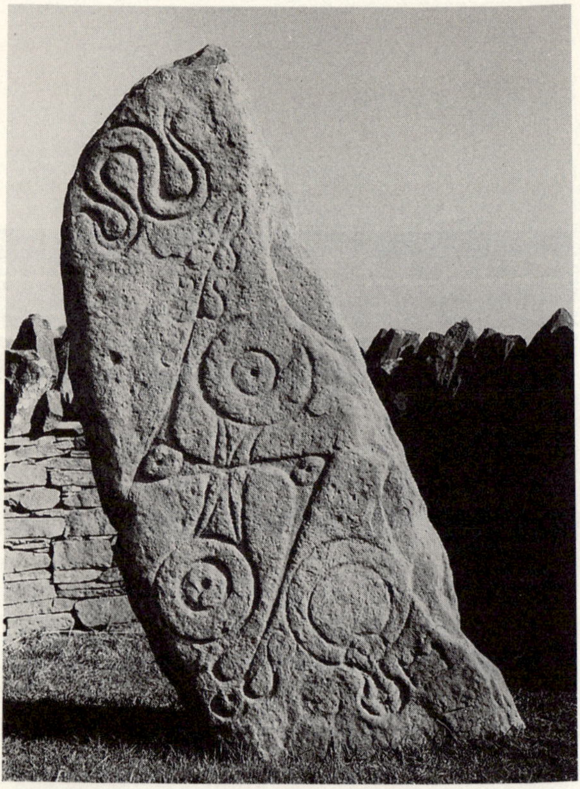

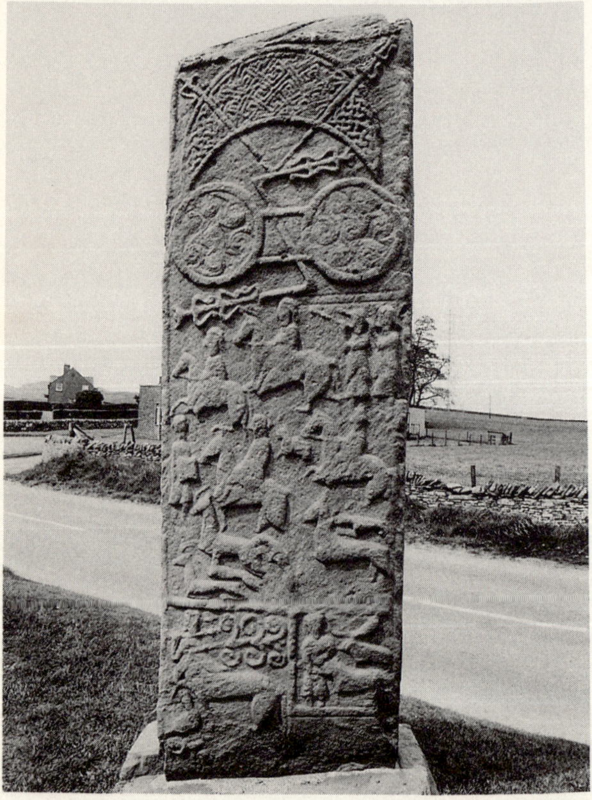

Frontispiece: Two of the stones beside the B9134 at Aberlemno (ANG); No.1 (above), a simply incised pillar (Class I), and No.3, a relief-carved cross-slab (Class II), are of different periods but they have a symbol in common. (See Introduction p.x and p.60)

FIELD GUIDE

TO THE

PICTISH SYMBOL STONES

Alastair Mack

THE PINKFOOT PRESS

BALGAVIES, ANGUS

1997

First published 1997 by
The Pinkfoot Press
Balgavies, Forfar, Angus DD8 2TH, Scotland

ISBN 1 874012 06 7

For a Bonny Lass

The author and publishers
gratefully acknowledge the help of Ann Ogle,
and the assistance of Historic Scotland.

Realisation – David Henry

Design, typesetting, illustrations, maps – The Pinkfoot Press

Printed and bound by Burns Harris & Findlay Ltd, Dundee

CONTENTS

ILLUSTRATIONS

Many of the illustrations are based on line drawings in Part III of *The Early Christian Monuments of Scotland* by J Romilly Allen and Joseph Anderson (Edinburgh, Society of Antiquaries of Scotland, 1903. Reprinted 2 vols, Balgavies, Angus, The Pinkfoot Press, 1993); in such instances, the source (ECMS fig.no.) is given in the captions. Most unattributed illustrations are based on drawings or photographs by the author. To keep this list concise only the names of stones are given; the captions contain fuller descriptions.

Frontispiece: *Top* Aberlemno 1 (ANG); *bottom* Aberlemno 3 (ANG). *Photographs reproduced by kind permission of Historic Scotland.*

Distribution Maps

AUTHOR'S ACKNOWLEDGEMENTS

This Guide has been helped in a hundred ways by a host of people throughout Scotland and I wish to extend my grateful thanks to all who have given me assistance, in particular:

Norman Atkinson : Anne Brundle : Jim Davidson
Stephen Driscoll : Eileen Eaton : Lesley Ferguson
Iain Fraser : Nigel and Patricia Dewar Gibb
Andrew Greaves : Jill Harden : David Henry
Charles Hunt : Jim Inglis : Stuart Kermack
Margaret Low : Eila Macqueen
Elizabeth Marshall : Alan Milne : Charles Orr
Walter Ottewill : Anna and Graham Ritchie
Susan Seright : Ian Shepherd : Mike Spearman
Matthew Stewart : Jonathan Williamson
John Wood : Margaret Wytrazek

My very special thanks are reserved for Julie Hunter Bennett.

PREFACE

Most of the stones are named as in *The Early Christian Monuments of Scotland* (ECMS) by J Romilly Allen and Joseph Anderson (see p.vi).

The stones are presented in a standard format, as in the following example, with a slight variation in layout for those in museum collections.

Aberlemno 1[1] ΔΔΔ[2] **C**[3] [4]

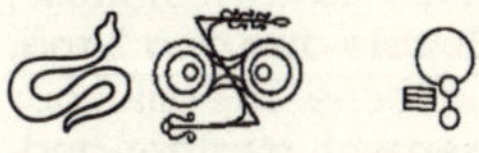

[5]

180 x 90 x 23cm **E**[6] NO 523 559[7]

ECMS III, 205[8]

KEY

1 *Name (and number) of stone:*

Class I *in normal type (upper and lower case) as above*

Class II *in capitals (e.g.* **ST VIGEANS 4***)*

2 *Clarity of carving (not given for stones in museum collections):*

ΔΔΔ *good*

ΔΔ *fair*

Δ *poor*

3 *Accessibility rating (rough guide only):*

A *easy for all*

B *not so good for wheelchairs*

C *restricted, but good view from nearby*

D *difficult (able-bodied only)*

4 *Cared for by Historic Scotland on behalf of the Secretary of State for Scotland*

5 *The stone's symbols (given left to right but generally read from top to bottom on the stone). For the symbols see Section 1, pp.1–28*

6 *Size in centimetres:*

E *exposed area only*

O *overall dimensions*

7 *Ordnance Survey six-figure grid reference*

8 *Principal reference/s (Section 17, pp.146–150)*

INTRODUCTION

WHAT ARE PICTISH SYMBOL STONES ?

The two stones shown in the frontispiece stand close to one another at Aberlemno in Angus. They are very different – one a natural pillar (Aberlemno 1), the other a shaped slab (Aberlemno 3) – but both are carved with distinctive designs which are known as Pictish symbols. The shaped stone has two of these, a **crescent and V-rod** over a **double-disc and Z-rod**, carved in relief above a hunting scene. The pillar has three symbols incised on it, a **serpent**, a **mirror-and-comb**, and between them yet another **double-disc and Z-rod**. The symbols on No.1 are simple and those on No.3 much-decorated, but it is clear that the second symbol on each is the same; these two stones are of the same culture.

Pictish symbols have also been found on objects of metal and bone and on the walls of caves, but they principally occur carved on stones, which have been grouped into two classes, Class I – natural slabs or pillars with incised symbols, and Class II – shaped slabs which are carved in relief with a cross and sometimes other sculpture in addition to the symbols.

Aberlemno 3, with a decorated cross dominating its other face, is one of the sixty-one known Class II stones. Aberlemno 1, with symbols only, is one of the one hundred and eighty-one Class I stones that have been found. It has the look of a prehistoric standing stone (which it once was – there are cup-marks on the reverse), but although Class I stones are certainly earlier than the Class II cross-slabs the symbols on them were not carved in prehistoric times.

It is not just these two Aberlemno stones that share a symbol. There are over forty different symbols and almost two-thirds of these appear on stones in both Classes. Class I and Class II are close in time, and the similarity of their symbols indicates that the period of the simpler stones was immediately before that of the Christian cross-slabs. It is likely that the transition from Class I to Class II began not very long after the introduction of Christianity to Pictland.

The ornamentation of some symbols has led some scholars to date Class I from *c*650 to *c*850 AD and Class II from *c*800 to *c*1000 AD, but both are earlier. Some Class I stones may have been carved before the Picts accepted Christianity, and the ClassII slabs are unlikely to have continued in use very long after the Picts lost their identity as a separate nation. Class I may be fifth or sixth-century to the eighth and Class II mid or late seventh to the ninth.

The stones themselves were designed to be set upright in the ground. Some were found standing, some still stand, and from the evidence of what remains of the rest most once stood erect. Their purpose may be indicated by their findspots. A majority come from old churches or graveyards or other burial places and, although many had been reused as building material, some were beside graves. One such, Dunrobin 2 (p.124) was discovered in 1977. It was lying just below ground on top of a low cairn built over a grave containing a skeleton contemporary with the type of carving on the stone. To judge from this example and from the findspots of many others (133 of a total of 242), the symbol stones were almost certainly gravestones.

There is a growing body of opinion that the stones were associated with burials, but even so the symbols are interpreted differently; for example, one view is that they were signs of rank or status with some being group emblems, another is that they are elements of personal names, and yet another is that each symbol represents a personal name. Others are that the symbols were not associated with persons but with religion or cults or that they were boundary markers or to do with land tenure. Another theory is that the stones indicated marriage alliances.

Very few of these interpretations adequately explains why there is almost always a pair of symbols on a stone – and *only* a pair (the mirror or mirror-and-comb being regarded as an 'additional' symbol) – but there is one solution that takes into account both the pairing and the likelihood that the stones were personal memorials. Whatever the origins of specific symbols, some perhaps derived from tribal emblems and others from artefacts which signified rank or status, by the time they were being carved on stone the majority had probably became family and therefore personal badges.

This would certainly explain their pairing and their occurrence on individual grave or memorial stones. A pair may be the family symbols of two individuals united by marriage, being either those of the parents of the person commemorated or the person's own symbol and the symbol of his or her spouse. Where there is only one pair on a stone it may have been for a man, and where a mirror (or mirror-and-comb) have been added it may have been for a woman – on almost every Class II stone carved with human figures and with a mirror the principal figure is female. Moreover, the symbols on Dunrobin 2, a Class I stone, include a mirror-and-comb and the skeleton found beneath it was female.

Some intact stones have only one symbol or one with a mirror-and-comb; some have more than one pair of symbols proper and a few have an odd number; there are also others with a symbol or set of symbols which is, like the mirror-and-comb, apparently additional to the conventional pair. Some explanations of these variations are attempted below, but, as symbol stones are a contentious subject, it may be best to reach one's own conclusions.

A.L.M.

June 1996 Glasgow

DISTRIBUTION MAP

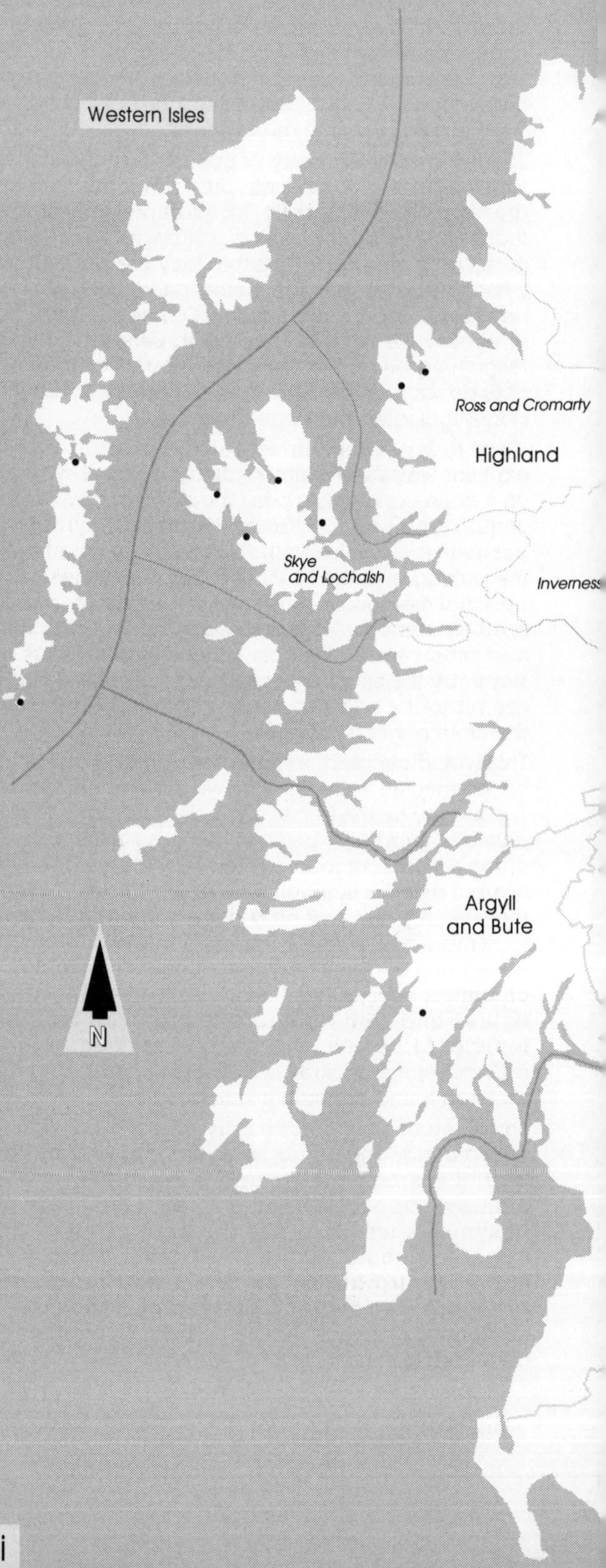

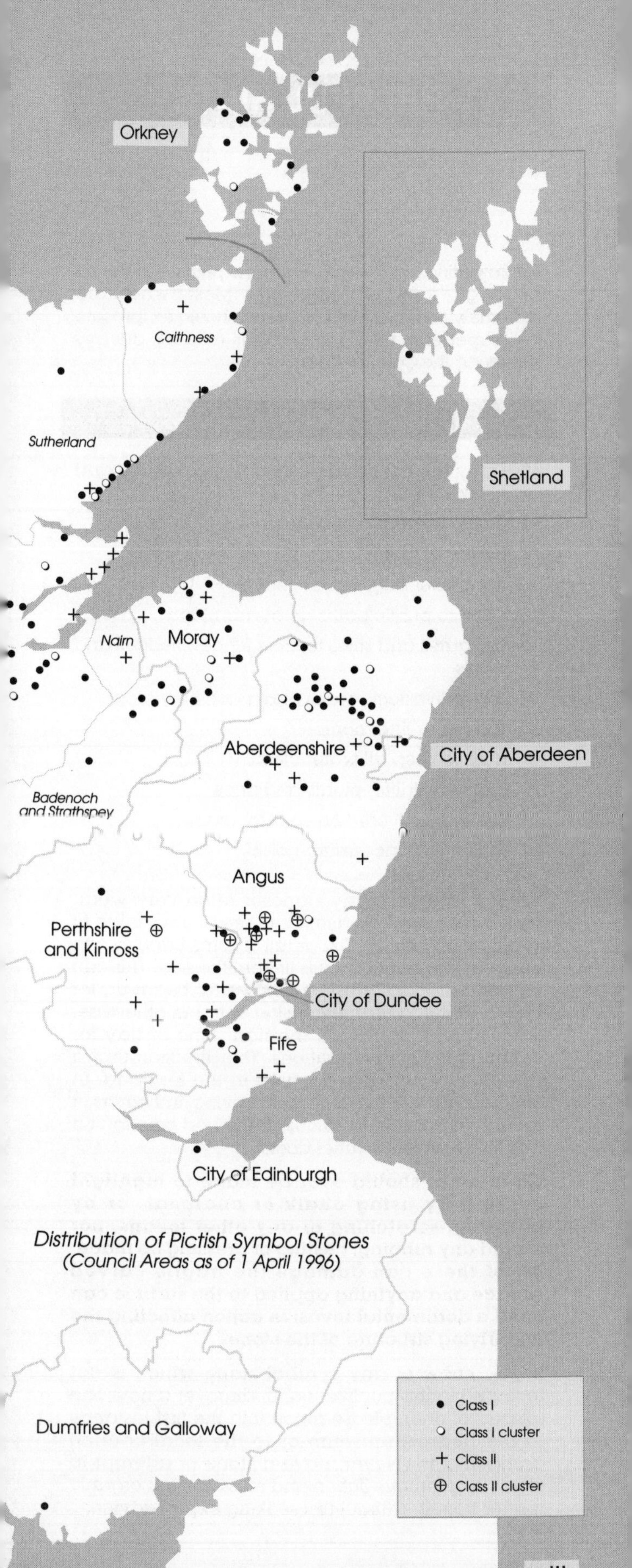

Distribution of Pictish Symbol Stones
(Council Areas as of 1 April 1996)

HELPFUL HINTS

Before visiting a stone on private land permission should be sought from the landowner. Most owners are extremely cooperative and visitors should reciprocate by respecting their instructions and by always observing the Country Code.

THE COUNTRY CODE

1 Enjoy the countryside, and respect its life and work
2 Guard against all risk of fire
3 Fasten all gates
4 Keep your dogs under control
5 Keep to public paths across farmland
6 Use gates and stiles to cross fences, hedges and walls
7 Leave livestock, crops and machinery alone
8 Take your litter home
9 Help to keep all water clean
10 Protect wildlife, plants and trees
11 Take special care on country roads
12 Make no unnecessary noise

The carving on many stones is often very worn, making the symbols difficult to see or impossible to photograph clearly. The detail of some carving can be greatly enhanced if it is lit from the side. This can be done artificially using a powerful beam or, for photography, a flash extension unit, but otherwise, it is essential to choose the right time of day for optimum viewing conditions. The direction that a stone's carving faces is given in the text and, in conjunction with the 'clarity of carving' indicators, it should be possible to calculate the best time to visit any stone which is out of doors.

No attempt should ever be made to highlight carving by using chalk or charcoal, or by brushing, scratching or any other means, nor should any rubbing, casting or pressing be made. All of these can damage the fragile carved surface and anything applied to the surface can have a detrimental invasive action affecting the underlying structure of the stone.

If you know of any symbol stone which is not recorded in this publication, or discover a new one (or part of one), please report it in the first instance to the nearest museum or to the local council archaeologist. Never move a stone or attempt to clean it, or remove lichen and moss or other organic matter from it, without first seeking expert advice.

THE SYMBOLS

If symbols were family badges, and some symbols for various reasons 'additional', their use must have been restricted to a fairly small proportion of the Pictish people – probably the aristocracy. Eastern Pictland, the most fertile part of the Pictish kingdom, may have supported a population of about 40,000 in Pictish times (Thomas 1963, 65–66), which would mean that over the probable three hundred years when Class I stones were carved, that is 400 to 700 AD, some half million Picts (ten or twelve generations), would have lived and died there. If it is assumed that stones with symbols were carved for every adult male the total number of Class I sets of symbols would be (estimating that one in three males would die young) about 160,000. The total from Eastern Pictland is, excluding a few untypical stones, about 160. These 160 sets, which include parts of single symbols on fragments, are of course only the survivors, and if the survival rate of symbol stones and fragments is taken as only ten per cent, the original total would be no more than 1,600. If such an arbitrary figure is accepted the symbol sets on stones would have been carved for a very few of the Pictish population, for only one in every hundred adult males – and for a smaller proportion if the stones were for females also. There is perhaps a total of forty-four individual symbols, including seven 'additional' ones. Here they are described more or less in their order of frequency of occurrence on the stones. Some, such as the less common animal symbols, have been grouped together for the purpose of showing their distribution.

COUNCIL AREAS

ABE	Aberdeenshire	
ABN	City of Aberdeen	
ANG	Angus	
ARG	Argyll and Bute	
DUM	Dumfries and Galloway	
DUN	City of Dundee	
EDI	City of Edinburgh	
FIF	Fife	
HIG	Highland	
BAD	Badenoch and Strathspey	Administrative Areas
CAI	Caithness	Administrative Areas
INV	Inverness	Administrative Areas
NAI	Nairn	Administrative Areas
ROS	Ross and Cromarty	Administrative Areas
SKY	Skye and Lochalsh	Administrative Areas
SUT	Sutherland	Administrative Areas
MOR	Moray	
PER	Perthshire and Kinross	
ORK	Orkney	
SHE	Shetland	
WES	Western Isles	

CRESCENT AND V-ROD

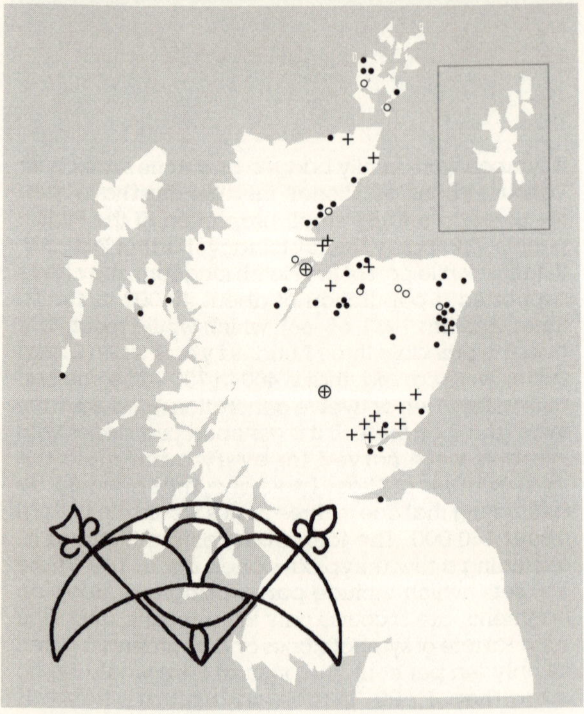

CRESCENT AND V-ROD — 66(62)|20(17) = 86(79)*

ABE 20|0; ABN 0|1; ANG 2|3; EDI 1|0; FIF 1|0; HIG 25(23)|8(6) (BAD 4|0; CAI 3|2; INV 3|0; NAI 0|1; ROS 4(2)|5(3); SKY 4|0; SUT 7|0); MOR 9(8)|1; ORK 6(5)|0; PER 1|7(6); WES 1|0

The V-rod is almost certainly an arrow, but the crescent itself is not a bow; its lower arc is curved, not straight like a bowstring. One possibility is that it is a small shield seen from the side, but there is no boss, as is common on the round shields carved on some Class II stones. A more likely solution is that the crescent is the representation of some adornment worn by ancestors of the Picts.

The majority of V-rods have one end, usually the right, like an arrowhead and the other like the flights of an arrow. Most also have twin curlicues behind each end-piece, but these are probably no more than decorative features.

Although the commonest symbol, with a Class I to Class II proportion of 66:20, one very like the proportion of Class I to Class II stones (181:61), the crescent and V-rod was thought by R.B.K. Stevenson to be post 600 AD (1980, 104), which may be late for a Class I symbol. Stevenson dated the crescent and V-rod symbol from the pelta patterns within some, a pattern derived from the peltae on sixth and seventh-century Anglo-Saxon hanging bowls, and said little about the 14 plain examples of the symbol. A number of the latter will owe their plainness to wear but four of the truly plain have equally plain V-rods which are more arrow-like than most. It is very

* *i.e. Class I total 66 (on 62 stones) | Class II total 20 (on 17 stones) = combined total of 86 examples (on 79 stones)*

possible that these at least are earlier and that the crescent and V-rod was one of the early Pictish symbols. To date a symbol by the patterns within it may be to date only similarly-patterned symbols rather than all of its general type.

Stevenson chose the pelta-decorated version as the first type of crescent and V-rod, but these are almost all from Orkney or the adjacent mainland and may be only a local type of decoration. If one wishes to pursue patterns to attempt to date the symbol the much commoner dome-and-wing may be a better target. This simpler design is not only less ornate but much more widespread, ranging from Caithness and Sutherland to Pabbay, back through Skye to Inverness, Moray and Aberdeenshire and down to Angus. Overall however it is likely that the various patterns within the Class I crescents and V-rods, whether they be dome-and-wing (20), spirals or scrolls (13 or 14), peltas (9 or 10) or 'others' (9), are only additions to what was originally a plain outline.

CRESCENT

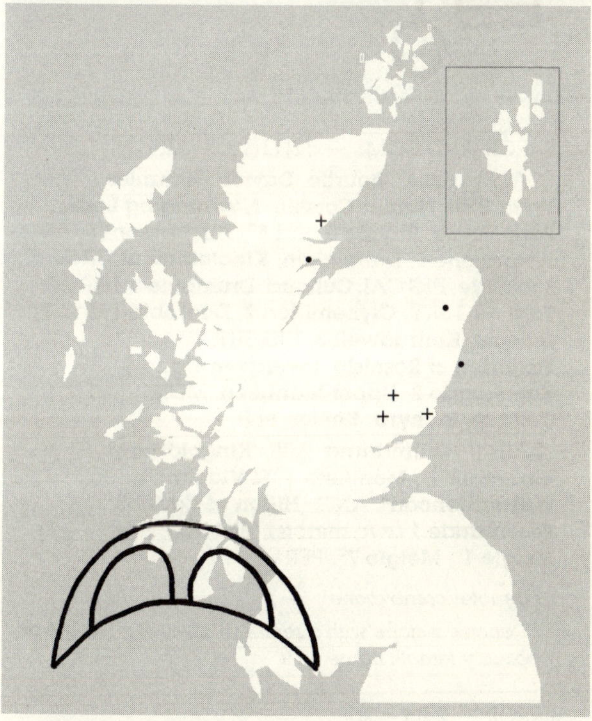

CRESCENT — 3|4 = 7

CLASS I: **Daviot**, **Dunnicaer 3**, ABE; **Roskeen**, HIG ROS

CLASS II: **Kingoldrum 1**, **St Vigeans 1**, ANG; **Craigton 2**, HIG SUT; **Meigle 6**, PER

This symbol is similar to the crescent of the crescent and V-rod symbol. Four are on Class II stones and three on Class I. The only certain example of the latter is at **Daviot** (ABE) – where it is paired with a similarly-domed crescent and V-rod.

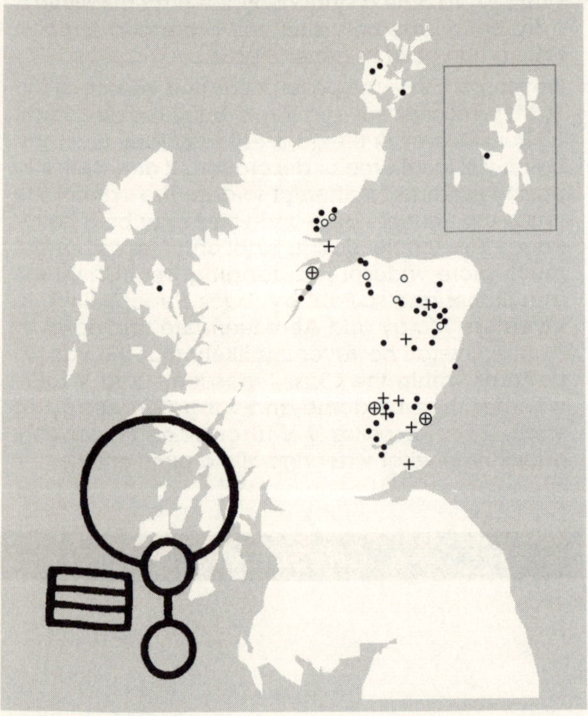

MIRROR-AND-COMB — 31|11(10) = 42(41)

CLASS I: **Birse**[c], **Bourtie**, **Daviot**, **Drimmies**, **Keith Hall**, **Nether Corskie**, **Newbigging Leslie**, **Park House**, **Rhynie 5** and **8**[c], **Tillytarmont 5**, ABE; **Aberlemno 1**, **Dunnichen**, **Kinblethmont**, ANG; **Sandside**, HIG CAI; **Cullaird**, **Drumbuie 2**, HIG INV; **Tote**, HIG SKY; **Clynemilton 2**, **Dunrobin 1** and **2**, **Golspie**, **Kintradwell 3**, HIG SUT; **Easterton of Roseisle**, **Inveraven 1** and **2**, **Knockando 2**, **Upper Manbeen**, MOR; **Collace**, **Inchyra**, **Keillor**, PER

CLASS II: **Drumdurno**, ABE; **Kingoldrum 1***, **Kirriemuir 1***, **Monifieth 1**, **St Vigeans 1**, **Wester Denoon***, ANG; **Hilton of Cadboll***, **Rosemarkie 1** (two mirrors), HIG ROS; **Meigle 1***, **Meigle 7**[c], PER

[c] *Denotes comb alone*

* *Denotes a stone with a representation of a female or possibly female figure on it*

MIRROR — 23|3 = 26

CLASS I: **Ardlair**, **Clatt 1**, **Dunnicaer 4**, **Fyvie 1**, **Inverurie 2**, **Kintore 2** and **4**, **Myreton**, **Rhynie 4** and **6**, **Tillytarmont 1**, **Tullich 1**, ABE; **Glamis 1** and **2**, ANG; **Lindores**, **Westfield 2**, FIF; **Clynekirkton 2**, **Clynemilton 1**, **Little Ferry Links 4**, HIG SUT; **Burrian**, **Greens**, **Sands of Evie**, ORK; **Sandness**, SHE

CLASS II: **Formaston**, ABE; **St Vigeans 2**, ANG; **Largo**, FIF

There are or were sixty-eight mirrors on sixty-seven stones – fifty-four Class I and thirteen Class II. The majority are in mirror-and-comb sets, but there is no apparent distinction between these sets (in three of which only the combs survive) and those with mirrors alone. The mirror or mirror-and-comb is almost always part of a set that includes a dominant pair of other symbols. It can therefore be said to be an additional symbol.

Why it has this complementary role may be shown by some of the thirteen mirror-bearing Class II stones. Seven are carved with human figures, and on all but two of these the principal figure appears to be female. If, as is likely, the principal figure represents the person for whom the stone was erected it is more than possible that mirror-bearing Class II stones were erected for women. Indeed the same may also be true of all stones with mirrors. Beneath one Class I stone with a mirror-and-comb was other evidence. When the site of the comparatively recently discovered (1977) **Dunrobin 2** (HIG SUT) (Dairy Park Stone) was investigated it was found to be over a grave containing a female skeleton.

If mirror-bearing stones were erected for females and those with no mirrors for males then there should presumably be about an equal number of both, but only just over a quarter of symbol stones have mirrors. The apparent imbalance can however be tentatively explained. If the stones were those of the aristocracy, this may be the reason why only one in four stones were for women. Perhaps the women so commemorated were heiresses, ladies through whom their family lands descended. As Pictish inheritance may have been largely matrilineal (through the female line) there would be a large proportion of heiresses in the Pictish aristocracy. That the proportion of mirror-bearing Class I stones was almost one third in Class I times (54:181) but only a fifth in Class II (13:61) may show that Pictish inheritance custom had changed through the centuries, from more commonly matrilineal in early times to more patrilineal in later.

Figure 1

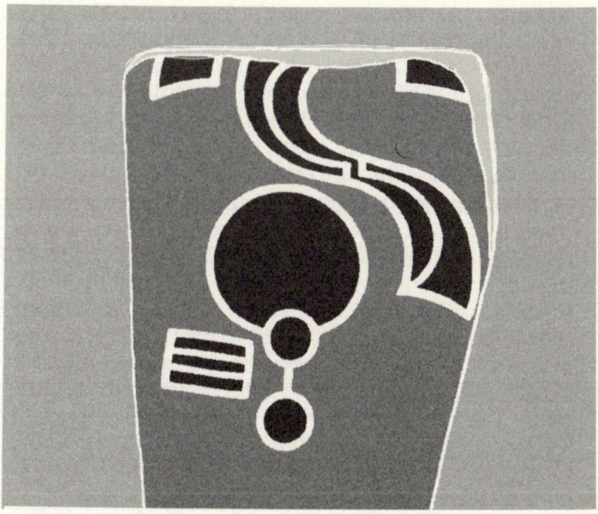

Drimmies (ABE), see p.74 (after ECMS fig.171)

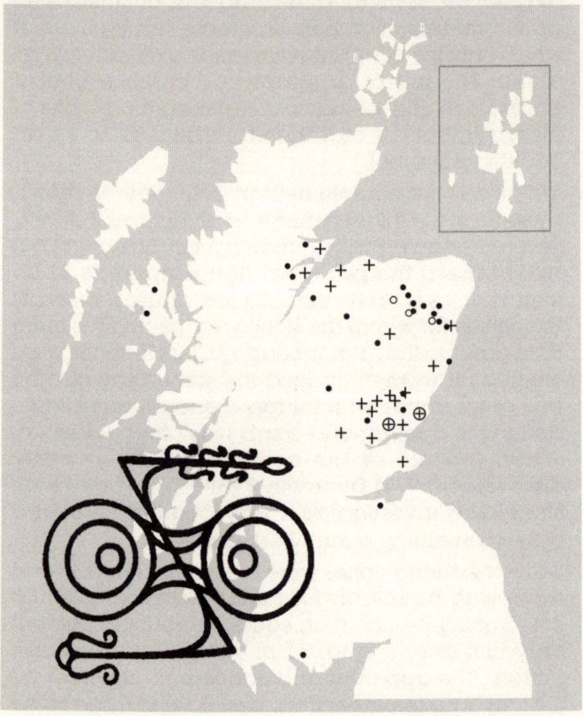

DOUBLE-DISC AND Z-ROD — 33(32)|24(23) = 57 (55)

ABE 18|2; ABN 1|1; ANG 2|11(10); EDI 1|0; DUM 1|0; FIF 0|1; HIG 8(7)|3 (BAD 1|0; INV 1|0; NAI 0|1; ROS 4(3)|2; SKY 2|0); MOR 0|2; PER 2|4

With fifty-seven examples on stones (and four more on silver or bronze objects) the double-disc and Z-rod comes second to the crescent and V-rod in frequency. Like that commonest symbol its origin is uncertain. It must certainly represent something specific; many of the Class I double discs and Z-rods are remarkably similar. The discs usually contain smaller concentric discs, often with a central dot, some are also rimmed, many of these have a smaller eccentric disc or discs, and the joining bars have concave sides. A concave-sided bar within the joining bar is also very common. Only five of the Class I double-discs and Z-rods on stones have other decoration within the discs, and only seven have other features within the bar, or oddly-executed bars.

More certain is the origin of the Z-rod. This resembles a spear bent into a backward Z-shape, a spear which is ball-ended like the 'bronze apple'-ended spears of the Caledonians of the third century (Thomas 1963, 51). If this is its origin the Z-rod is archaic – but more recent perhaps than the double-disc it adorns. The rod usually has a spearhead at the upper end and a ball at the other – although a few have 'flights' there. The ball or flight end is usually twin-curlicued, but the spearhead is seldom so; on the shafts behind many spearheads are sets of 'floriations', that is curlicue-like shapes which are forward-facing.

The double-disc and Z-rod continued late into Class II times and disproportionately so, its Class I: Class II proportion being 33:24 and not 3:1 as are Class I to Class II stones.

DOUBLE-DISC

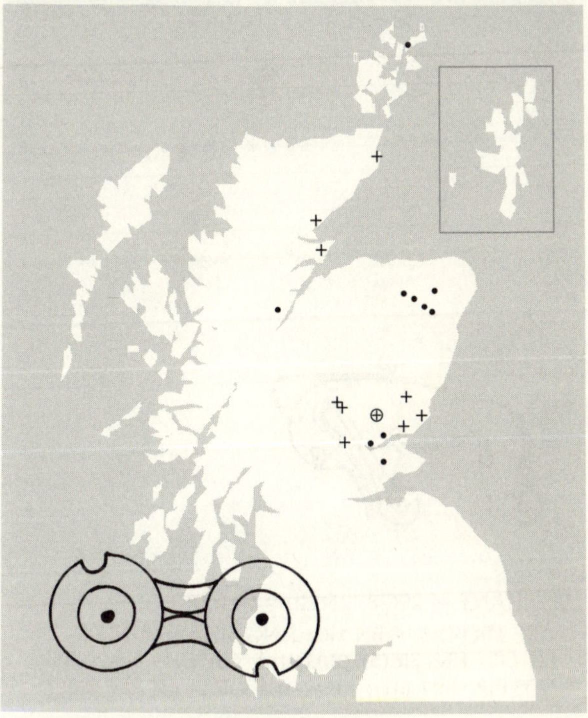

DOUBLE-DISC — 10|11 = 21

CLASS I: **Fyvie 2**, **Huntly 1**, **Logie 1**, **Newton House 1***, **Tillytarmont 3**, ABE; **Westfield 1***, FIF; **Drumbuie 1**, HIG INV; **Pool**, ORK; **Inchyra***, **Longforgan**, PER

** Denotes 'notched' disc*

CLASS II: **Monifieth 1**, **St Vigeans 4**, **Woodrae**, ANG; **Ulbster**, HIG CAI; **Shandwick**, HIG ROS; **Craigton 2**, HIG SUT; **Dunfallandy**, (?)**Fowlis Wester 1**, **Logierait 2**, **Meigle 3** & **6**, PER

This fairly common symbol is much the same as the double-disc and Z-rod but with no rod. Three of the Class I double-discs are 'notched' in one or both discs – a variant that does not appear in any double-disc and Z-rod symbol. Despite the considerable proportion of Class II examples, the double-disc could be a remarkably early symbol; a possible example is pecked on a small slab which was found in use as a floor stone in a fifth or sixth-century building at Pool on Sanday.

Figure 2

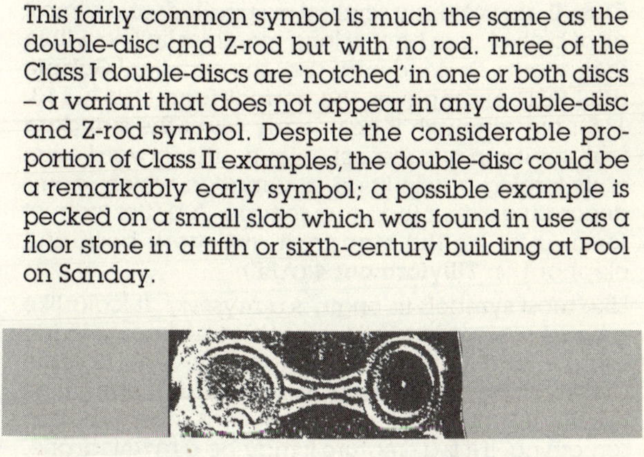

Notched double-disc: Newton House (ABE) see p.85

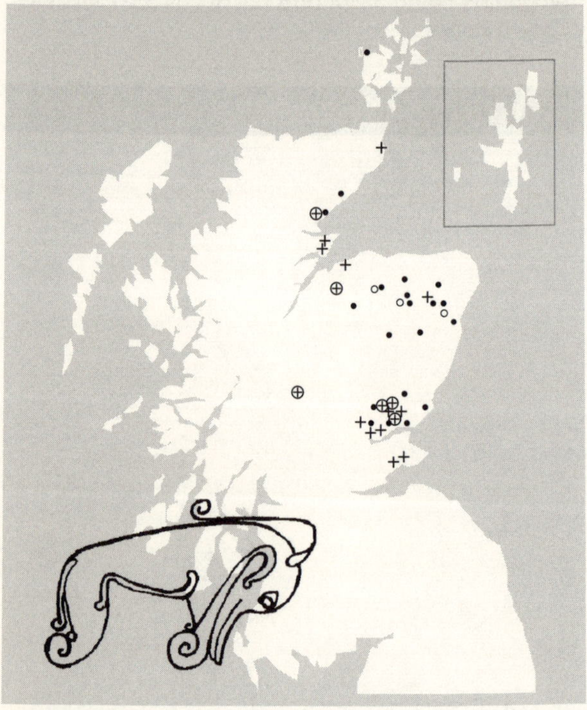

ELEPHANT — 29(28)|25(22) = 54 (50)

ABE 15(14)|1; ABN 1|0; ANG 3|7(6); DUN 1|0; FIF 0|2; HIG 3|6(5) (BAD 1|0; CAI 0|1; NAI 0|2(1); ROS 0|2; SUT 2|1); MOR 3|1; ORK 1|0; PER 2|8(7)

The name 'elephant' is not popular with many students of symbol stones. There are alternative names, one of which is 'Pictish beast', but this author prefers the old term.

The 'elephant' is a long-snouted beast with spiralled feet, a spiral-ended antenna thrusting back from its brow and a drooping but usually spiral-ended tail. All but two of Class I face right, but more than half of Class II face left. Some, of both classes, have small 'additional' fore and rear 'paws', and many Class I have scrolls within their bodies – although some have only a loop or spiral at the shoulder. A number of Class II are variously scrolled or spiralled, and almost all of both classes have a long mouth or lip line within their snouts. Dr Henderson uses the excellent **Golspie** (HIG SUT) example as the correct form (1967, 113, 115), but although it has nearly all of the standard features it is in one respect unique – the forward edge of its foreleg is twin-lined, a variation which seems decorative rather than true to type. A better 'correct form' may be the standard and very beautiful elephant on **Tillytarmont 4** (ABE).

Like most symbols its origin is a mystery. It looks like a beast of some kind but resembles no known living thing – and yet on many stones, even on some Class II stones, it is almost as standard in pattern as the Burghead bulls. It must represent a very specific something. If it is a creature it may be a mythical one, but if so what is or was its source? It may be an object symbol rather than an animal one. That there is no known object with which it can be matched does not necessarily condemn this; the same is true of the majority of object symbols. In addition, a very valid point was made by Joseph Anderson in the Rhind Lectures of 1892, which became Part I of *The Early Christian Monuments of Scotland*. Anderson remarked that unlike the animal symbols which appear on Class II stones the Class II elephants are sometimes filled with interlace or fretwork or spirals as are, for example, many of the Class II crescents and double-discs (ECMS I, lxii-lxiii). The origin of the elephant is therefore more likely to have been an object, not an animal.

R.B.K. Stevenson described the elephant as an imaginary animal and considered that it was derived from certain designs, the most 'elephant'-like of which are on the eighth-century Hunterston Brooch. This silver brooch of Hiberno-Saxon style has panels containing beasts which although curled or contorted do have much in common with the Pictish elephant. The Hunterston beasts however seem derived from the symbol rather than vice-versa. Their bodies contain late Class II-like decoration, their feet are opened spirals, the whorls within their bodies have become spirals at the top of both legs, their eyes are dots, their necks are long, and their snouts are spiral-ended and lack the almost universal mouth line. They look like fanciful copies of the Pictish elephant and can by no means be its source.

From his argument that the brooch beasts may have been the elephants' progenitors one of Stevenson's deductions was that the elephant could not have been earlier than the eighth century (1955, 108–110). It was in any case in his view a late symbol, it being almost as common on Class II as on Class I stones. The Class II total is considerable, but so also is the Class I total of twenty-nine examples which makes it the third most common Class I symbol, with ten more occurrences than the next, the horseshoe. It cannot therefore be easily argued that the elephant was a late entrant to the Pictish symbol set. It is more likely to be one of the earliest, there being quite possibly other factors responsible for its proliferation in Class II times.

Figure 3

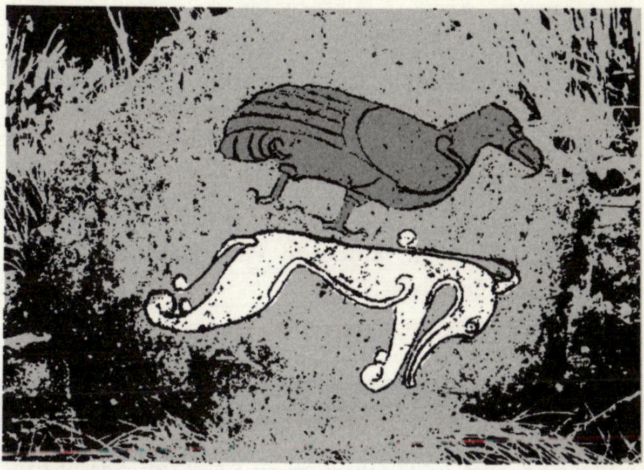

Eagle (p.14) and Elephant: Tillytarmont 4 (ABE), see p.94

HORSESHOE

The horseshoe is one of the commoner symbols and one of the very few object symbols that can pretend to a recognisable origin. Two of the Class I horseshoes, **Rothiebrisbane** (ABE) and **Crosskirk** (HIG CAI), have on the lower part of the apex a semicircular shape, and Charles Thomas argues that these two may be representations of an early adornment, a hinged bronze collar of the second century (1963, 57). The same artefact could well have been the origin of the other horseshoe symbols also. Some have the remnants of what may have been a 'hinge'.

The horseshoe may be a very early symbol. There is only one Class II example, and the horseshoe appears on two stones which are probably of Pictish pagan times. On these it is beside what may be a Pictish warrior-god figure, on the **Newton of Collessie** (FIF) stone and on **Rhynie 3** (ABE).

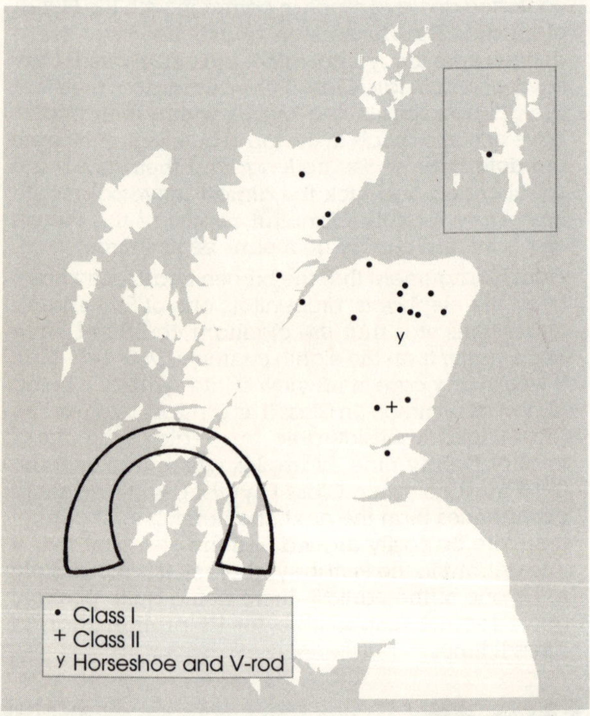

HORSESHOE — 19|1 = 20

CLASS I: **Drimmies, Clatt 3, Huntly 1, Percylieu, Rhynie 3, Rothiebrisbane, Tillytarmont 5**, ABE; **Aberlemno 5**, ANG; **Newton of Collessie**, FIF; **Congash 1**, HIG BAD; **Crosskirk**, HIG CAI; **Cullaird**, HIG INV; **Strathpeffer**, HIG ROS; **Clynemilton 1**, **Langdale**, **Little Ferry Links 2**, HIG SUT; **Easterton of Roseisle**, MOR; **Bruceton**, PER; **Sandness**, SHE

CLASS II: **Eassie**, ANG

HORSESHOE AND V-ROD — 0|1 = 1

HORSESHOE AND V-ROD

The one example, which may be a variant of the horseshoe proper, is on the **Migvie** (ABE) cross-slab.

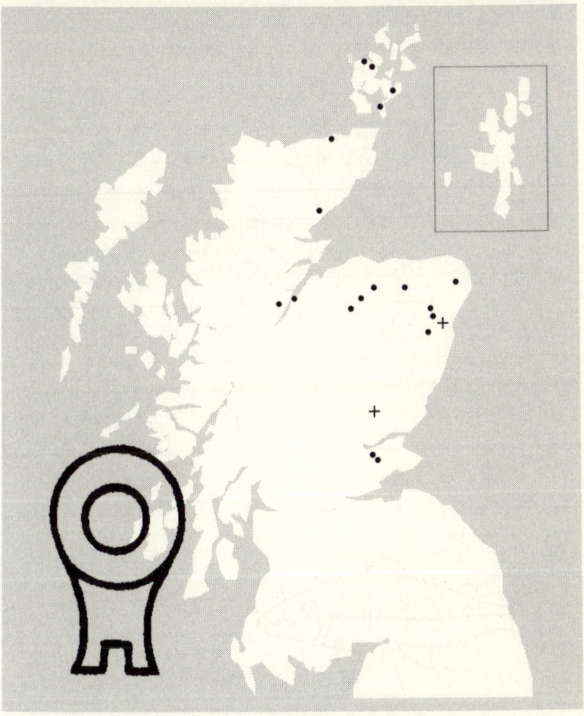

MIRROR-CASE — 18|2 = 20

CLASS I: **Fetterangus**, **Inverurie 1**, **Nether Corskie**, **Newton of Lewesk**, **Tillytarmont 1**, ABE; **Strathmiglo***, **Westfield 2**, FIF; **Advie**, HIG BAD; **Sandside***, HIG CAI; **Drumbuie 2**, **Knocknagael**, HIG INV; **Kintradwell 1***, HIG SUT; **Arndilly**, **Inveraven 1**, MOR; **Birsay**, **Greens***, **Gurness***, **South Ronaldsay***, ORK

CLASS II: **Dyce 2**, ABN; **Meigle 5**, PER

* *Denotes divided mirror-case*

Like most symbols the mirror-case appears to lack a recognisable origin. No known artefact resembles it, and it is called the mirror-case only because it looks a little like one, a circular head on a wide base.

Almost all the mirror-case heads are rimmed, and some have decoration within them. The bases, about half of which are also decorated, are approximately rectangular, most with sides of concave arcs and some slightly wider at the very base. Some also have a re-entrant in the baseline's centre and are called 'divided mirror-cases'. This feature, the flared bases and the symbol's shape may show that the origin was indeed a case for a mirror. If made of leather or textile such cases could have been pulled over mirrors as protective coverings. The lower edge of the base of the **Advie** (HIG BAD) mirror-case appears to be pleated or gathered as if it represented something made of fabric. Another interesting example is the mirror-case on **Inveraven 1** (MOR) (see p.100). It and the mirror on the same stone are very similar in shape, the peculiarly-shaped handle-end of the mirror being repeated in outline by the mirror-case base (Close-Brooks 1989, 15).

SALMON

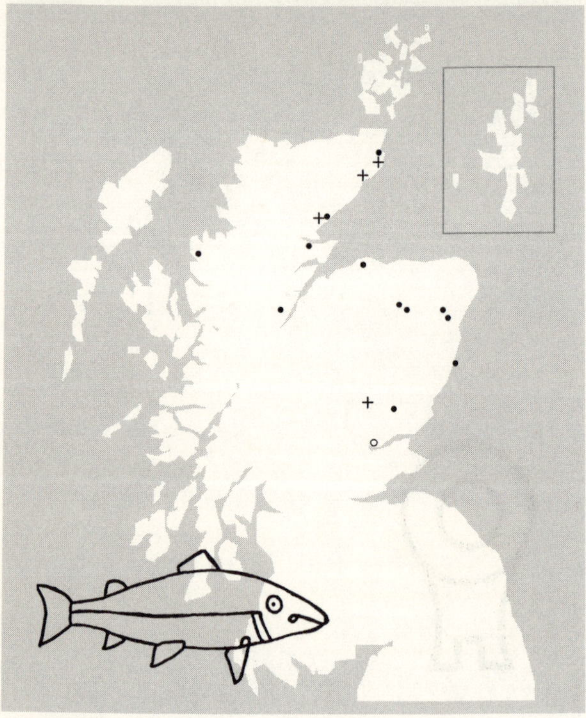

SALMON — 14(13)|4 = 18(17)

CLASS I: **Dunnicaer 2**, **Keith Hall**, **Kintore 1**, **Percylieu**, **Rhynie 1**, ABE; **Glamis 2**, ANG; **Ackergill 1**, HIG CAI; **Drumbuie 2**, HIG INV; **Edderton 1**, **Gairloch**, HIG ROS; **Dunrobin 1**, HIG SUT; **Easterton of Roseisle**, MOR; **Inchyra** (two), PER

CLASS II: **Latheron 1**, **Ulbster**, HIG CAI; **Craigton 2**, HIG SUT; **Meigle 1**, PER

Nine of the Class I examples swim or leap to the right and only five to the left, but the Class II salmon are equally divided. The salmon is regarded by some as a purely Christian emblem, but it is rather more likely to be a symbol as such. All but one are in symbol pairs or sets.

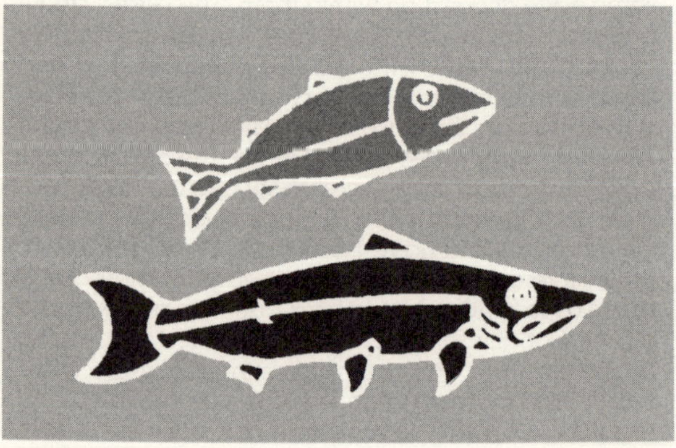

Figure 4

Two types of fish: Ulbster (HIG CAI) Class II (upper), see p.131, and Dunrobin 1 (HIG SUT) Class I (lower), see p.124 (after ECMS figs 31A & 39)

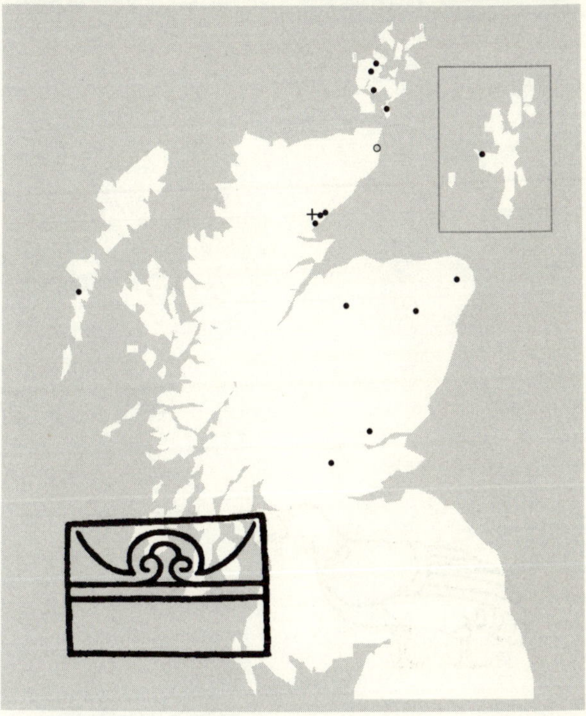

RECTANGLE — 16|1 = 17

CLASS I: **Newbigging Leslie**, **Old Deer**, ABE; **Grantown**, HIG BAD; **Ackergill 1** and **2**, HIG CAI; **Clynekirkton 1** and **2**, **Little Ferry Links 1**, HIG SUT; **Firth**, **Gurness**, **Orphir 2**, **South Ronaldsay**, ORK; **Cargill**, **Peterhead**, PER; **Sandness**, SHE; **Benbecula**, WES

CLASS II: **Craigton 2**, HIG SUT

This may be an early symbol. There are only two in the south and only one Class II rectangle. The rectangle is usually horizontal, simple in shape and almost always bisected within or decorated or both. It may represent some kind of container with a flap (Thomas 1963, 56).

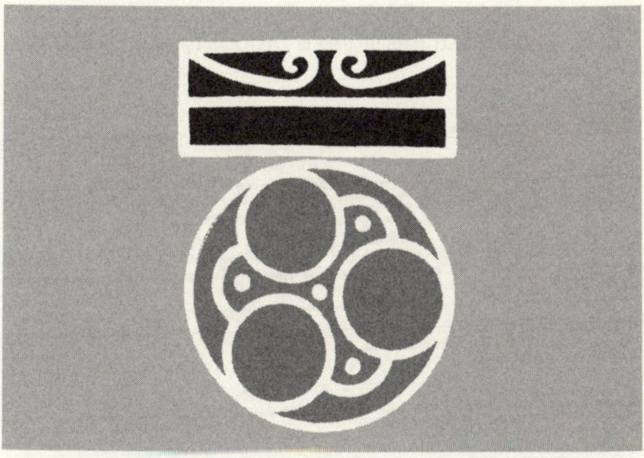

Figure 5

Rectangle and disc (p.20): Benbecula (WES), see p.30 (after ECMS fig.114)

EAGLE

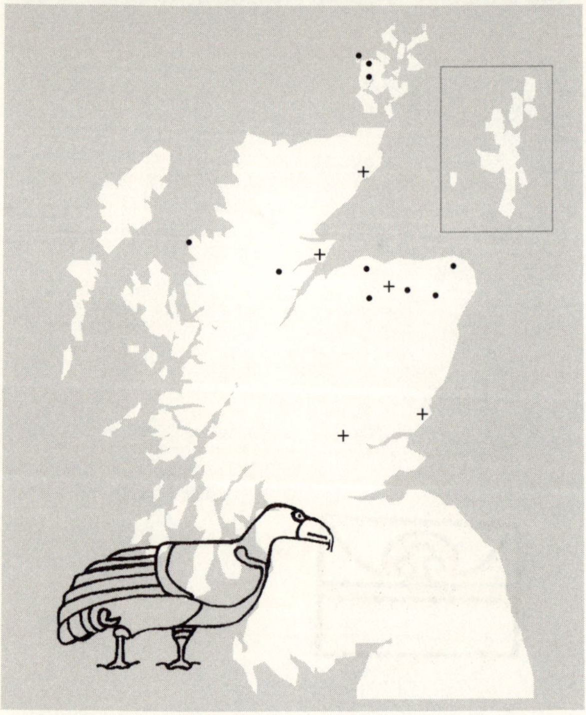

EAGLE — 10|5 = 15

CLASS I: **Fyvie 2**, **Tillytarmont 4**, **Tyrie**, ABE; **Gairloch**, **Strathpeffer**, HIG ROS; **Birnie 1**, **Inveraven 1**, MOR; **Birsay**, **Burrian**, **Oxtro**, ORK

CLASS II: **St Vigeans 2**, ANG; **Latheron 1**, HIG CAI; **Nigg**, HIG ROS; **Mortlach 1** (?symbol), MOR; **Fowlis Wester 1**, PER

The Class II eagles face left, but the majority of the Class I are right facing and almost half have neck or leg scrolls (or spirals) or both. As all but two of the eagles are on northern stones the symbol may have originated from the emblem of a tribe or group of northern Pictland. The two southern examples, which are both Class II, may be in comparison outliers. (A fragment from Walton in Fife is incised with some of an eagle, but this stone is probably not Pictish.)

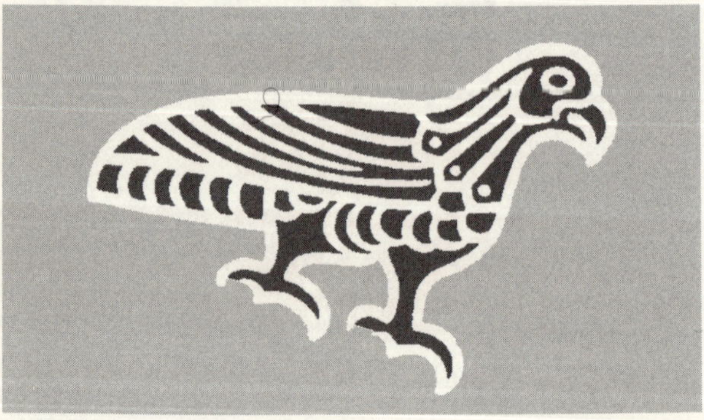

Figure 6

Eagle: Strathpeffer (HIG ROS), see p.120 (after ECMS fig.114)

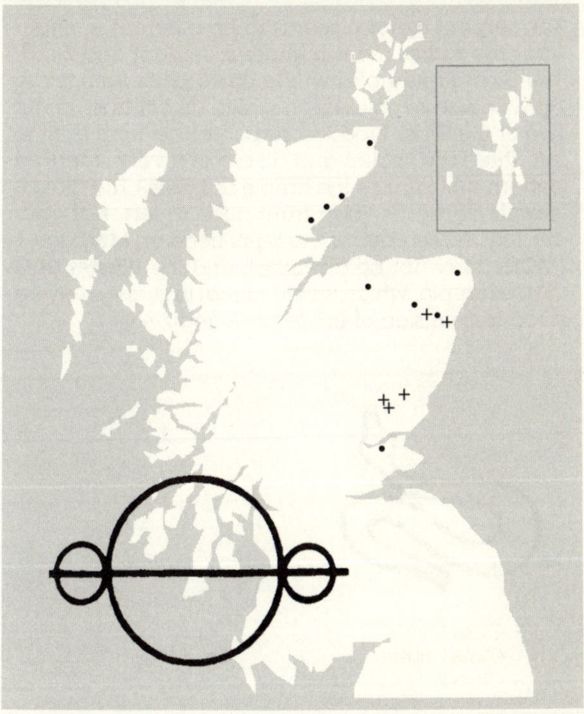

TRIPLE-DISC — 9|5 = 14

CLASS I: **Clatt I**, **Fetterangus**, **Kintore 1**, ABE; **Lindores**, FIF; **Keiss**, HIG CAI; **Kintradwell 2**, **Little Ferry Links 3**, **Navidale**, HIG SUT; **Inveraven 2**, MOR

CLASS II: **Monymusk**, ABE; **Dyce 2**, ABN; **Aberlemno 2**, **Glamis 1** and **2**, ANG

This symbol, which consists of a large ring with a smaller at each side (or above and below), could represent a cauldron seen from above. Five of the nine Class I examples have a transverse bar which can be interpreted as a suspension bar; in certainly one of these (**Kintore 1**) and possibly in others the bar goes through the small rings. In addition, in two of the Class I and three of the Class II examples the small rings appear to be linked to the large as would be the suspending rings of a cauldron.

Figure 7

An ornate Class II triple-disc: Monymusk (ABE), see p.84 (after ECMS fig.209)

SERPENT

The serpent symbol seems to be different in origin from the rather more numerous serpent and Z-rod. The Class I examples writhe upwards or from left to right and have no evident scales. (In contrast all but two of the Class I rodded serpents loop from right to left, three are scaled and all are of a very standard pattern quite unlike the simple serpents.) The Class II 'simple serpents' loop from right to left, but one, crudely incised below the bull's head on **Mortlach 1** (MOR), may not be a symbol, and the **Ulbster** (HIG CAI) example, which is very formal in shape, may be a rod-less version of the serpent and Z-rod.

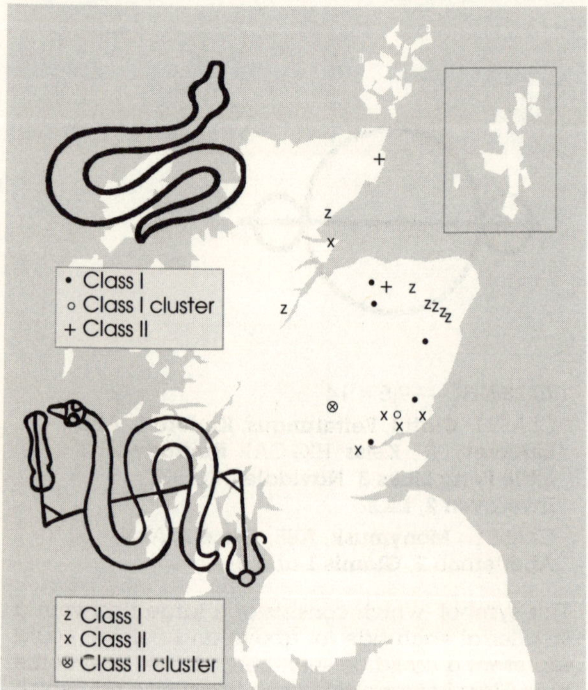

SERPENT — 7|2 = 9

CLASS I: **Craigmyle**, ABE; **Aberlemno 1**, **Glamis 1** and **2**, ANG; **Knockando 2**, **Tom na Heron**, MOR; **Inchyra**, PER

CLASS II: **Mortlach 1**, ABE; **Ulbster**, HIG CAI

SERPENT AND Z-ROD — 7|7 = 14

CLASS I: **Brandsbutt**, **Inverurie 1**, **Myreton**, **Newton House 1**, **Tillytarmont 5**, ABE; **Drumbuie 1**, HIG INV; **Dunrobin 2**, HIG SUT

CLASS II: **Balluderon**, **St Vigeans 2**, ANG; **Tarbat 1**, HIG ROS; **Gask**, **Meigle 1**, **Logierait 1** and **2**, PER

SERPENT AND Z-ROD

The serpents and Z-rods, whether Class I or II, are very similar in appearance and their serpents, three of which are scaled, are rather more formally laid out than the 'simple serpents'. The majority loop across the stones, most of these from right to left, and across or through their loops runs a Z-rod, usually a backwards Z. This is not unlike the spear of the double-disc. One end is sometimes a spear-point with curlicues, sometimes a 'flamboyant' spearhead (Thomas 1963, 51), and the other is often a curlicued ball. In one Class II example, **Logierait 1** (PER), the rod, which is straight, is a ball-ended spear running through the serpent's coils. Some have two 'ball-ends' and one a 'flight'.

The origin of the serpent and Z-rod could be an object as formal and unvarying as the symbol itself. It may be the bronze serpentine armlet common in eastern Scotland in the second century, which would have been worn by many of the Pictish nobility's ancestors. In Pictish symbol-carving times, this would be a memory contemporary with the bronze-apple-ended spear that apparently became the Z-rod.

DIVIDED RECTANGLE (AND Z-ROD)

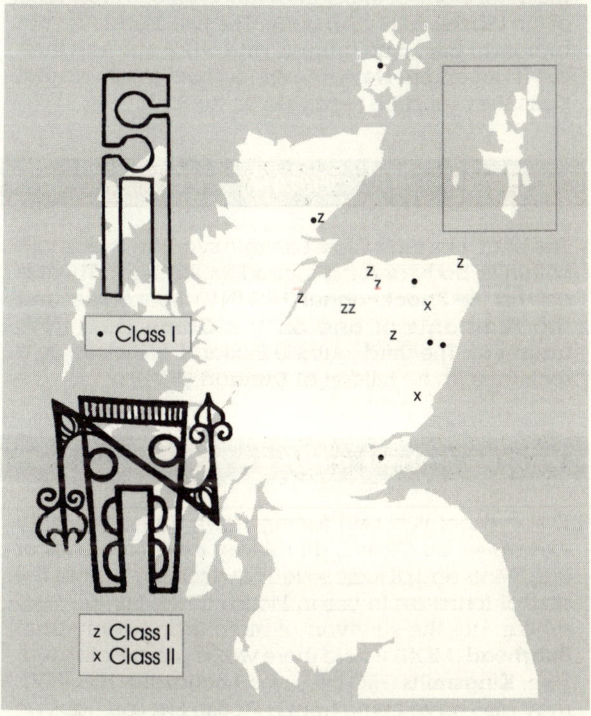

DIVIDED RECTANGLE AND Z-ROD — 8|2 = 10

CLASS I: **Mill of Newton**, **Tyrie**, ABE; **Finlarig**, **Inverallan**, HIG BAD; **Cullaird**, HIG INV; **Clynemilton 2**, HIG SUT; **Arndilly**, **Birnie 1**, MOR

CLASS II: **Drumdurno**, ABE; **Aberlemno 2**, ANG

DIVIDED RECTANGLE — 6|0 = 6

The divided rectangle might represent a chariot (Thomas 1963, 53-54). The majority of the more intact examples have circular or semicircular re-entrants that may represent wheels, and four of the Class I examples have in each projection a pair of closed semicircular re-entrants which may represent the bodies of horses.

The Z-rod might be a spear (like the Z-rod of the double-disc), but some look more like flighted arrows.

Two of the six rod-less examples are uncertain, **Gurness** (ORK) and **Craigmyle** (ABE), and one is very incomplete, **Park House** (ABE). A topless and almost featureless type appears on the large crescent-dominated **Craigton 1** (HIG SUT) stone, and most of a peculiarly-decorated one remains on the **North Redhill** (MOR) fragment. The only 'classic' example is on **Westfield 2** (FIF). It is 'chariot-like', if without the 'horse body' semicircles. (The Westfield symbol is very like one of the two symbols on the silver joining-ring of a great silver chain found at Whitecleuch in South Lanarkshire (ECMS I, fig.17).)

BEAST

This term is used to describe animal symbols on two stones. One is on the Class I face of **Glamis 1** (ANG), the other is one of the eight symbols on one cross-face of the **Ulbster** (HIG CAI) stone. The two 'beasts' do not represent the same animal, and what animals they are is uncertain. Nevertheless, as both are in symbol pairs they must be regarded as symbols.

BOAR

The boar, like most Class I animal symbols, has scrolls within its body and it is incised facing right. There is one on the **Knocknagael** (HIG INV) 'Boar Stone' and the remnants of one on the **Clune** (HIG INV) fragment. The third, outside Pictland, is incised on a rock-face in the hill-fort at **Dunadd** (ARG).

BULL

This symbol is a bull facing right. There are nine examples, all Class I, all solitary on their stones or fragments and at least seven of which came from the sites of fortresses in use in Pictish times. Six, all very similar, are the survivors of more than twenty from **Burghead** (MOR) where there was a great Pictish fort. Two, **Kingsmills** (HIG INV) and **Lochardill** (HIG INV), may also have come from a Pictish fort (perhaps on Inverness's Alde Castlehill), and the ninth bull stone was found in the fort on **East Lomond Hill** (FIF).

FISH-MONSTER

The fish-monster is somewhat sea-horse-like – although the ones with spiralled tails have tails that spiral backwards.

This rare symbol should not be confused with decorative sea-horses or fish-monsters, like the pair on the **Brodie** (MOR) cross-slab. The latter are not symbols.

GOOSE

The three goose symbols are all Class I and incised from left to right. The two clear examples are not like one another in appearance or stance but both are certainly geese. One is on **Tillytarmont 1** (ABE) and the other on a reused stone, **Easterton of Roseisle** (MOR). The latter looks backwards – as does the third, which is on the **Peterhead** (PER) standing stone.

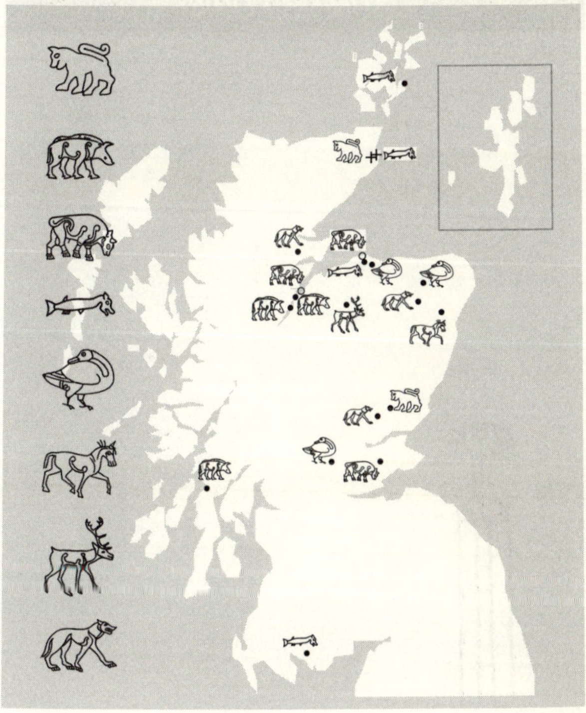

BEAST — 1|1 = 2 BOAR — 3|0 = 3 BULL — 9|0 = 9

FISH-MONSTER — 3|1 = 4
CLASS I: **Anwoth**, DUM; **Ness**, ORK; **Upper Manbeen**, MOR
CLASS II: **Ulbster**, HIG CAI

GOOSE — 3|0 = 3 HORSE — 1|0 = 1

STAG — 1|0 = 1 WOLF — 3|0 = 3

HORSE

The horse symbol is not only unique but is the only symbol on its stone, **Inverurie 4** (ABE). Nevertheless the horse does appear to be a symbol. It is incised facing right and within its body is a long scroll.

STAG

There is only one of this symbol, an antlered stag incised facing right on a Class I stone found near **Grantown** (HIG BAD). Within the body are scrolls, and below the stag is a simple rectangle.

WOLF

Two of the three wolf symbols are very similar, one on a fragment, **Ardross 1** (HIG ROS), and the other on a more complete stone, **Newbigging Leslie** (ABE). Very much less survives of the only southern wolf, the topmost symbol on the worn **Keillor** (PER) stone. All are incised from left to right.

TUNING-FORK

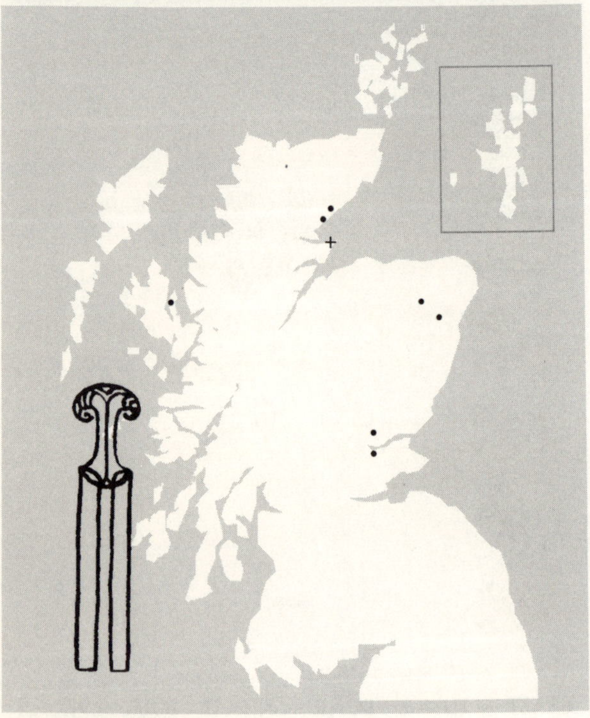

TUNING-FORK — 7|1 = 8

CLASS I: **Ardlair**, **Kintore 3**, ABE; **Raasay**, HIG SKY; **Dunrobin 1**, **Kintradwell 4**, HIG SUT; **Abernethy 1**, **Collace**, PER

CLASS II: **Tarbat 1**, HIG ROS

This fairly common symbol may represent a 'broken' or 'divided' sword (Thomas 1963, 52-53) of a type that reached Scotland in the first century. The tuning-fork's 'pommel' is, in four of the five more complete symbols, pelta-like and therefore similar to the first-century swords, but the blade is invariably divided, usually for almost its entire length.

DISC

Four of the eight examples of this exclusively Class I symbol contain three smaller discs in triangular formation, another is of three small discs with no enclosing disc about them, two are of concentric circles, and one on a fragment is only a part. The spoked 'disc' on another stone is more likely to be a wheel symbol. (The small 'disc' on a stone at Corrachree (ABE) is not considered to be a symbol.)

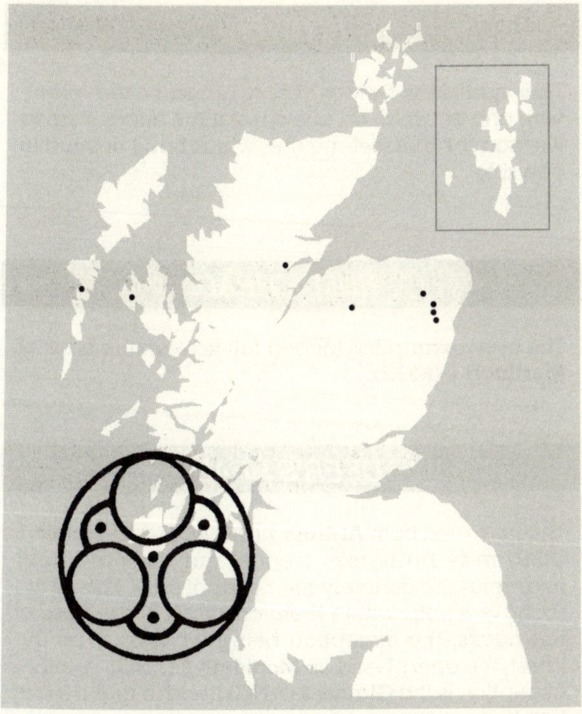

DISC — 8|0 = 8

CLASS I: **East Balhalgardy**, **Inverurie 3**, **Kinellar**, **Rothiebrisbane**, ABE; **Dingwall**, HIG ROS; **Dun Osdale**, HIG SKY; **Balneilan**, MOR; **Benbecula**, WES

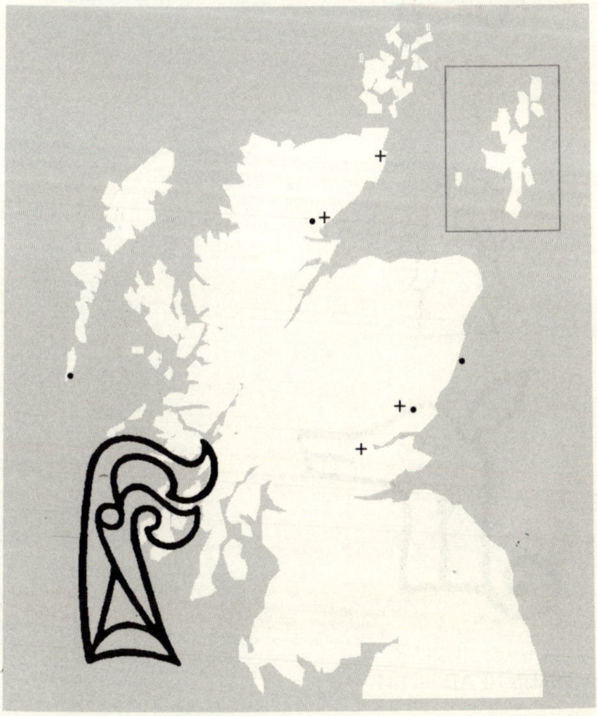

FLOWER — 4|4 = 8

CLASS I: **Dunnicaer 4**, ABE; **Dunnichen**, ANG; **Craigton 1**, HIG SUT; **Pabbay**, WES

CLASS II: **Glamis 1**, ANG; **Ulbster**, HIG CAI; **Craigton 2**, HIG SUT; **Gask**, PER

FLOWER

This symbol is flower-like, a broad-based 'plant' with one or two or (in one case) three heads shaped like convex trumpet-mouths, which hang or thrust to one side.

BULL'S HEAD

The only example is incised full-face on the back of **Mortlach 1** (MOR).

DEER'S HEAD

The heads on both **Ardross 1** (HIG ROS) and **Meigle 1** (PER) may be horses' heads, but the other four examples are certainly the heads of deer. Five of the six have scrolls within them or spirals at the base of the necks, the exception being what may be the latest, the deer's head on **Monifieth 2** (ANG). Another exception is the **Glamis 2** (ANG) head in that it faces left; the rest face right.

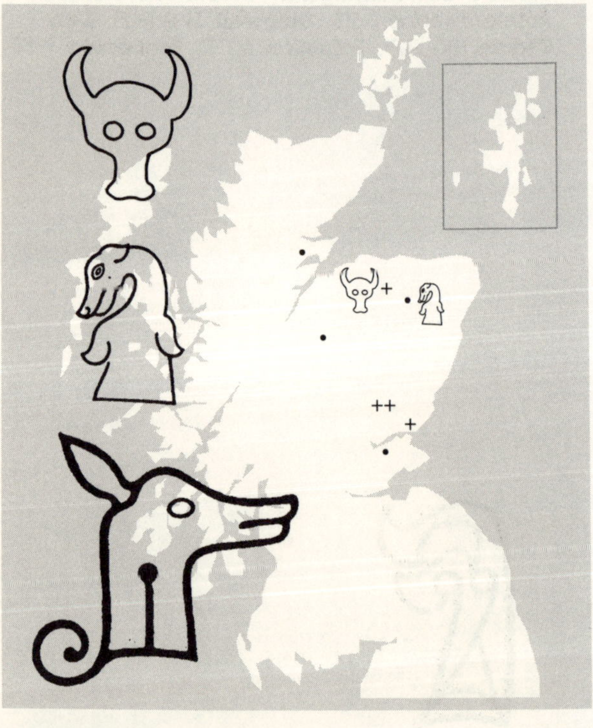

BULL'S HEAD — 0|1 = 1

DOG'S HEAD — 1|0 = 1

DEER'S HEAD — 3|3 = 6

CLASS I: **Strathmiglo**, FIF; **Dunachton**, HIG BAD; **Ardross 2**, HIG ROS

CLASS II: **Glamis 2**, **Monifieth 2**, ANG; **Meigle 1**, PER

DOG'S HEAD

The one example on a stone is on **Rhynie 5** (ABE). Facing left and without decoration it resembles a dog-headed glove-puppet. A similar symbol is engraved on two leaf-shaped silver plates from the Norrie's Law, Fife, hoard, and another was on a now-lost crescent-shaped plate from Monifieth, Angus (see p.89 fig.22).

STEP

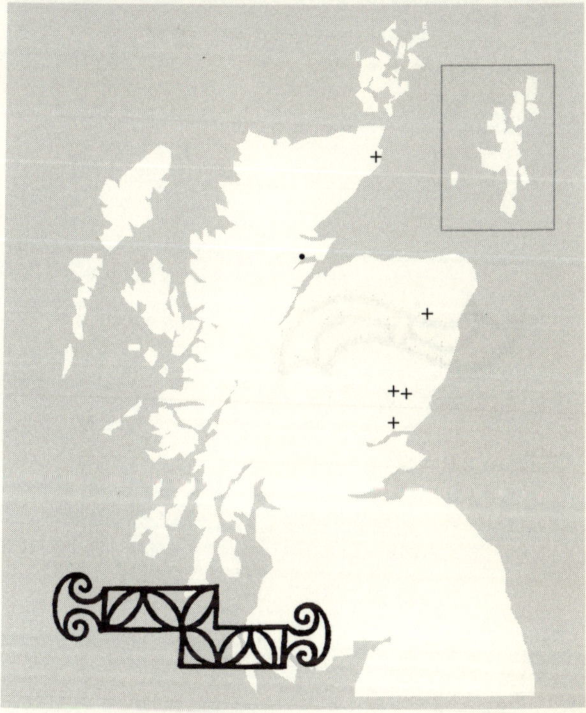

STEP — 1|5 = 6

CLASS I: **Roskeen**, HIG ROS

CLASS II: **Monymusk**, ABE; **Kingoldrum 1**, **Strathmartine 3**, **Woodrae**, ANG; **Ulbster**, HIG CAI

There are only six examples of this step-shaped symbol, five of which are Class II. The only Class I step, which is incised on the **Roskeen** (HIG ROS) standing stone, is plain, but the rest are decorated. That on the **Monymusk** (ABE) cross-slab also has pelta-like projections at its ends.

OGEE

Three examples of the ogee, one on the **Drimmies** (ABE) stone and those on **Kintradwell 1** and **2** (HIG SUT), are very similar, with internal lines and collars around their centres, while the example on **Mortlach 2** (MOR), resembles a double snap-hook. Only the upper part of a very plain ogee remains on the fifth stone, **Rhynie 8** (ABE).

(An ogee symbol as plain as the Rhynie remnant is engraved on the joining-ring of a silver chain found at Parkhill, also in Aberdeenshire (ECMS I, fig.15).)

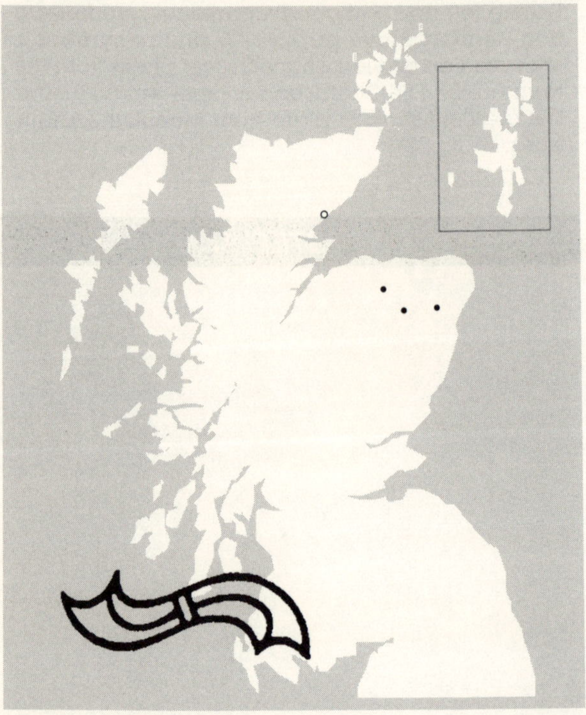

OGEE — 5|0 = 5

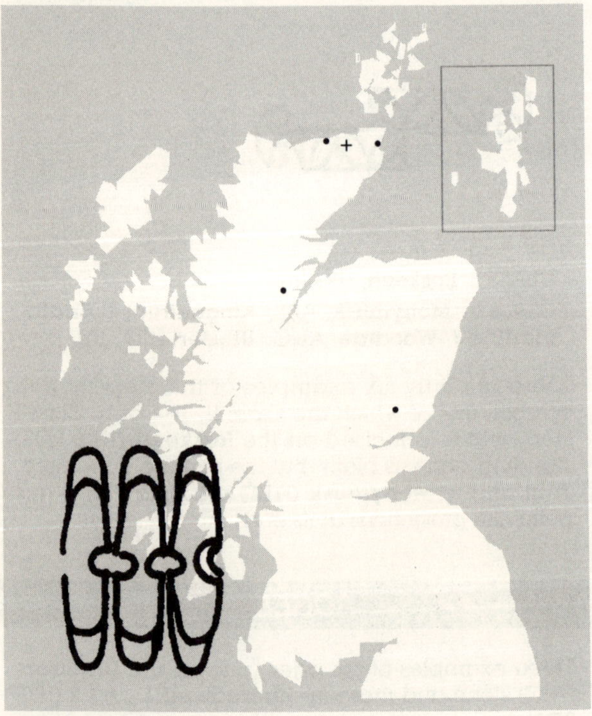

TRIPLE-OVAL — 4|1 = 5

CLASS I: **Glamis 4**, ANG; **Keiss**, **Sandside**, HIG CAI; **Wester Balblair**, HIG INV

CLASS II: **Skinnet**, HIG CAI

TRIPLE-OVAL

This symbol may represent an armlet – but if so one of unknown type. Until 1984 it was thought to be a northern symbol, but in that year the fourth Class I example was found, in Angus.

Figure 8

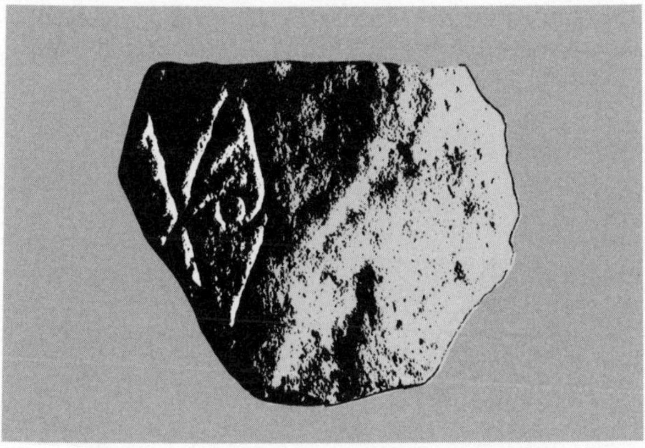

(?) Triple-oval: Glamis 4 (ANG) fragment, see p.66

DOUBLE-CRESCENT

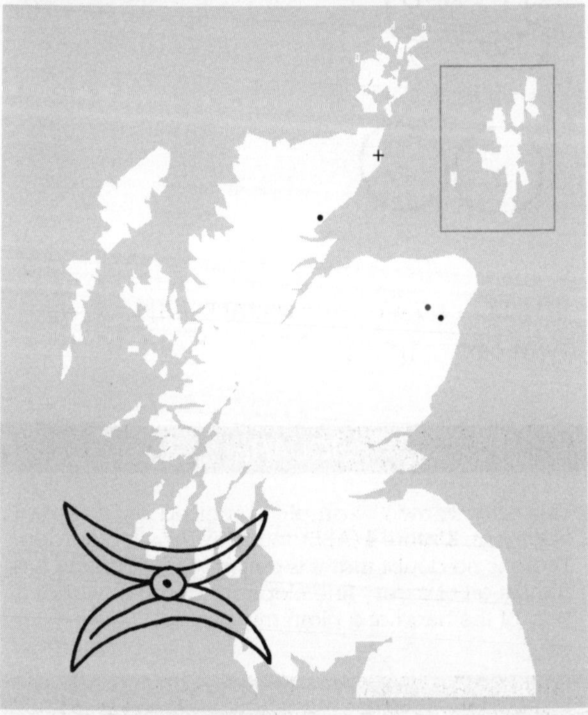

DOUBLE-CRESCENT — 3|1 = 4

This symbol may be of the same origin as the crescent and V-rod, but its crescents are usually longer and more slender. One is on **Dunrobin 2** (HIG SUT), another two are on Aberdeenshire stones, **Kintore 3**, and **Newton of Lewesk**, and the only Class II example is on the **Ulbster** (HIG CAI) stone.

HELMET

This symbol looks something like a late nineteenth-century spiked helmet. As the 'spike' is the point of a vertical shaft that runs downwards right through the symbol it may instead be the head of an arrow and the symbol may be related to the crescent and V-rod. Its only example, which is on **Congash 2** (HIG BAD), is paired with the crescent and V-rod's most frequent partner, the double-disc and Z-rod.

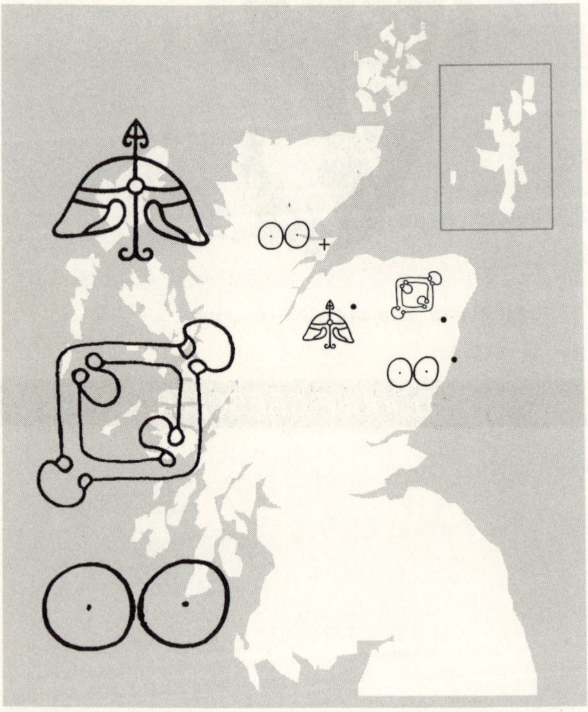

HELMET — 1|0 = 1 SQUARE — 1|0 = 1

TWIN-DISC — 1|1 = 2

SQUARE

The only known example is incised on a Class I fragment, **Kintore 4** (ABE), found in 1974 in a garden. There is no doubt that it is a symbol; just below it is almost all of a very fine elephant and below that is part of the head of a plain mirror.

TWIN-DISC

This may be not be a symbol. There are only two examples, the 'pair of discs' on **Dunnicaer 5** (ABE), and the great pair on **Hilton of Cadboll** (HIG ROS). Dunnicaer 5 is one of the strange 'small stones'; the Hilton of Cadboll discs may be a corrupt copy of the double-disc and Z-rod on **Aberlemno 3** (ANG).

ANVIL

This 'additional' symbol appears on two stones. On both it is in a set of smith's tools. On the Class I **Abernethy 1** (PER) stone, it is to the right of the main symbols, on the other side of which is a great hammer. On the **Dunfallandy** (PER) cross-slab, the anvil is between a hammer and a pair of pincers, and above the tools is the stone's principal figure, a mounted Pict. Beside him are what may be his main symbols, a crescent and V-rod over an elephant.

HAMMER

The two hammer symbols are on the two stones with anvils, **Abernethy 1** (PER) and **Dunfallandy** (PER).

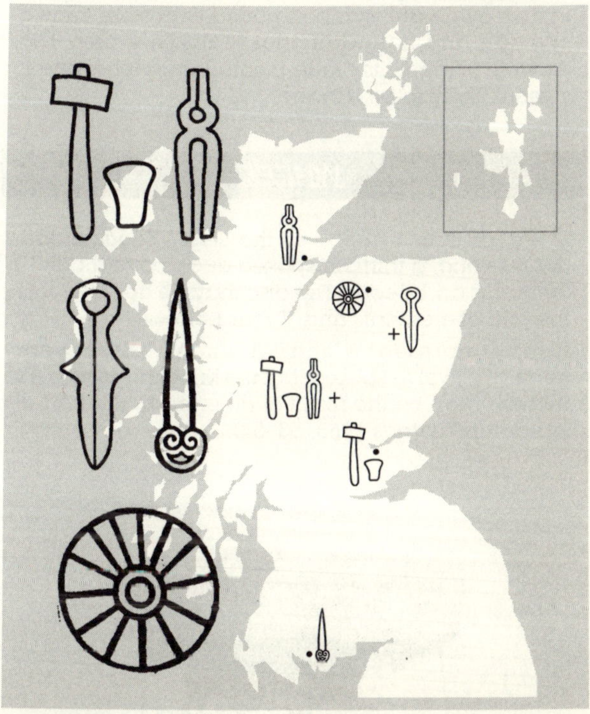

HAMMER — 1|1 = 2	ANVIL — 1|1 = 2
PINCERS — 1|1 = 2	SHEARS — 0|1 = 1
SWORD — 1|0 = 1	WHEEL — 2|0 = 2

PINCERS

There are only two examples of this additional symbol, one Class I and one Class II. One of the tools in the set of smith's tools on the **Dunfallandy** (PER) cross-slab is the huge horizontal pair of pincers, which is to the right of the hammer and anvil. The other pair, which is on the **Roskeen** (HIG ROS) standing stone, is vertically-incised. The Roskeen pincers are presumably in addition to the stone's two other symbols.

SHEARS

Shears appear only on one stone, the **Migvie** (ABE) cross-slab. As they share the stone's cross-face with two other symbols, a double-disc and Z-rod and the one known example of the horseshoe and V-rod, the shears are apparently an additional symbol. They could be another of the smith's tools.

SWORD

The only 'sword' is on the rock-face on Trusty's Hill near **Anwoth** (DUM). As it is between a double-disc and Z-rod and a fish-monster and is also smaller it seems to be another additional symbol. It has been considered by Charles Thomas to be a tuning-fork or broken sword symbol, but tuning-forks are symbols in their own right, symbols paired with other known symbols and not additional to another pair. The Anwoth symbol, its blade pointed and not divided, is more likely to be a sword.

WHEEL

There are three symbols on the Class I **Knockando 1** (MOR) stone, a thirteen-spoked disc above a pair of crescents and V-rods. The disc may be additional to the pair of crescents and V-rods below it.

It may represent a chariot wheel. These were generally twelve-spoked, but the Knockando wheel's thirteen may be the result of an error on the part of its carver (Thomas 1963, 53–54).

Figure 9

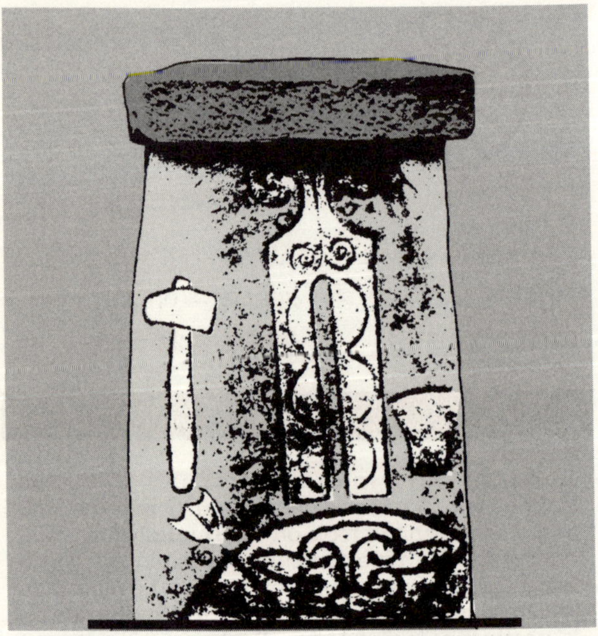

Hammer and anvil (p.27) flanking a tuning-fork: Abernethy 1 (PER), see p.44

MUSEUM OF SCOTLAND

Chambers Street, Edinburgh, EH1 1JF **A**
Tel: 0131 225 7534

Mon–Sat	1000–1700
Sunday	1400–1700
Free	

The new 'Museum of Scotland' should open towards the end of 1998. All the thirty-one symbol stones in its collection are described below in alphabetical order. The IB numbers are those in the museum catalogue.

Which stones will be on display is not yet known, but any not on view can usually be seen (by appointment) in the Museum's Leith store.

Ackergill 1 HIG CAI IB168

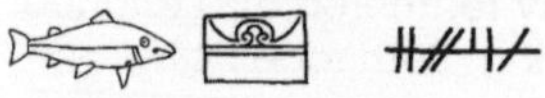

104 x 66 x 8cm **O** ECMS III, 28–29 (Links of Keiss Bay)

Only the lower part of the stone was found. It stood at one end of a long burial-mound at ND 348 550.

It has two symbols, a **salmon** over a **rectangle**, and a slanting Ogam inscription to their left. Not much of the salmon survives, but the rectangle is intact. It is laterally divided and contains spiral and whorl decoration. The Ogam also may be complete. It reads (upwards) NEHTETRI.

Ackergill 2 HIG CAI IB206

32 x 42 x 4cm **O** Edwards 1926, 179

This fragment lay not far from the mound, at ND 349 550 close to a long cist which had been disturbed.

On it is a **rectangle** with a U-shaped re-entrant in the centre of the top line. Below the rectangle is a small convex curve.

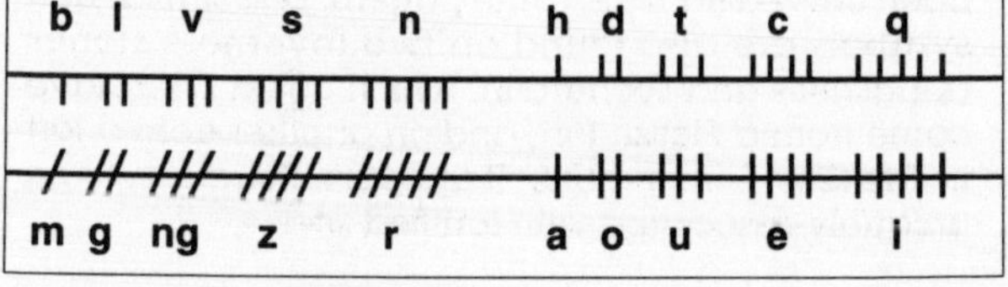

Figure 10

The Ogam alphabet

Benbecula WES IB37

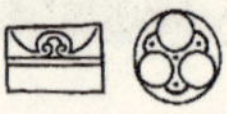

90 x 75 x 22cm **O** ECMS III,110–111

Both symbols, a **rectangle** and a **disc**, are very faint. The rectangle is divided down its length, and although decorated with spirals in one half only it is displayed vertically. The disc contains three smaller discs in triangular formation. (See p.13 fig.5)

The stone was found lying on the seashore at NF c803 566, near the remains of an ancient building.

Birsay ORK IB243

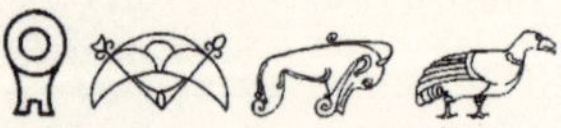

182 x 84 x 3cm **O** Simpson 1959, 17

The surviving fragments of this stone show three marching warriors and parts of four symbols. The missing parts of the symbols, a **mirror-case**, a **crescent and V-rod**, an **elephant** and an **eagle**, have been outlined on the board about the remains of the stone. The mirror-case and the crescent and V-rod, the two upper symbols, are rimmed and decorated with whorls. The elephant, a finely incised creature, has linked scrolls above its hind and forelegs, and the eagle below it, which is fully-feathered and taloned, has a whorl behind its left leg. Both face right.

The fragments were found during the excavation of a Norse burial-ground at Birsay which had graves, presumably Pictish, below the Norse levels. A complete reconstruction of the stone now stands there, at HY 240 285 (see p.132).

The Birsay stone is the only Class I stone (other than Inverurie 1 (ABE), which is a reused stone) with four symbols on one face and one of only three carved with a figure or figures. As the Birsay figures are relief-carved and some of the eagle is also in low relief this stone may be late in the Class I period, or the fragments could actually be from one face of a Class II cross-slab.

Burghead 1 MOR IB95

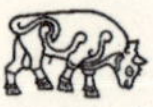

68 x 43 x 8cm **O** ECMS III, 118–120

Burghead was a fortress in Pictish times. About twenty stones incised with bulls were found there (NJ 109 691), but only six survive – this intact stone, another in the British Museum, and four fragments. The bulls on all are so alike that they could have been carved from the same pattern. Less similar **bull** symbols are also found on two Inverness stones (Kingsmills and Lochardill), which could both have come from a Pictish fort, and on another from a fort in Fife (East Lomond Hill). It appears, therefore, to be uniquely-associated with fortified sites.

Clune, Dores HIG INV IB38

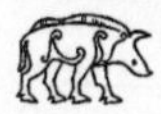

56 x 42 x 20cm **O** ECMS III, 97–98

Much of a stylised **boar** can be seen on this rectangular fragment. Only two other boar symbols are known, one on the Knocknagael (HIG INV) Boar Stone, the other incised on rock at Dunadd (ARG).

This stone was found near Loch Ness at NH c605 354.

Drumbuie 1 HIG INV IB287

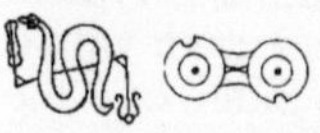

76 x 76 x 6cm **O** ECMS III, 98–99

Both this and No.2 are fragments found during ploughing at NH 51 31 on Upper Drumbuie Farm, which is on the north side of Urquhart Bay, Loch Ness. They covered a cist-like construction.

The symbols on No.1 are a **serpent and Z-rod** over a **double-disc**. The serpent loops very formally from right to left, and the Z-rod has a 'flamboyant' head and a curlicued ball-end. The discs of the double-disc, one of which is slightly damaged, are rimmed and have small central discs. The joining bar has concave sides and a narrower 'bar' within it.

Drumbuie 2 HIG INV IB288

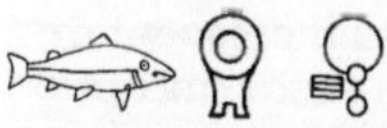

112 x 86 x 6cm **O** ECMS III, 99–100

This is the lower part of a slab. Incised on it is part of a **salmon**, a **mirror-case** below it and a **mirror-and-comb** to the right. Only the tail-end of the salmon, which swims from left to right, remains on the stone, but it can be seen that its upper body was scaled – with diamond-shapes. The mirror-case head has a narrow rim and a small dotted central disc about which are four almost circular shapes and four dots, a design very like that on Inveraven 1 (MOR). The base is rectangular, with two vertical arcs inside it. The comb is double-sided and toothed, and the mirror below it is small and rimmed, its handle like an inverted keyhole.

East Lomond Hill FIF IB205

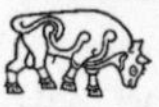

43 x 30 x 8cm **O** Corrie 1926

This stone came from a hill-fort at NO 244 062.

Its **bull** is more natural in appearance than the stylised Burghead bulls, and the hooves are not shown – as if concealed by grass or other vegetation.

Easterton of Roseisle MOR IB226

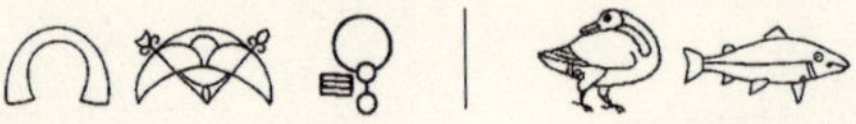

120 x 56 x 7cm **O** ECMS III, 124–126

This stone has been used twice as a symbol stone. One set, a **goose** over a **salmon**, appears on one face, and an earlier set, a **horseshoe** over a **crescent and V-rod** with a **mirror-and-comb** below them, is incised the other way up on the other face.

The goose, carved from left to right but peering backwards, has a small whorl or spiral behind the left leg. The salmon, also from left to right, is a typical example. The horseshoe is crescent-shaped, with a small necked re-entrant, and is quite plain, as is the crescent and V-rod below it. The left end of the V-rod is flighted, with open 'flights', the right end is arrow-headed, and both are curlicued. The mirror, which is rimmed, has an unusual feature – its handle begins outside the mirror-head. To the right of the handle is the comb, single-sided with a three-pointed top.

The stone was found on farm land at NJ c144 647, in a field containing burials. It had been reused yet again – as one side of a stone coffin.

Edinburgh IB1

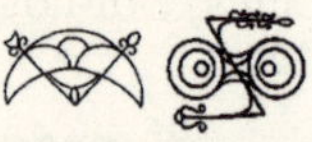

112 x 68 x 18cm **O** ECMS III, 421

On this fragment are most of a plain **crescent and V-rod** and the upper part of a vertical and plain **double-disc and Z-rod**. Both are somewhat faint. Nothing of the rod-ends can be made out, but the left arm of the Z-rod is floriated.

This stone was found in use as a footbridge in Princes Street Gardens (NT 250 736). It is possible that it had been brought there when the gardens were being laid out in the early nineteenth century. Before then the site lay under the Nor' Loch, and earlier still was marshy waterlogged ground.

Finlarig HIG BAD IB11

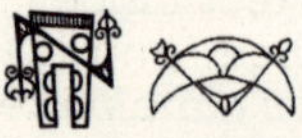

106 x 43 x 6cm **O** ECMS III, 101

This fragment was dug up at NH 991 254 on the Farm of Finlarig near Grantown-On-Spey, beside a circular enclosure containing a ruined chapel.

On it is part of a **divided rectangle and Z-rod** with below it the left half of a **crescent and V-rod** decorated with interlocking spirals and curved lines. The left end of the V-rod is a leaf-shaped arrowhead with curlicues below it. Most left ends are flighted (see p.140, **Lynchurn**).

Firth ORK IB24

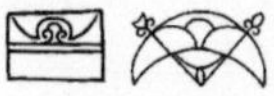

114 x 53 x 8cm **O** ECMS III, 20

This trimmed stone was once built into the inside wall of a cottage at HY 378 171 in Firth and is said to have come from an older cottage close by.

Some of its symbolled surface has flaked away. All that remains on it is the central part of a horizontal **rectangle** over more of a **crescent and V-rod**. The ornamentation within the crescent is pelta-shaped.

Fiscavaig HIG SKY IB213

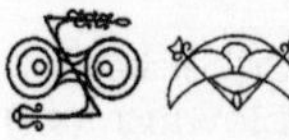

90 x 50 x 26cm **O** Callander 1927, 241–243

This is one of the three known Skye mainland stones. Its symbols are a very plain **double-disc and Z-rod** and a **crescent and V-rod** containing some dome pattern. The latter may be unfinished.

The stone, which was found on the seashore, at about NG 33 34, is on display in the third-floor ante-room at the St Mungo Museum in Glasgow.

St Mungo Museum of Religious Life and Art 2 Castle Street, Glasgow G4 0RH Tel: 0141 553 2557	**A** (lift)
Mon–Sat 1000–1700 Sun 1100–1700	Free

Grantown HIG BAD IB10

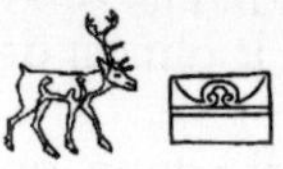

120 x 25 x 23cm **O** ECMS III, 126–27

This pillar-like stone was found in a knoll called Cnoc-an-Fruich (Heather Hill) at NJ 045 301.

It is incised with the only known **stag** symbol. The stag, with antlers, faces right and has leg and shoulder scrolls. The **rectangle** below it is laterally divided into two parts and has a spiral or circle outside the top right and bottom left corners.

Greens ORK IB203

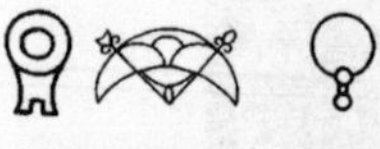

185 x 56 x 17cm **O** Marwick 1924

Finely incised on this tall slab are a divided **mirror-case**, a **crescent and V-rod** below it and a **mirror** below that. The mirror-case has a rimmed head with small central disc, and its divided base is decorated with arcs and horizontal lines. The central decoration of the crescent and V-rod is an inverse pelta, there are arcs in the wings, and the rod is flighted and arrow-headed. The mirror is plain-headed and has a twin-bossed handle.

The stone was found below ground at HY 542 032, near the farm buildings of Greens.

HILTON OF CADBOLL HIG ROS IB189

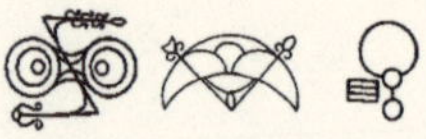

236 x 140 x 24cm **O** ECMS III, 61–63

(1993 edn fig.59 faces p.55)

There was once a cross on one face of this stone, but it was stripped off in the seventeenth century and replaced by a burial inscription. On the other face are the symbols and a hunting scene whose principal figure is a Pictish lady on horseback. Grandly dressed in a pleated plaid and a long gown she sits side-saddle and is presented full-face. Her hairstyle is ornate, and she wears a large penannular brooch at her breast.

Behind her is one of her hounds, and further behind stand a pair of plaid-clad musicians blowing long horns. In front of her is a **mirror-and-comb**, and at her right side is another almost hidden horse and rider. This individual appears to be male as a large nose and what may be the tip of a beard project to the left from behind the lady's hair. Below are two more Picts on horseback, each in a plaid and with a spear and shield, and below them a hind is savaged by two more hounds.

In the panel above the scene are two large interlace-filled discs with above them an oddly shaped **crescent and V-rod** decorated with key pattern and whorls and with its rod-ends floriated. The two discs are probably not symbols, and what may be the crescent's partner is above it. Within the top of the ornate frame that surrounds the panels is a **double-disc and Z-rod.** Its joining bar is long and its Z-rod short with floriations on both arms. It is almost as corrupt as the crescent and V-rod.

The scene is very like the hunting scene on Aberlemno 3 (ANG), and the crescent and V-rod and the two discs are similar in position to the Aberlemno symbols. The Hilton of Cadboll stone, which is later, may be in part a copy of the Aberlemno slab, made perhaps without full understanding of its meaning.

Before the Hilton of Cadboll stone lost its cross it stood near the ruins of a chapel at NH 873 769, on the north side of the Moray Firth.

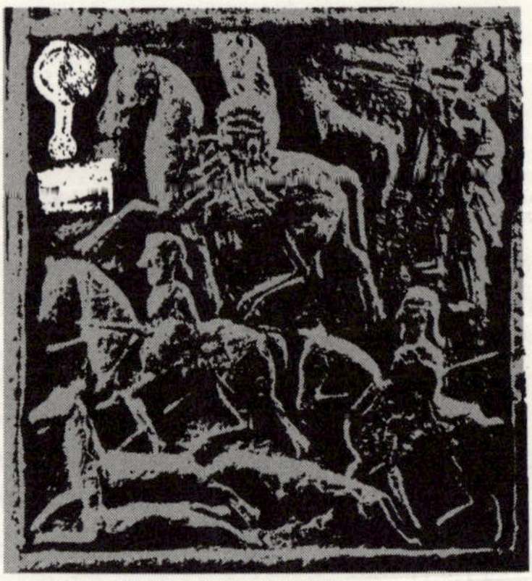

Figure 11

Mirror-and-comb prominently displayed before the principal horse and (female) rider in the Cadboll hunt scene

Huntly 2 ABE IB179

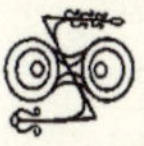

78 x 61 x 38cm **O** ECMS III, 167

This is one part of a stone found at NJ 558 376, in a field on the Farm of Leys of Dummuies near Huntly. The farmer used explosive to break it into two pieces one of which is said to be still buried in the field.

On the surviving fragment is most of a **double-disc and Z-rod**. The discs are rimmed, with small rimmed circles in the centre of each, and the joining bar is concave-sided with a similar bar within it. There are additional arcs at the ends of the inner bar, a feature which is almost unique, and the one pair of 'floriations' on the Z-rod's upper arm are reversed, looping away from the point. Of the point itself only a pair of curlicues survives on the broken stone.

Invereen HIG INV IB227

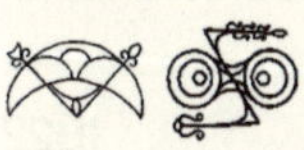

117 x 66 x 19cm **O** PSAS 68 (1933–34), 56

This virtually intact slab is incised with a **crescent and V-rod** above a **double-disc and Z-rod**. The left end of the V-rod is a curlicued arrow-flight, the other a curlicued head, and the ornamentation within the crescent's centre is of dome-and-wing pattern. The double-disc and Z-rod has a spear-pointed upper arm, with reversed floriations behind the point, but its angled arm is twin-lined, a very uncommon feature. There is also a circle incised near the top left corner of the stone with a vertical line running down from its centre. This may be a later addition.

The stone was found at NH 797 311, during ploughing at Invereen near Moy.

Keiss HIG CAI IB188

? 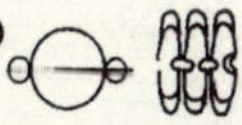

96 x 53 x 7cm **O** ECMS III, 27–28

This fragment was found during the excavation of two sand mounds at ND 339 585, on Keiss Links north of Wick. In one were the foundations of a rectangular building, and the fragment was one of its floor-slabs.

There are two symbols on it, an almost complete **triple-oval** linked by overlapping circular shapes and to its left what Romilly Allen described as a "mirror". If this is a mirror it is on its side and has no more than a single disc for a handle. As the 'mirror head' contains a pattern, and as the small disc is joined to the larger by a link this symbol may be a **triple-disc** with one disc missing.

KINGOLDRUM 1 ANG IB39

60 x 38 x 7cm **O** ECMS III, 226

On the reverse of this small cross-slab a long-gowned figure sits in a great chair. As the top of the stone is missing the figure is headless but, dressed as it is, is probably female. There is also a **mirror-and-comb**.

The mirror, which is upside down, is in front of the enthroned figure's feet and above a vertical **crescent**. Under the figure is a large **step** symbol and a large double-sided comb. Both crescent and step are rimmed and also decorated, and the long-handled mirror has a rim about its entire outline. The comb is like a bone comb of the period.

On the other face is a long-shafted cross with a square centre and interlaced serpentine creatures at each side of the shaft.

The cross-slab was found in the old church at Kingoldrum (NO 334 550).

Kintore 2 ABE IB22

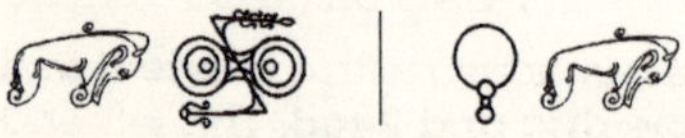

150 x 90 x 22cm **O** ECMS III, 172–74

This very large slab, which is in two pieces with the bottom right-hand corner of the lower missing, is a reused symbol stone. There are symbols on both faces, one set upside-down in relation to the other.

Figure 12

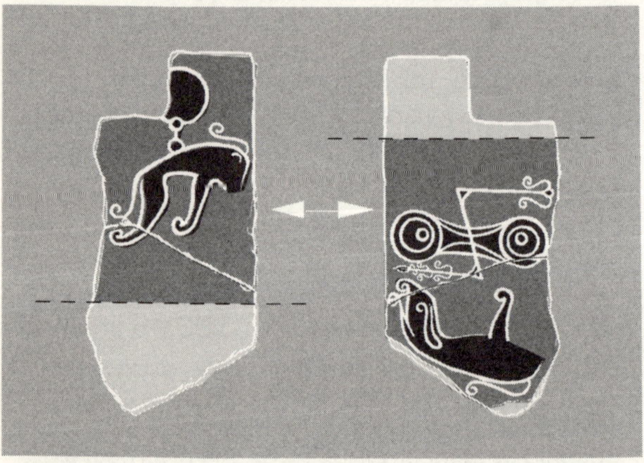

Kintore 2 (ABE) (after ECMS figs 106 & 186A)

On one face is a very faint **elephant** incised facing left with below it a much clearer **double-disc and Z-rod** the joining bar of which is unusually long. The rod, its upper arm floriated, is spear-pointed and has a ball-end decorated with a huge pair of curlicues.

On the other face is most of a plain **mirror** over an **elephant** which faces right. This is an unusual arrangement. For some reason the mirror has been given pride of place.

This stone and Kintore 3 were found in the Castle Hill, an artificial mound of earth and stones on a natural base which was at NJ 794 163.

Kintore 3 ABE IB23

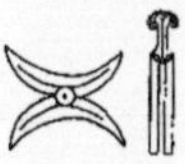

106 x 91 x 23cm **O** ECMS III, 174–175

This is the other stone from the Castle Hill. Some of the top is missing, but on it are two almost complete symbols, a **double-crescent** decorated with arcs and to its right the remains of a **tuning-fork** with the upper part of the handle missing.

LATHERON 1 HIG CAI IB183

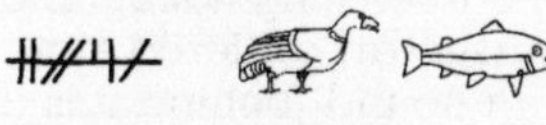

90 x 43 x 10cm **O** Anderson 1904

Found in a byre wall at ND 198 332, this is part of a cross-slab which was carved on one face only.

Its two symbols, an **eagle** and a **salmon**, are very like their Class I counterparts but are incised facing left. In front of them is an Ogam inscription, which Anderson read as DUNNODNNATM?QQNETO.

MONIFIETH 1 ANG IB26

76 x 37 x 15cm **O** ECMS III, 228–229

On one face is a cross with a square centre and rectangular arms. On the other is a **double-disc** with below it a double-sided **comb** and a **double-disc and Z-rod**, both vertical. The stone's base has been broken off, but just above the break is part of what may be a rimmed **mirror**. The double-disc and the double-disc and Z-rod are well-shaped and also rimmed and decorated. One Z-rod end is pointed, the other apparently a stub, and there are two sets of curlicues at or near each end. The comb is an accurate representation of a contemporary bone comb.

This cross-slab and Monifieth 2 were found in the foundations of the old parish church of Monifieth at NO 495 324 and later built into a wall of the new.

MONIFIETH 2 ANG IB27

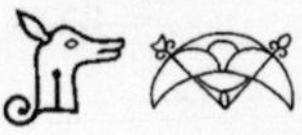

45 x 30 x 9cm **O** ECMS III, 228–230

In the bottom left panel on the back of this very small cross-slab is a figure which appears to be female. Carved full-face, she wears a gown with a penannular brooch, and what look like horns about her head may be an elaborate hairstyle. The symbols on the stone, a **crescent and V-rod** and a **deer's head** above this, include no mirror-and-comb, but there could have been one on the stone's base. This has been broken off.

SCOONIE FIF IB110

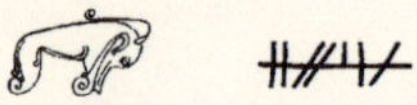

106 x 71 x 10cm **O** ECMS III, 347

(1993 edn fig.360 faces p.346)

The top, bottom and one side of this cross-slab are missing. The cross is very worn, but the carvings on the reverse are still clear. At the top is most of a large **elephant**, and below it is a hunting scene. The elephant is scrolled above both legs, like Birsay's, but it also has the rather commoner scroll down the inside of the hind leg. In the scene three long-haired and large-nosed horsemen pursue an antlered stag. Below the stag is a leaping hound, behind it is a smaller one, and in front of the scene a line of Ogam runs upwards near the edge of the stone. The Ogam reads EDDARRNONN, which may be the Pictish name Etheman or Itheman. It appears very similarly spelt in one of the Ogams on the Rodney Stone in Moray.

The Scoonie stone was found in the old churchyard at Scoonie (NO 384 017).

South Ronaldsay ORK IB2

150 x 48 x 8cm **O** ECMS III, 20–21

This reused stone was later trimmed and used yet again – as a window sill in St Peter's Church on South Ronaldsay (ND 471 908).

On one face are most of two symbols one above the other. The upper is a **rectangle** decorated with pelta-like dome-and-wing patterns and scrolls. The lower is a **crescent and V-rod** with similarly-styled ornamentation. The one visible V-rod end, the left, is flighted and curliced.

On the reverse are the remains of a plainer **crescent and V-rod** and a simple divided **mirror-case**. The V-rod's visible end is an arrowhead with curlicues. Less of these two symbols is left on the stone than of the other pair. In addition to the trimming that removed part of both sets some of the surface of this face has flaked away.

STRATHMARTINE 4 ANG IB47

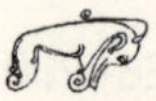

38 x 18 x 6cm **O** ECMS III, 230–233

Four symbolled fragments, Strathmartine 3, 4, 5 and 6, were found in the old church at Strathmartine or in the churchyard (NO 378 353, north of Dundee), but three of these have been lost.

This, the sole survivor, is probably from one side of a cross-slab. On one face are relief-carved spirals with part of a border of interlace beside them. On the other is some of what may be an incised **elephant** symbol.

TARBAT 1 HIG ROS IB90

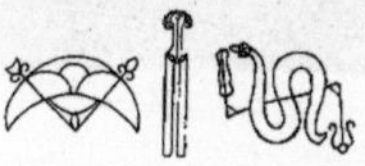

63 x 112 x 15cm **O** ECMS III, 73–75

This fragment is part of the base of a cross-slab. One face is missing, but on the other are the remains of figures, including part of a horse and rider, which are within a scrolled frame very like that from nearby Hilton of Cadboll. On the left side is incised interlace, and on the right side are three symbols in relief, one above the other. These are some of a **crescent and V-rod**, most of a much smaller **tuning-fork** pointing left, and an almost complete **serpent and Z-rod**. The visible (left) end of the crescent's V-rod is flighted, and the tuning-fork has very distinct prongs, but the serpent and Z-rod is unusual. The serpent's shape is a reversed S, its head at the bottom and facing right. The Z-rod is an upright and true Z, the end of the upper arm like an arrow-flight and the end of the lower missing.

The fragment lay in Tarbat churchyard at Portmahomack (NH 915 840) until about 1850.

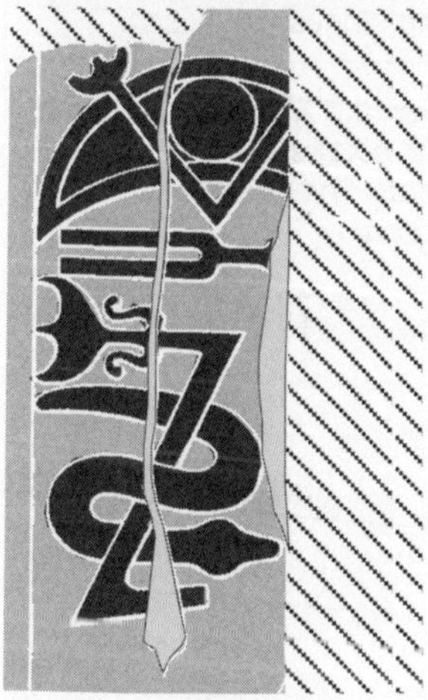

Figure 13

Tarbat 1 (HIG ROS) : detail of the symbols (after ECMS fig.71A)

WOODRAE ANG IB202

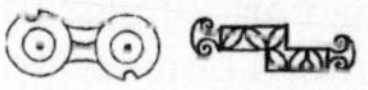

175 x 101 x 13cm **O** ECMS III, 242–245

The relief-carved equal-armed cross on this slab has been deliberately removed leaving only its outline. The cross and the other carvings are framed by a wide border of interlace which is also incomplete, as the bottom of the slab has broken off and the base strip is missing. Above and below the cross is a vertical band of similar interlace which together with the remains of the cross divides the face into four quadrants containing fabulous creatures one of which devours a human figure.

The reverse is also badly damaged, only the top panel being more or less intact. In this a bearded Pict rides from right to left, and behind him are symbols, a **double-disc** over the upper part of a **step**. Both are rimmed, and the step is decorated with leaf-shapes.

The stone was found built into the kitchen floor of the now-demolished Woodray Castle (NO 519 566).

FALKLAND PALACE MUSEUM

Falkland Palace, Falkland, KY7 7BU **B**
Tel: 01337 857397

Apr–Oct	Mon–Sat	1100–1730
	Sunday	1330–1730
	(Free – if viewing stones only)	

This National Trust property on the A912, not far south-south-east of Auchtermuchty, houses a museum which has been closed for some years. The two stones can be seen only by prior arrangement.

Westfield 1 74 x 42 x 16cm **O**

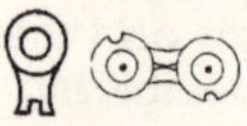

Westfield 2 50 x 41 x 15cm **O**

Stevenson 1971

Both are trimmed and broken Class I fragments found built into a steading at Westfield Farm (NO 238 073).

The symbols on No.1 are most of a small-based **mirror-case** over a **double-disc** with a large part of the right-hand disc missing. The mirror-case head and the discs of the double-disc are very similar in size and design, each plain with a smaller dotted disc in the centre, and the mirror-case base is also similar in decoration to the double-disc's joining bar. The discs of the double-disc are 'notched' with a closed U-shaped re-entrant on the inner edge of each.

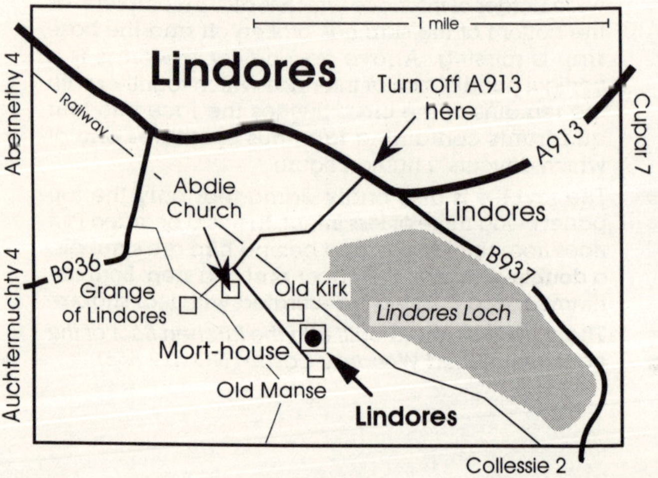

On No.2 is the greater part of a **divided rectangle** with some of a rimmed disc to the right. The divided rectangle is very like the one engraved on the joining ring of a silver chain found near Crawfordjohn in Lanark (ECMS I, Fig.17). In the upper part are necked circular 'chariot wheel' re-entrants, and there are no 'horse body' semicircles in the lower projections. The other symbol was probably part of a rimmed **mirror.**

LARGO — Δ B

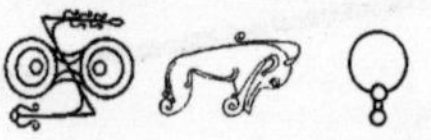

198 x 76 x 15cm **E** — NO 423 035
ECMS III, 344–347

This cross-slab stands under cover outside Largo Parish Church, Upper Largo, which is close to the junction of the A915 and A917. The stone, which was found in two pieces on the Largo estate, was at first moved to Midlothian but later returned to Largo.

The carving on both faces is worn and defaced. On the reverse, the surface of which is also flaking, are three horsemen, one above the other and riding from right to left. Below the first are what remains of two hounds, in front of the lower horsemen is a vertical **double-disc and Z-rod**, and below them is a large **elephant**. The elephant has an additional 'forepaw', a small spiral above the curled front foot. Under the elephant are two deer-like creatures with much of their legs flaked away, and behind the lowest horseman is what may be a small rimmed **mirror**. The lower part of its handle is missing.

Lindores — MAP opp ΔΔΔ A

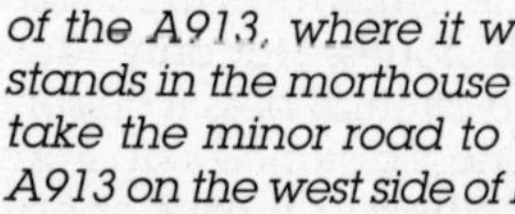

137 x 57 x 45cm **O** — NO 260 163
ECMS III, 343–344

This Class I stone once stood at NO c263 172, on Kaim Hill north of Lindores. Later built into a wall at the side of the A913, where it was used as a sundial, it now stands in the morthouse of Abdie Old Kirk. To reach it take the minor road to Grange of Lindores from the A913 on the west side of Lindores. Less than half a mile down this, beyond the railway bridge and just before Abdie Church, turn left up the track to Abdie Old Kirk. The morthouse, which is just past the old kirkyard entrance, is open-fronted, facing west.

On the stone's north face are two symbols, a plain horizontal **triple-disc** and bar above a **crescent and V-rod**. The V-rod has an arrow-flight at the left rod-end and an arrowhead at the other, both curlicued. The decorations within the crescent include a central pelta flanked by two crescent shapes, but the pelta itself is somewhat obscured by a surveyor's bench-mark, probably carved when the stone was in the roadside wall. The triple-disc too is defaced, by the socket for the sundial's gnomon and by some of its Roman numerals. On the west face is a large rimmed **mirror**. It is the only example of a mirror not carved on the same face as the other symbols in its set.

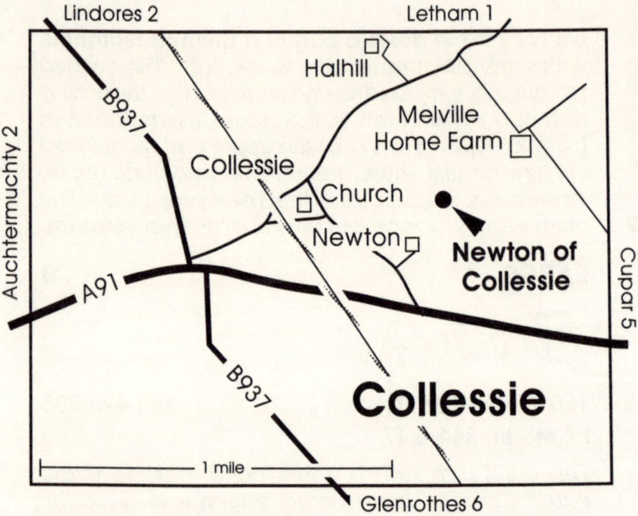

Newton of Collessie MAP above Δ **D**

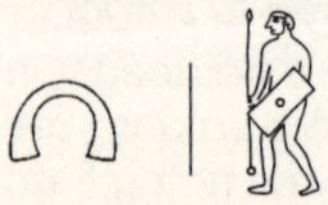

ht. *c*305cm **E**, circ. *c*220cm NO 293 132
Lines 1989

The Newton stone stands in a field of Melville Home Farm, which is half a mile east of Collessie, a village six miles west of Cupar by the A91. The stone fell in 1994 but has been re-erected. The best approach is from Melville farm steading. Permission should be asked at Halhill.

Incised on the upper part of the south-east face is the faint figure of a man walking from right to left. Although naked the figure, who is large-nosed and has curling hair, has the look of a Pict. He also carries weapons. At his left side is a rectangular shield inclined downwards and forwards, and his right hand holds a spear vertically. In front of him is a symbol – a small **horseshoe** on the adjacent south-west face. The spear is ball-ended, like the spears which may be the origin of the Z-rods, and the shield is unlike any on the Class II stones. Not only rectangular but small and with a circular boss it closely resembles one on the Bridgeness distance slab from the Antonine Wall. The Collessie man's spear appears to be a representation of the 'bronze apple'-butted spear of the second/third century, and his shield may also be of second-century type.

It is unlikely that the carving is contemporary with the period of the sword and shield. The presence of the horseshoe suggests that it was done within the symbol stone period, and that the figure carrying weapons which are therefore archaic is not a contemporary Pict but the representation of some ancient hero or mythical being, perhaps a Pictish warrior-god.

A similar but cloaked figure was on the now almost featureless Rhynie 3 (ABE). He carried a similar shield and what may be a similar spear – and beneath him was an arch-like symbol. As the figures and the symbols on the two stones are virtually the same it is unlikely that they represent two different Picts who had by chance the same symbol or that the stones were the grave or memorial stones of real persons. Although many miles apart both stones may have been incised for the same purpose. Both may also indicate that the carving of symbols on stones began in Pictish pagan times.

Perhaps an Angus standing stone should be added to these two. It is in a field at Westerton of Balgavies (ANG) (NO 536 521), near the crossroads on the B9113 five miles east of Forfar. On its broad (*c*140cm) south-west face are the remains of a male figure incised from right to left who is not only apparently naked but whose jaw-line and chin and what can be seen of his hair style are very reminiscent of the Collessie Pict's. Because of the heavy flaking of this layered and very irregular sandstone slab half of the figure, almost all of what he may have been holding and anything else that may have been in front of him (for example a symbol) has disappeared; but from what is left it looks as if he may have represented the same being.

Figure 14

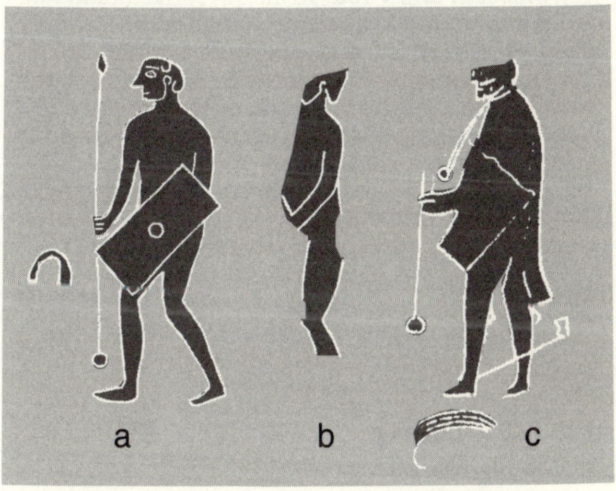

Warriors compared: a) Newton of Collessie (FIF); b) Westerton of Balgavies (ANG); c) Rhynie 3 (ABE), *see p.88*

Strathmiglo ΔΔΔ **A**

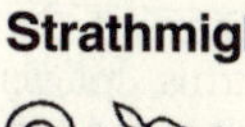

167 x 58 x 40cm E NO 217 102

Stevenson 1969

Strathmiglo is less than two miles west of Auchtermuchty by the A91. Kirk Wynd runs south from the east end of the High Street to the Church, where the stone stands at the right-hand side of the kirkyard entrance. It had been used as a gatepost at NO 209 101.

The symbols, which are on the west face, are a divided **mirror-case** over a **deer's head**. The mirror-case, which is unusually small-headed and long-based, is very like the one on the small Gurness (ORK) stone. The deer's head, which looks right and has whorls at the neck-base, is longer in the neck than any other example.

Abernethy 1 ΔΔΔ **A**

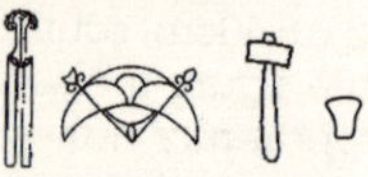

86 x 66 x 18cm **O** NO 190 164
ECMS III, 282

In Abernethy, which is eight miles south-east of Perth by the A912 and the A913, is a trimmed Class I stone that was found in the village. It is set up facing south-east, against the foot of Abernethy Round Tower.

On the stone is most of a vertical **tuning-fork** over part of a **crescent and V-rod**. To the left of the tuning-fork is a **hammer** and to the right a small **anvil**. The only other examples of these additional symbols are on the Dunfallandy (PER) cross-slab. At the top of the tuning-fork are the remains of its whorl-ended handle, and there are spirals above the prongs, each containing three vertical arcs one above the other. The crescent and V-rod's central decoration is a twin-pelta pattern, and the surviving (left) end of the rod is arrow-flighted and curlicued. (See p.28, fig.9)

ALYTH ΔΔΔ **B**

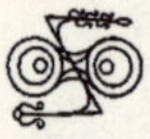

138 x 43 x 13cm **O** NO 243 488
ECMS III, 286–287

This stone is in the inner porch of Alyth High Kirk, which is at the north end of Alyth, five miles east of Blairgowrie. It was found near the old kirk ruins.

The stone, a natural slab carved in relief on one face and incised on the other, has one side broken off. On the front is a small cross with rectangular arms, spirals in each quadrant and a narrow base. Half of the left arm is missing. On the reverse, which is close to the wall and difficult to see, is an incised **double-disc and Z-rod**, the right hand disc lost with the breakage. The left disc has a smaller disc in its centre with spokes about it, a unique form of decoration for this symbol. The Z-rod, its remaining (left) end spear-pointed, is a true Z.

Bruceton MAP opp ΔΔ **D**

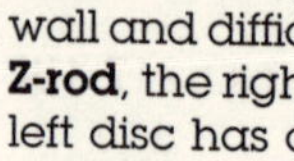

137 x 91 x 28cm **E** NO 290 504
ECMS III, 282–283

Bruceton Farm is about three miles east-north-east of Alyth by the B952, the B954 and a minor road. The farm buildings are about two hundred metres north of the minor road, and permission to visit the stone should be requested there. On the south side of the road is a long field stretching south. The stone stands three hundred metres down this. About 1840 a number of stone coffins were dug up some twenty metres north-east of the stone (Jervise 1857, 188).

It is a natural slab incised on the south-south-east face with two symbols, a **horseshoe** over an **elephant**. The horseshoe is without decoration, the elephant carved facing right. Lichen obscures parts of the symbols, and they are worn in places. The elephant's tail and some smaller details are not now visible.

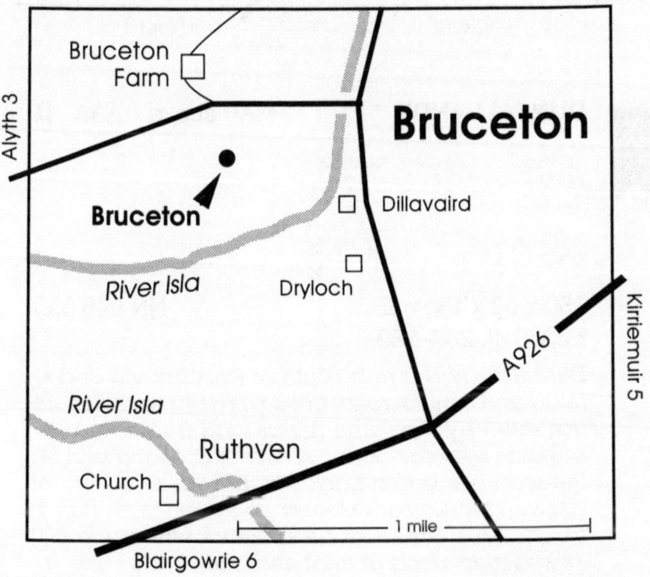

Cargill ΔΔ **A**

91 x 66 x 25cm **E** NO 148 362

ECMS III, 283–284

This stone stands at the corner of a rockery close to the front of Balholmie House, which is on the west side of the A93 about eight miles north of Perth. There is no sign at the entrance drive to the house, but Balholmie Farm, which is on the other side of the road and less than two hundred metres further on, is signed. Permission to see the stone should be asked at the house. The stone once stood in a plantation wall at NO 160 345.

The stone is an apparently intact slab incised on its north face with a finely decorated vertical **rectangle**, and a later addition (a small rectangle at the top of a vertical line) to its left. Despite the stone's being lichened most of the symbol's details can be made out – most easily when the sun is low in the west.

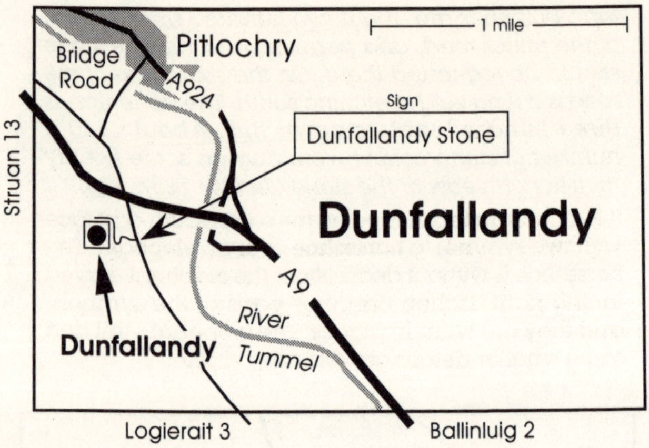

DUNFALLANDY MAP above ΔΔΔ **D**

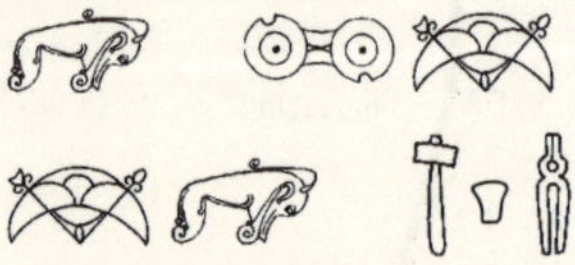

150 x 66 x 13cm **E** NN 946 565
ECMS III, 286–289

Dunfallandy is a mile south of Pitlochry via Bridge Road and a minor road. (It can also be reached from the south by the same minor road from the A827 opposite Logierait Hotel.) A Historic Scotland sign on the road points to a track which leads to a flight of steps up Mausoleum Mound, on top of which stands the stone. It is in a stone structure with huge but locked glass doors at front and back.

Although the stone is said to have come from an old chapel (?NH 90 61) near Killiecrankie (Stuart 1856, 15) and to have later been moved (ECMS III, 286–287) to behind Dunfallandy Cottage (NN 950 560) it is probable that these reports are inaccurate. The stone, *Clach an t'Sagairt* or 'The Priest's Stone', was standing on Mausoleum Mound when it was surveyed in 1863 (and in 1898 and 1938) and is earlier referred to, in the *New Statistical Account* (1845), as "the stone of Dunfallandy, which was long the object of much superstitious attention of the natives." It was even then "much sunk" into the ground. As Mausoleum Mound is not only a burial site but also the site of an ancient chapel it is very likely that the mound was the stone's original site. Nor does it seem that the stone was ever moved.

A great equal-armed cross, with a square centre and on a long shaft, fills one face of the stone. Bosses and key pattern or whorls decorate the arms, and around the cross and shaft are beasts and angels.

The reverse is framed by two beast-headed and fish-tailed serpents, and in its upper part two men sit facing each other. They wear long gowns or robes and are seated in elaborate chairs, and between them a small cross rests on a legged pedestal. Perhaps this scene represents the meeting of Saint Anthony and Saint Paul (Henderson 1967, 148–149), but the two may be Picts. The man on the left has a single symbol, an **elephant**, above his head. The one on the right has in front of him a pair of symbols comprising a **double-disc** over a **crescent and V-rod**.

In the stone's centre is a figure on horseback. Not only are there two symbols before him, a **crescent and V-rod** over an **elephant**, but below is a great set of smith's tools, a **hammer**, an **anvil** and a pair of **pincers**. The tools may be a mark of additional status. It is also to be noted that the horseman shares a symbol with each of the two seated figures. Perhaps he was related to both.

FOWLIS WESTER 1 ΔΔ A

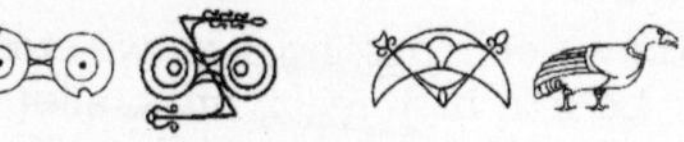

314 x 84 x 15cm E NN 928 241
ECMS III, 289–290

This stone once stood in the middle of Fowlis Wester, five miles east of Crieff, but is now in Fowlis Wester Parish Kirk. A replica has been erected on its former site, which is quite close to the church. The replica is excellent, and many details are much clearer than those on the slab proper. The latter is well-lit, but a light near the top makes it hard to see the very top of the reverse face. The replica stands with the cross-face to the west.

The Fowlis Wester stone is the tallest known symbol stone and is further unique in that the horizontal arms of its cross project beyond its edges. All four arms are rectangular, with square-cut re-entrants where they meet, and the cross has a square centre adorned with nine great bosses. The horizontal arms are decorated with key-pattern, there is some interlace on the shaft and there are parts of various animals below this, but the rest of the face is so weathered that little else can be made out.

The details of the worn reverse are slightly clearer. Near the top is a **double-disc and Z-rod** with rimmed discs, the left-hand disc containing seven bosses, and with a V-shape or flight at the end of the Z-rod's lower arm. The upper arm is missing. Above the symbol is what may be a smaller **double-disc**, now a plain relief shape, and below are various figures or groups all one above the other and all carved from right to left. The upper three are the remains of a horseman, a large but headless hound and a pair of horsemen, one of whom has a hawk perched on his outstretched arm. Below the hawk-bearing horseman is a cow with a bell tied to its neck, the cow led by one long-gowned man and followed by six more. The six, who are bearded, march abreast and carry small square shields. The horsemen, all of whom are bearded, have long and wide saddle-cloths shaped to lie beneath their legs. Below the figures are two symbols side by side, the left-hand a **crescent and V-rod** and the other an **eagle**. The crescent is rimmed and whorl-decorated and lies over the V-rod, the ends of which are missing. The eagle is no more than an outline. Below these symbols a lion consumes a man.

GASK ΔΔ B

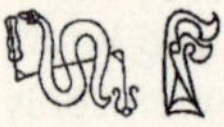

184 x 109 x 23cm **E** NO 138 194

ECMS III, 290–291

The 'Bore Stone', as it is known, once stood in a field near Gask House (NN 996 189), some miles east of Perth. It now stands beside Moncrieffe House, which is three miles south of the city, the entrance drive being on the east side of the A912 a mile before Bridge of Earn. Permission to look at the stone should be asked at the house.

The stone, the top of which is missing, has two cross-faces. The crosses, both in high relief, are similar in design with long shafts and great rings of glory. Their semicircular re-entrants are cut right through the stone and correspond exactly.

The cross on the north face is very worn and the carvings about it almost obliterated, but on the other face more can be seen. Animal and other figures, including two centaurs, are carved to the left of the shaft, and to the right are other animals, two horsemen and two symbols, all in relief and from right to left. A **serpent and Z-rod**, its curlicued rod-ends apparently similar, is above the upper horseman, while behind him is a two-headed **flower**.

Keillor Δ C

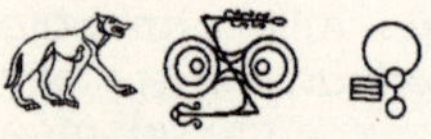

198 x 86 x 30cm **E** NO 273 398

ECMS III, 207–208

Three miles south-east of Coupar Angus by the A923 is a crossroads from which the road to the right leads to Collace and the left to Newtyle. Two and a half miles along the Newtyle road is the entrance to High Keillor Farm and on the roadside opposite is a small mound crowned with a symbol stone. The mound is the stone's original site. In it cists and bones were found (Stuart 1856, xxv).

On the convex south-east face of this natural pillar, are the remains of a **wolf** symbol above a **double-disc and Z-rod.** Below these is most of a rimmed **mirror** and perhaps part of a **comb**. All are very worn. Romilly Allen's drawing shows the wolf to be snarling but there is no sign of this now. It has a pointed snout with no trace of open jaws. The double-disc and Z-rod is of a fairly standard pattern, each disc rimmed and with a smaller dotted circle in the centre and the bar concave-sided and containing a narrower bar. The rod is spear-pointed but without floriations. Its other end is indistinct.

Figure 15

(?)Wolf: Keillor (PER) (after ECMS fig.224)

Logierait Church — NN 967 520

Logierait is on the A827, which crosses the Tummel beside Ballinluig on the A9, and the church is not far beyond Logierait Hotel. Logierait 1 stands outside the church and Logierait 2 is inside. A board beside the steps down to the church tells where keys are available. Requested entry times are 1000–1600 – except when services are being conducted. The churchyard is open at all times.

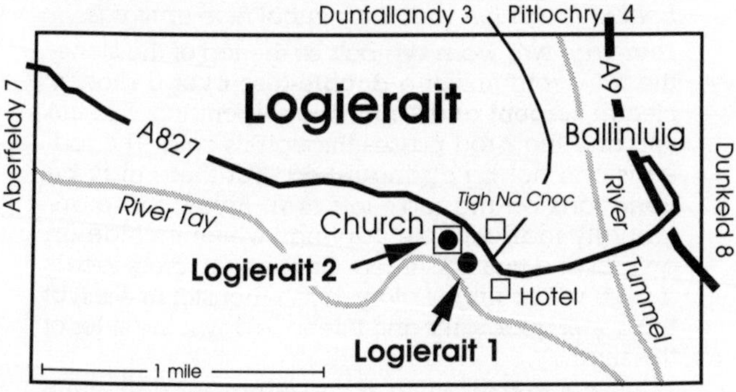

LOGIERAIT 1 125 x 58 x 11cm **O** ΔΔΔ **D**

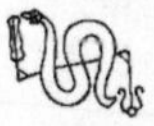

ECMS III, 291–292

Logierait 1, a partly-shaped stone with some of its top and right side missing, was discovered in the churchyard.

On the south-south-east face is most of a small cross in heavy relief on a plain rimmed background. On the reverse, more of which is lost, is part of a spear-carrying horseman who rides from right to left. He is long-cloaked, and his horse, which has a disproportionately large head, has a full bridle. Below the figure is a single symbol, a large-headed serpent looping to the left with a straight and spearheaded rod through its coils. Behind the spearhead are forward-facing curlicues, and the butt is a curlicued ball-end. This unique symbol is presumably a late version of the **serpent and Z-rod**.

Figure 16

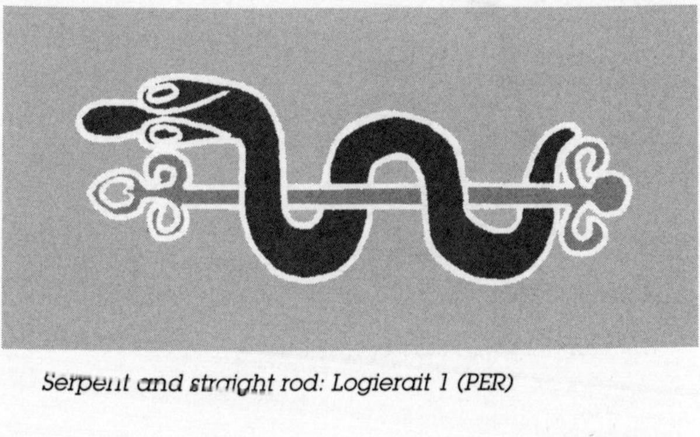

Serpent and straight rod: Logierait 1 (PER)

LOGIERAIT 2 168 x 52 x 14cm **O** Δ **D**

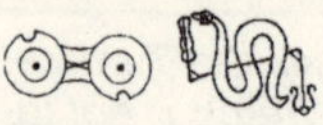

Robertson 1989

Logierait 2, a shaped slab, was found some years ago in the churchyard by Niall Robertson of the Pictish Arts Society and was investigated in 1989. After the slab had been turned over it was found to be a symbol stone. It is now inside the church, lying behind the pulpit with the symbol face upwards.

There are two worn symbols at the top of the stone, the faint remains of a **double-disc** over a slightly clearer **serpent and Z-rod**. The serpent loops to the left, and the Z-rod passes through its coils. The rod-ends can not be distinguished, but there may be floriations on the rod's left arm. Below these are virtually indiscernible carvings which include an animal and two horsemen. On the worn cross-face is a cross with a ring of glory, a fish-monster in each of the upper quadrants and interlace down the sides of the shaft.

There are various plans for the future display of the stones. Up-to-date information can be had from the Minister, the Rev Irene Miller, at 01887 840251. Donations to assist the stones' display should be made out to 'Pictish Stone Account' and sent to Strathtay Manse, Pitlochry, PH9 0PG.

Longforgan ΔΔ **A**

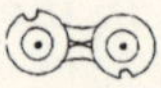

20 x 25 x 11cm. **O** NO 310 300

Taylor 1966

This fragment is in the back of the church in Longforgan, which is six miles west of Dundee by the A90. It was found in a nearby field, at NO 306 299.

It appears to have been part of a shaped and dressed slab, but its one symbol, most of a very small **double-disc**, is incised.

Figure 17

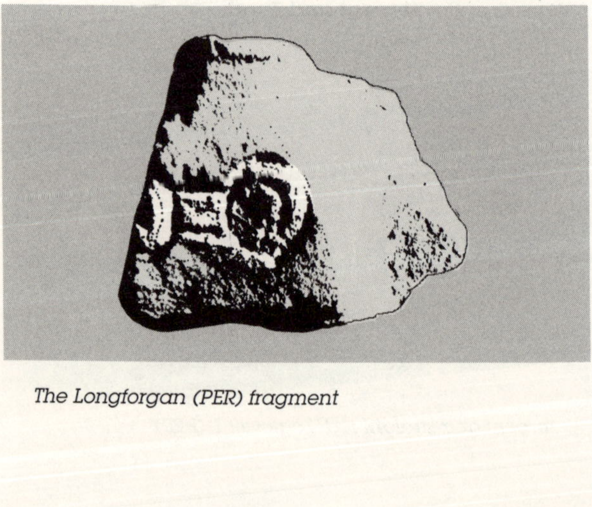

The Longforgan (PER) fragment

MEIGLE MUSEUM

Dundee Road, Meigle, PH12 8SB **B**
01828 640612

April–Sep	Daily	0930–1230
		1330–1800
	Sunday	1400–1800
Oct/Nov	*Autumn Gold* special opening	
	Mon–Wed	0930–1600
	Thursday	0930–1230
	Saturday	0930–1600
	Sunday	1400–1600
	£1.20; pen/child 75p; conc 60p	

This Historic Scotland Museum contains a large collection of Pictish stones found in or close to Meigle's old church. The stones are well displayed, and the custodians are extremely helpful.

MEIGLE 1 182 x 103 x 18cm O

ECMS III, 296–297 (1993 edn figs 310a & b face p.295)

On one face of this shaped slab is a long-shafted cross in high relief. About it are beasts and monsters, some intertwined. On the other face are symbols and figures. There are cup-marks in the base.

The symbols are in two distinct sets. A huge **salmon** swims across the top of the stone, below it is an equally large **serpent and Z-rod** and below that a massive **mirror-and-comb**. Under the salmon is a pair of smaller symbols, a (?)**deer's head** and an **elephant**. Between them is a small triquetra knot.

The salmon is a fine example, and the serpent is as natural – although the Z-rod, a true Z on its side, has virtually similar ends, both curlicued ball-shapes. The mirror, which lies on its side, is rimmed and has a boss-ended bar handle, and the comb is double-sided with very clear teeth. Although horse-like the head could be the head of a deer. Like most of the deer's head symbols it has spirals at its neck-base, and it looks to the right as do all but one. The elephant is simply-carved. The symbols and the cross place this stone early in the Class II series.

Below the symbols are various worn figures. Five are human, of different sizes and all on horseback. They ride upwards and to the left in two columns. Although there are odd figures between and behind them (an angel with widespread wings, a kneeling camel and a strange beast with coiled body – very like one on the other face) the riders are hunting. No deer can be seen, but behind the largest mounted figure is a hound. Although now indistinct, the mounted figure is carved full face and rides side-saddle. It is a lady. Perhaps the principal set of symbols with its massive mirror-and-comb are hers.

The stone once stood in the churchyard, and beneath it was a skeleton (Stuart 1856, xxiv). Unfortunately there is no record as to whether it was a male or female skeleton.

MEIGLE 3 40 x 35 x 6cm **O**

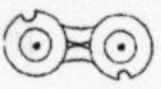

ECMS III, 298–299

This fragment, which was found built into the church wall, is the upper part of a small cross-slab. Its one surviving symbol, half a vertical **double-disc**, is on the cross-face. Symbols on Class II stones are usually on the reverse and are carved on a cross-face only if the back of the stone is unworked or if there are two cross-faces. The back of this stone is carved but contains only a figure.

A bearded Pict mounted on a small splay-eared horse rides from right to left. He carries a long spear, which is incised, he wears a pointed shoe and he sits on a saddle-cloth with a pleated fringe. Behind him projects the scabbard of a short sword. Although something of a caricature the figure is a valuable close-up of a mounted Pict. Little detail remains of the bridle or the man's dress, but the way that the saddle-cloth is shaped to lie under his leg can be clearly seen and it is as clear that there is no stirrup.

MEIGLE 4 152 x 89 x 15cm **E**

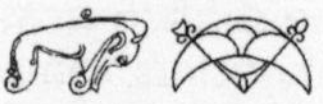

ECMS III, 299–300

The upper and lower parts only of this stone were found, both built into a kiln near the church. The missing segment has been replaced with cement. On one face is a cross filled with interlace and surrounded by long-tailed long-necked beasts, interlaced serpents and the remains of a long-haired Pict who grasps the forelegs of a rearing horse. On the other are the symbols as well as more beasts and serpents and two mounted Picts. The Picts, both wearing short fringed cloaks and with swords at their sides, sit on shaped saddle-cloths one at least of which must be a true saddle. The upper rider's is over a long and wide saddle-cloth proper, and hanging from the saddle is a shaped flap that lies under his leg. He also has a spear. An incised spearhead and some of the shaft can be seen projecting in front of his horse. Below him are the symbols, an **elephant** over a **crescent and V-rod**. The elephant is fairly standard in pattern (and has additional fore and rear paws), but is somewhat long-legged and listless in appearance. The crescent is decorated with interlocking whorls, and the V-rod has the usual ends, the left flighted, the right with an arrowhead and both curlicued, but there is one perhaps late feature. The arrow-headed arm of the V-rod runs under the crescent, and the flighted arm is crossed by some of the whorl decoration.

Symbol stones in Historic Scotland's museum of early carved stones at St Vigeans, Arbroath, Angus are described on pages 69 and 70

MEIGLE 5 76 x 53 x 16cm **E**

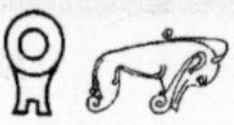

ECMS III, 300–301

Part of the top of this small stone, which was found built into the kiln, has been damaged. On the front is most of a high-relief equal-armed cross with ringed re-entrants. It is decorated with fret work, key pattern and whorls and is on a round-topped broad base which is filled with circular interlace and adorned with deer's heads. In the quadrants are strange beasts and a bird which is swallowing a serpent.

On the reverse is the lower part of a horseman who wears a shoe and whose saddle, which is vertically pleated, has a wide but carefully shaped flap. His horse's tail is cropped, a feature almost unique among the horses on Pictish stones.

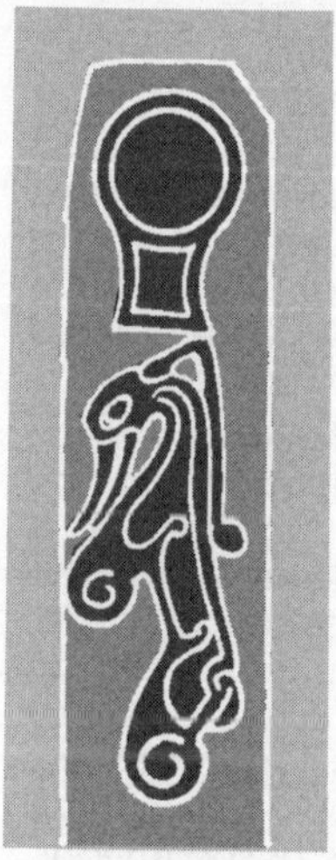

Figure 18

Meigle 5 (PER): symbols on the side (after ECMS fig.314c)

The symbols are incised on a side of the stone. Both vertical, they are a simple rimmed **mirror-case** over an **elephant**, which is well-shaped but has untypical internal decoration. The cross-face occupies more of the stone's height than do the symbols or the horseman, under whom is a considerable plain base. It is possible that the cross, which seems late in pattern compared to the figure and symbols, was a later addition. Its very high relief mayhave been used to obliterate earlier carvings.

MEIGLE 6 56 x 43 x 12cm **O**

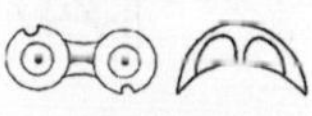

ECMS III, 301–302

This fragment, found built into the old church, is the centre part of a small cross-slab. On the front is some of the cross-shaft and on the reverse a small horseman and a **double-disc** over a **crescent**. The caricature-like style of the figure and the clumsiness of the symbols indicate that this is a late Class II stone.

MEIGLE 7 43 x 53 x 8cm **O**

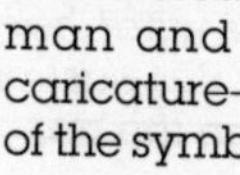

ECMS III, 302–303

Also found built into the church, this fragment is the upper part of a small cross-slab. On the reverse is a **double-disc and Z-rod** (a true Z) of late and corrupt style and part of a double-sided **comb**.

PERTH MUSEUM AND ART GALLERY

78 George Street, Perth, PH1 5LB **A**
Tel: 01738 632488

Mon–Sat 1000–1700
Free

The St Madoes slab is in the entrance hall; the others are in 'The Time of Our Lives' display, under 'Power and Authority' and 'Transport and Communication'.

GELLYBURN 2 80 x 25 x 10cm **O**

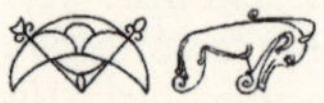

Calder 1951

Found in the wall of a house (NO 094 392) at Gellyburn, Murthly, this is the lower part of a small cross-slab; it was in two pieces but they have been joined. On one face is all of a cross-shaft and parts of two re-entrants which were cut right through the stone between the arms of the cross; there are also the remains of a cross on the face on display.

This second cross was composed of interlace within a circular rim. Below it is a **crescent and V-rod** and below that an **elephant**, both in pseudo-relief. Under them is a roughly-worked irregular base. The crescent, rimmed and decorated with central whorls, is well-shaped, as is the elephant which has an additional rear 'paw' and incised scrolls within its body. The symbols are of early Class II type, but there is certainly one corrupt feature – the V-rod ends are similar, both being curlicued arrow or spearheads. The pierced re-entrants are, however, unusual and indicate a later date for this beautifully carved stone.

Inchyra 160 x 40 x 10cm **O**

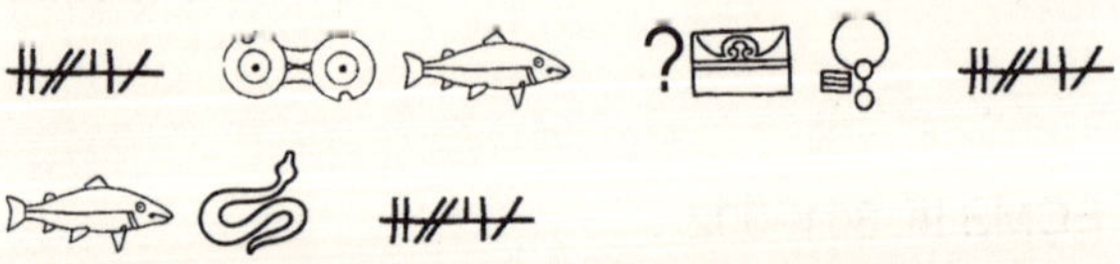

Wainwright 1961

This stone, which was found at NO 190 212 during ploughing, lay just below the surface in what had been the park of Inchyra House a few miles east of Perth. Below the stone was a grave, and on the stone are three sets of symbols.

The stone, which is set on its side in a double-sided case, is a flat sandstone slab narrower at one end and with some of the broader end broken off. At the narrow end is a notched **double-disc** over a leaping **salmon**. Both are incised with rounded grooves that were probably first pocked out. On the edge of the stone to the left of (above) these symbols is an Ogam which, read towards the narrow end, is INEHHETESTIETD. It continues along the end as INNE.

On the same face but near the broad end and the other way up is the pocked outline of a **mirror** with the remains of a similarly-worked symbol (?**rectangle**) above it. The upper part of this other symbol is missing. There is also part of a **comb** on a fragment. These symbols were never finished. There is also a faintly-scratched Ogam on the edge to the right of (above) the mirror. There is another poorly-cut Ogam on the edge opposite.

On the other face of the broad end is the third set of symbols, which are partly hidden by the adjoining case and a label. A headless **salmon** swims off the broken stone, and beside it is a **serpent**, its head stretched upwards and its tail curled. This pair's incisions are V-shaped grooves. On the face beside the two is a short Ogam of strokes which are also V-cut. It reads SETU.

It is likely that the Inchyra Stone was first set up with the broad end as its base and the stone incised with only the double-disc and salmon and their related Ogams. Not so very long after that the stone may have been taken down and the symbol set including the mirror started – and its scratched Ogam. It was presumably after this that the salmon and serpent set was cut – and its V-cut Ogam. The stone would then have been re-erected with the double-disc and the salmon submerged in the ground. They are its clearest symbols.

The stone was found as the capstone of a grave, probably a Bronze Age burial, and may have been placed there in relatively recent times, after the grave had been disturbed. As there was no trace of most of the stone's broken-off pieces at the grave site the stone may have come from elsewhere.

ST MADOES 1 175 x 91 x 20cm E

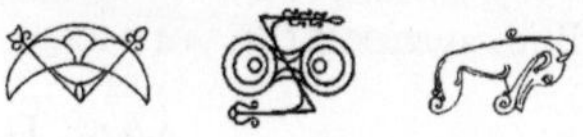

ECMS III, 292–296

This Class II cross-slab came from beside the Church of St Madoes (NO 197 212). First recorded as lying in the churchyard, it was re-erected in 1853 in a roofed verandah against the outer wall of the church. In 1991 it came to the Museum.

The stone's front face, most of which is carved in high relief, is filled by a square-bossed cross with a ring of glory and with climbing animals about the cross and shaft. On the reverse, which now can only be seen in the mirror behind the stone, are (or were) three symbols and three horsemen, each in lower relief and each in a separate panel. Almost all the panels are now damaged. A crack or fissure begins at the base of the top panel and spreads, angling downwards and to the right, through most of the others. The horsemen's panels are in column, and two of the symbolled panels are side by side below them. In the left is a very faint **crescent and V-rod**, and in the right, which is now flaked away, was a **double-disc and Z-rod**. Under these is a panel containing an **elephant** which is not only very worn but lacks its hind legs.

There is no apparent principal figure on the stone. The three separately panelled figures are more or less similar in size. As the symbols are also separately-panelled they may be the symbols of the three men, one symbol to each rider.

The horsemen are squat figures on elongated horses and seem rather caricature-like, but despite the damage the detail of some of their horse harness is easy to make out. The horses' bridles and reins, including the bit-rings and joining-rings, are clear, and so too are the long-flapped saddles. It is also clear that the riders are stirrup-less. Even at the time of this late stone the Picts may have not known of the stirrup. An additional point of interest is that the horse of the uppermost rider has a cropped tail.

Peterhead Δ **D**

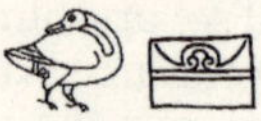

150 x 75 x 90cm **E** NN 924 098
Calder 1947

This stone stands in a field bounded on the north by a short stretch of the old A9 to Perth (alongside the new road) and on the east by the A823 into Glen Eagles. The old road can be entered from the A823 or from the Peterhead Farm road off the new A9. Permission to enter the field should be asked at the farm. The stone stands on what may be a submerged low cairn.

Incised on the north-north-west face are the symbols, a **goose** over a small **rectangle**. The goose is carved from left to right but peers backwards – as does the goose on the Easterton of Roseisle stone in the Museum of Scotland. The rectangle is laterally divided into three parts by parallel lines and is without other decoration. Both symbols are very faint.

ROSSIE ΔΔΔ **D**

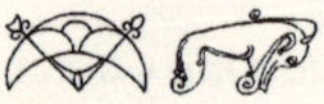

168 x 116 x 30cm **E** NO 292 308
ECMS III, 306–308 (1993 edn figs 322a and b face p.305)

This Class II stone is another of those with two cross-faces. Found originally in the churchyard it stands in the old church about half a mile east of Rossie Priory and can only be visited with permission. Rossie Priory itself is just over a mile north and east of Inchture, along the first turning to the right off the B953 which runs north from the A90 eight miles west of Dundee.

The symbolled cross-face is carved in low relief with an interlace and key-pattern-filled cross within a wide border of interlace. The stone's principal figure, a mounted Pict, is in the lower arm of the cross, and below him are two Pictish riders within the shaft and two more to its right. Above the right-hand pair are two hounds, and in the upper quadrants are a winged angel full-face and a running figure who clasps two large birds by their necks. To the shaft's left are the symbols – above a two-headed beast. The upper is a vertical **crescent and V-rod** and the lower an **elephant**. Although raised in relief both symbols are plain, with some details incised, and are very standard in form – but the V-rod itself is not. While the right end is broad-bladed like the head of an arrow the other has a curlicued ball-end.

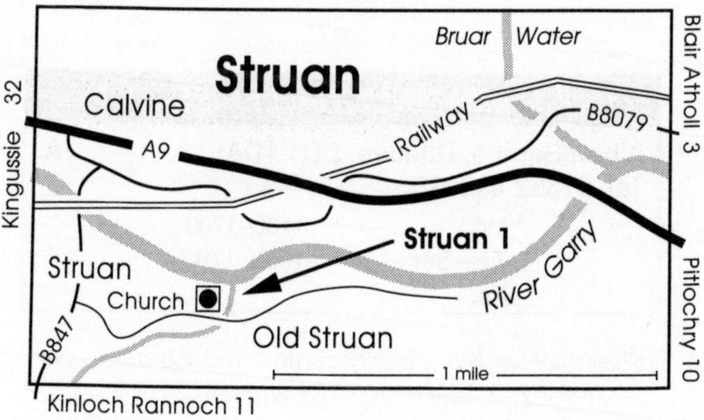

Struan 1 MAP above ΔΔ **B**

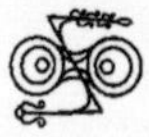 ?

132 x 80 x 11cm **O** NN 809 653

ECMS III, 285–286

This stone is in Struan Church south of Calvine, which is about four miles west of Blair Atholl by the A9. It was found in the churchyard.

Figure 19

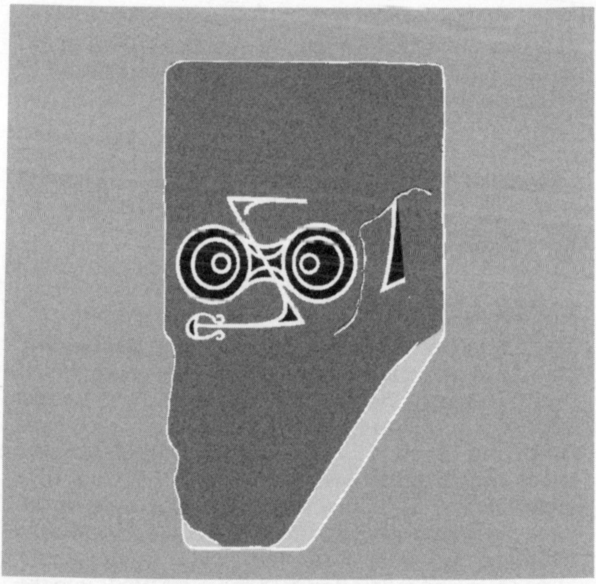

Struan 1 (PER) (after ECMS fig.303)

Incised on one face is a **double-disc and Z-rod** and the remains of another symbol. The discs are rimmed and have smaller eccentric discs within them. The rod is without floriations, and the upper end, once pointed, is now plain. At the other end are two long curlicues which meet to form a ball-end.

5 CITY OF DUNDEE

MCMANUS GALLERIES

Albert Square, Dundee, DD1 1DA **A**
Tel: 01382 432020

Mon	1100–1700
Tue–Sat	1000–1700
Free	

The museum is in the city centre, and the stones are on display in its archaeology section.

Aberlemno 5 ANG 173 x 52 x 36cm **O**

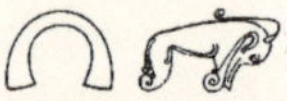

Boyd 1962

This stone is a natural pillar incised with two symbols, a **horseshoe** decorated with two curving lines that end in spirals and below it a slightly larger **elephant**. The elephant has a somewhat stubby tail but seems otherwise to be a good example, one with an extra hind 'paw'. Parts of it have been defaced by score-marks.

The stone was found during ploughing at Flemington farm at NO 524 556, about thirty metres east of Aberlemno Church.

Dunnichen ANG * 136 x 69 x 25cm **O**

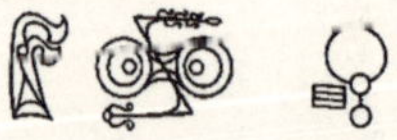

ECMS III, 206–207

This pillar stone is incised with a **flower**, a **double-disc and Z-rod** and a **mirror-and-comb**. The flower, which has two heads hanging to the right, is the most beautiful of all the flower symbols. The double-disc and Z-rod below it has almost uniquely-decorated discs, each centred with a small dotted disc surrounded by seven whorls. It also has an exceptionally wide joining bar (and an oddly-placed narrower bar within), but the Z-rod is more typical. The upper arm is floriated and spear-pointed, and the lower ends in something like a curlicued ball. Under the Z-rod is a small mirror with a single-sided and clearly-toothed comb.

This fine stone was found in 1805 on the lower slopes of Dunnichen Hill, at about NO 516 496, and "a stone coffin and bones were got below it" (Jervise 1857, 189). A replica now stands at the road junction beside Dunnichen Church (NO 509 488).

** On display at the Meffan Institute, Forfar (see p.67)*

Strathmartine 1 ANG 95 x 90 x 22cm **E**

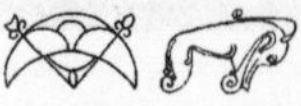

ECMS III, 208-209

This irregular slab once stood in a field at NO 374 361.

The upper symbol is a **crescent and V-rod,** the crescent decorated with spirals and curved lines and the left end of the V-rod curlicued and flighted. The right end is missing. Below is a fine **elephant** the body of which contains no less than three scrolls. It also has additional fore and hind 'paws', both minuscule in size.

TEALING ANG 72 x 24 x 18cm **O**

ECMS III, 234-235, Hutcheson 1911, 420-423

This fragment, the lower right part of a small cross-slab, was once built into an outside wall of Tealing Church (NO 403 379) and later lay in the churchyard.

On one face is some of the right arm and side of the shaft and base of a small cross. The shaft has traces of key-pattern, and beside it is a fish-monster – which is probably not a symbol. What is more likely to be a symbol was discovered only after the stone was removed from the wall. On the reverse is the head of a peculiar **elephant** symbol looking left.

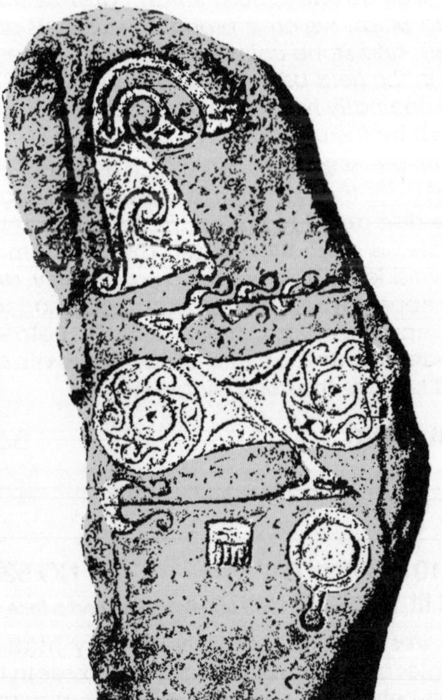

Figure 20

Dunnichen (ANG): Now on long-term loan to Angus Council, it will be displayed in the Meffan Institute (see p.67) from February 1997.

6 ANGUS

ABERLEMNO

Aberlemno is midway between Forfar and Brechin on the B9134. At the time of writing, Aberlemno 1 and 3 stand at the roadside near the village hall and Aberlemno 2 is in the churchyard, standing near the west gable of the church. Historic Scotland propose to protect these stones by removing them to a stable environment indoors. A study is being undertaken to assess the possibility of housing the stones in a new building on a site beside the village hall. While the stones remain outside, however, they can not be seen during winter as they are protected by wooden boxes from October to April. A fibreglass cast of Aberlemno 2 is on display at the Meffan Institute in Forfar (see p.67).

Aberlemno 1 ΔΔΔ C

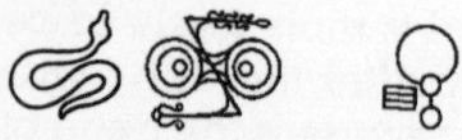

180 x 90 x 23cm **E** NO 523 559
ECMS III, 205 (1993 edn fig.221 faces p.203)

There was at one time a small cairn beside this leaning pillar, which is probably still in its original position, and stone coffins and human bones were found in the field behind it (Jervise 1857, 192). That it may originally have been an older standing stone is shown by the cup-marks on its base.

Near the top of the north-west face a deeply incised **serpent** loops from left to right, and under it is a large **double-disc and Z-rod** at an angle. In the centre of each disc is a smaller dotted disc, the long and concave-sided joining bar has a bar within it, and the Z-rod's upper arm is floriated and spearheaded. The lower ends with a curlicued ball. Below is a **mirror-and-comb**. the mirror rimmed and with a twin-bossed handle, the comb single-sided.

ABERLEMNO 3 ΔΔΔ C

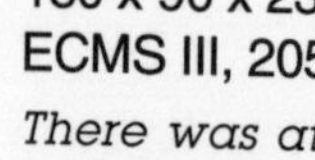

282 x 101 x 28cm **E** NO 523 559
ECMS III, 214-215 (1993 edn figs 228a and b face p.211)

On its west face is a cross with very high relief rectangles on the arms and rimmed bosses in the re-entrants between the arms. A greater boss forms the centre of the cross, and about it is an interlace-filled ring of glory. Key-pattern decorates the long shaft, more key-pattern and interlace are on either side, and about the cross and shaft are figures, which include two bowing angels. Its complex yet matching carvings place the stone at earliest at the very end of the eighth century. On the stone's reverse four mounted Picts, each with a shaped saddle, hunt deer with hounds, two on foot blow long horns, and in the lower panels a centaur bears an axe and tree and David rends the lion's jaw. David may also be the figure who stands with a spear and small shield in front of the lower horsemen. At the top of the stone are the symbols, a huge **crescent and V-rod** above a **double-disc and Z-rod**. Both are ornate but are well-shaped and not unduly corrupt. The scene and symbols on the Hilton of Cadboll stone (see p.34) seem to be copied from this slab.

Aberlemno 3 could also be in its original position. In 1569 it apparently stood where it is now, then "with ane cairn of stones beside it".

ABERLEMNO 2 ΔΔΔ A

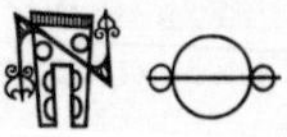

198 x 127 x 29cm **E** NO 522 556
ECMS III, 209–214 (1993 edn fig.227a faces p.207)

On the west face of this cross-slab is a long-shafted cross in very high relief and decorated with interlace and key-pattern less fine than that on the roadside slab. The re-entrants, in one of which is a hole bored through the stone, are rimmed, the outer parts of the rims also forming a ring of glory. The cross's round centre is filled with whorls, and about the cross are hinds and intertwined beasts. On the other face, in a great panel below the symbols, is a battle scene. The battle is possibly the Battle of Dunnichen (or Nechtansmere) between the Picts and the Northumbrians, which was fought in 685 AD. On the left are the Picts, who are bareheaded with long queues of hair, on the right the helmeted enemy. At the top a helmeted horseman gallops to the right, apparently fleeing from the Pictish rider behind him, who could represent the Pictish left-flank cavalry. Behind the fleeing figure are a shield and a sword, presumably his discarded weapons. Immediately below the mounted Pict is a battle-line of Pictish infantry, its ranks shown by two spearmen with a sword-bearer in front of them. The three advance steadily, despite the attack of the enemy centre cavalry, represented by a helmeted horse-man about to hurl a spear. Below them the Pictish right-flank cavalry, again shown by one mounted man, rides forward to meet the charge of the enemy left, another helmeted rider ready to throw his spear.

To the right of this pair a great carrion bird (probably a raven) strikes at a fallen warrior. He has no horse but is helmeted and wears a split hauberk, indicating that he must once have been mounted. Perhaps he was the leader of the enemy, the Northumbrian king Ecgfrith who was killed on the field of battle – and a great host with him.

The Northumbrians are identified by their helmets which have nasals and mail neck-guards and are of a similar type to the Coppergate Helmet from York, which although found during the Viking excavations is Northumbrian.

Above the scene are the symbols, a **divided rectangle and Z-rod** with a **triple-disc** beside it. The divided rectangle and Z-rod may be a late version, but this does not mean that the Battle Stone was carved very much later than the Battle depicted on it. This symbol did not survive long into the Class II period, there being only one other on a Class II stone. The Aberlemno symbol may be late but only in comparison to the Class I majority. In any case these are all on stones far north of Aberlemno; it is distant enough from its Class I fellows to have lost in accuracy. Besides, its arrow-like Z-rod is not corrupt and much of the symbol is incised or in low relief – as is the triple-disc to its right.

This stone was once set very deeply into the ground in the kirkyard, perhaps because earth from later graves had been piled around it. It is also possible that the stone originally stood beside the roadside stones; the hole in it may have been made so that drag-ropes and lifting ropes could be attached for its move and re-erection.

BALLUDERON (*St Martin's Stone*) MAP ΔΔ **D**

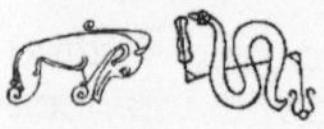

116 x 70 x 18cm **E** NO 375 376
ECMS III, 215–216

Leave the A90 Dundee ring road at Downfield roundabout, go through Bridgefoot and pass Wynton farm. The stone is 150 metres north of the sharp bend half a mile further on. It can also be easily reached leaving the A90 at Tealing. Permission should be sought at South Balluderon.

The stone, which faces east, is the lower part of a cross-slab carved on one face only. Of the cross only some of the high-relief and rimmed base remain,

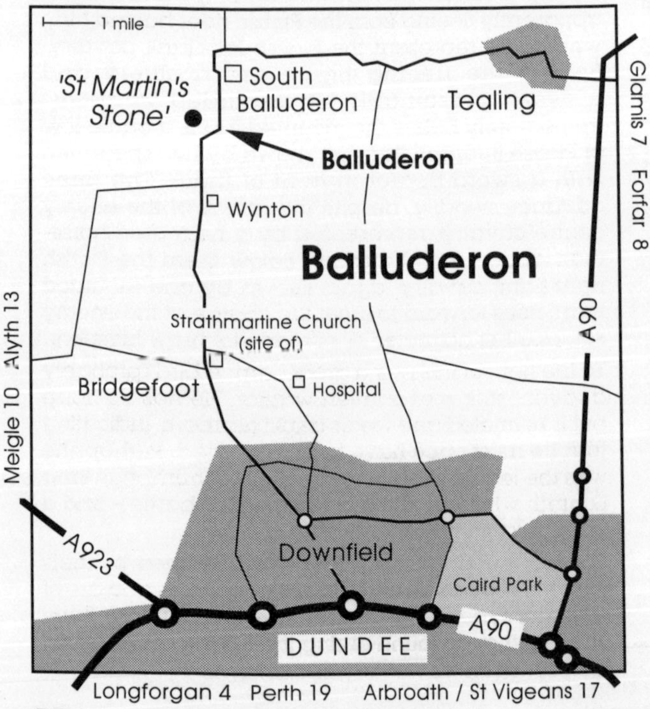

within which is a now-headless horseman riding from right to left. His leg and foot rest on a wide shaped saddle-cloth and behind his leg is what may be a sword scabbard. Below the base are the remains of another mounted figure and two symbols, all carved in lower relief. In front of the second horseman is a slender **elephant** and below that a **serpent and Z-rod**. Both ends of the Z-rod are curlicued, and the upper is spear-pointed.

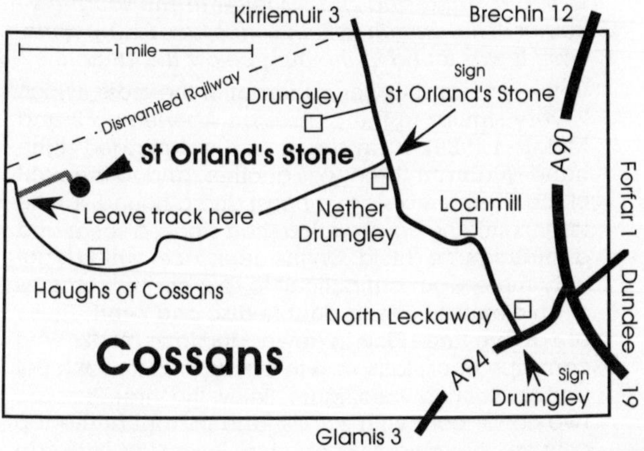

COSSANS (*St Orland's Stone*) MAP ΔΔ **D**

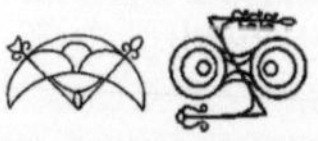

236 x 71 x 25cm **E** NO 401 500

ECMS III, 216–218

The best approach to St Orland's Stone is by the Drumgley road which runs north from North Leckaway on the A94 a mile and a half south-west of Forfar. The route is signposted and the stone is fairly prominent, standing in an enclosure on a low mound about four hundred metres to the east of the track, but there is no footpath to it. Five short cists containing skeletons were found close to the stone (Jervise 1857, 248–249).

The stone, which was broken and pinned together, faces east, and bears a high-relief cross with a ring of glory within a high-relief frame.

The reverse, in a frame that ends at the top with snapping monster heads, is divided into five panels. Above two beasts in the bottom panel is a ship sailing right with five long-haired figures behind its sail and a faint steering oar at the stern. In the second panel are two riders with hounds, two more riders are in the panel above, and in the fourth panel, where the stone was broken, is what appears to be a cut out segment. In the fifth are the symbols. These are a **crescent and V-rod** above a **double-disc and Z-rod**. The crescent is whorl-decorated and is over the V-rod, which is standard, its right end curlicued and pointed, the left apparently curlicued and flighted. The decorated double-disc is also over its rod, which is a 'standard' Z-rod, the upper arm spearheaded and floriated, the lower ball-ended and curlicued.

It is possible that the stone will be moved into either Kinnettles Kirk or Glamis Parish Kirk.

EASSIE ΔΔ B

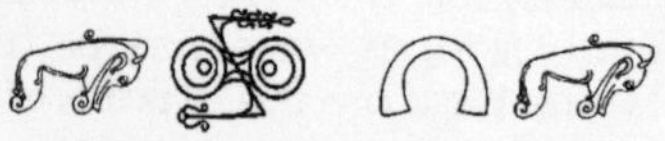

202 x 101 x 23cm **O** NO 353 475

ECMS III, 218–219 (1993 edn figs 231a, b and c face p.217)

This stone stands within the ruins of Eassie Church, which is just off the A94 two miles west of Glamis. It is in a stone and glass shelter in the south-east corner of the church with the cross-face facing north-east. It was found in the burn below the church.

In the left-hand upper quadrant of the cross, which is very similar to the crosses on Aberlemno 2 and Meigle 1 (PER), is an angel, in the damaged right-hand quadrant there was another, and to the right of the shaft are a stag, a beast and a hound. To the left is a striding figure with a short cloak, a spear and a small square shield. On the other face, which is not only more worn but difficult to see, are the remains of an **elephant** over a **double-disc and Z-rod**. These are above three Picts in gowns and long cloaks who carry spears or staffs, and to the right is a tree in a pot and another gowned figure. Below the three Picts are two cows, both with scrolls, and in front of the top cow are the remains of another. Below this little can be seen because of damage to the stone, but above it are parts of more symbols, a **horseshoe** over an **elephant**. Both elephants and all the figures face right. The horseshoe is one of only two on Class II stones, the other being the V-rodded version at Migvie (ABE).

GLAMIS

GLAMIS 1 Δ D

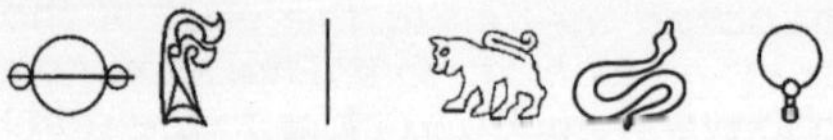

150 x 72 x 14cm **E** NO 394 465

ECMS III, 221 (1993 edn fig.233a faces p.220)

This is a Class I stone reused as a cross-slab. It stands beside a track on the north side of Hunter's Hill, the wooded hill south-east of Glamis. The track runs east-south-east from the A94 at NO 390 467, not far from where the eastern road from the village meets the A94. The stone is about three hundred metres up the track, in a small railed enclosure behind a fence on the left side. It is possible that it will be moved to Glamis Parish Kirk.

The cross, on the east face, has a circular centre and is decorated with interlace and key-pattern. In the left-hand upper quadrant is an angel, and in the damaged right-hand quadrant are two tunic-clad figures, one beast-headed and with an axe, the other with most of its body broken off. To the left of the shaft are two deer and to the right a pair of four-legged three-toed beasts. Below these are two symbols, a **triple-disc** over a single-headed **flower.** The cross and figures are in fairly low relief, the symbols little more than incised. The stone's Class I symbols are on the west face. About halfway up this and slightly to the right are the remains of a faint **beast** symbol incised from left to right, and below it is an upwards-looping **serpent**. Under the serpent's tail are the remains of a plain **mirror**. This had a bar handle with a boss at the upper end. Not all of the mirror (nor all of the flower on the other face) is exposed.

GLAMIS 2 ΔΔΔ **A**

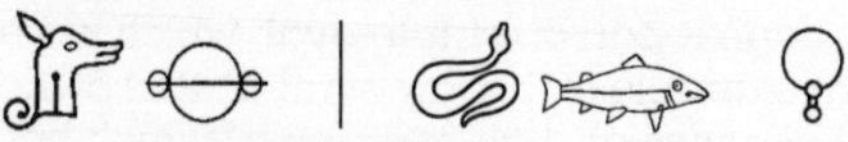

276 x 150 x 24cm **E** NO 386 469
ECMS III, 221–223

This massive stone, the only other known Class I stone reused as a cross-slab, stands in the garden of Glamis Manse. It can be viewed at all reasonable times, but please shut the gate behind you.

The cross, its re-entrants each of three adjacent arcs, is on the relief-carved west face. It is decorated with heavy and some finer interlace and stretches almost to the top of the stone. There is a four-legged three-toed beast above the cross's left arm, and below it is a cauldron out of which project two pairs of human legs. Below this are two tunic-clad figures fightingwith axes. Above the right arm of the cross is a long-haired centaur with two axes. Below it is a **deer's head** above a **triple-disc**. The latter demonstrates that this symbol could indeed be the representation of a cauldron seen from above. The outer rings pass through much smaller rings or collars projecting from the inner – just as a cauldron's suspending rings are attached to its rim. As both symbols are simply carved in the lowest of relief and very like some of their Class I counterparts this face of the stone is an example of early Class II work. (It is also notable that some of the figures and symbols are like some of the carvings on Glamis 1.)

The east face is natural and very irregular, but its symbols, which are incised, are beautifully fitted in between the irregularities – and are beautifully carved. An S-shaped **serpent** writhes up the stone, below it leaps a great **salmon** with a rimmed **mirror** below. There are also a number of earlier cup-marks sunk into the undressed base of the cross-face.

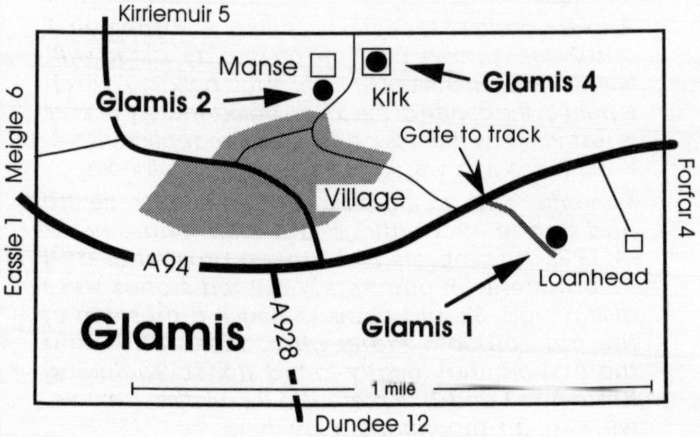

Glamis 4 ΔΔΔ A

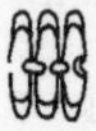

29 x 34 x 5cm **O** NO 387 469

RCAHMS 1994, 21

This fragment, which was found in the manse garden's rockery (NO 386 469), is in the Kirk, in the passage to the right immediately inside the door.

Near the left edge is part of a **triple-oval**, which is the only southern example of this rare symbol. Part of the central oval survives and all of another, which has a circular central decoration linked to the sides by short arcs or 'commas'. Both 'ovals' are straight-sided, and the intact one is flat-topped and flat-bottomed.

Kinblethmont ΔΔΔ B

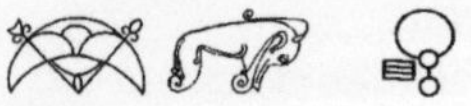

85 x 70 x 21cm **O** NO 641 472

Wainwright 1951

Kinblethmont House is about a mile east of the road that leads north from St Vigeans (see map p.68). The stone is in the entrance hall of this private residence and cannot be seen without the owner's consent. It was found during ploughing nearby, at NO 638 473.

The base of the stone is missing, but on one face are a **crescent and V-rod**, most of a fine **elephant**, most of a rimmed **mirror** and the three-pointed top of a single-sided **comb**. The crescent, which has an almost straight lower arc, is decorated with dome-and-wing pattern, and the left-hand end of its V-rod is flighted, the other pointed. The elephant, which has linked scrolls within its body, has an additional 'forepaw'. At the bottom right of the stone is what may be a cup-mark.

KIRRIEMUIR

Tourist Information Centre			D
1 Cumberland Close, Kirriemuir, DD8 4EF			
Tel: 01575 574097			
Apr/May/Sep	Mon–Sat	1030–1700	
Jun–Aug	Mon–Sat	0930–1700	Free

*Angus Council's fibreglass replicas of **Kirriemuir 1** and **2** (see opposite p.67) are on display, along with Nos.3 and 5, on the upper level of this building, which is right in the centre of the town. Unfortunately access is restricted as there is no lift. Another replica, No.4, is exhibited in a window of the nearby Tolbooth.*

*Kirriemuir was an important Early Christian centre and during excavations in the old churchyard in 1995 a complete but broken cross-slab and 11 fragments of other early carved stones were discovered. Should plans to house a museum in the old Tolbooth materialise, these finds and the five original locally-found stones (including **Kirriemuir 1** and **2**) at present in the Meffan Institute, will form an important display there.*

MEFFAN INSTITUTE

20 West High Street, Forfar, DD8 1BB **B**
Tel: 01307 468813

Mon–Sat 1000–1700
Free

'The Forfar Story', an outstanding permanent display, opened in March 1995. It includes an impressive collection of Early Christian carved stones. The Dunnichen Stone (see p.58) will be exhibited from February 1997.

KIRRIEMUIR 1 58 x 46 x 10cm **O**

ECMS III, 226–227

This stone and Kirriemuir 2 were discovered in 1787 in the foundations of an old church in Kirriemuir and later lay for many years in a cemetery.

On one face, the base and top-left corner of which are missing, is a square-centred and rectangular-armed cross filled with thick interlace and with a figure in each quadrant.

The reverse is divided into two panels, in the upper of which are three human figures. Two, facing one another and clasping a round object, probably represent St Anthony and St Paul in the desert breaking the bread brought to them by the raven. Tho third stands full-face. In the lower panel is an enthroned female figure, also full-face. On one side of her throne is what has been called a 'cased sword' but which may be a loom. On the other is a small upside-down **mirror** with below it a large and vertical double-sided **comb**. There may have been other symbols on the lost lower part of this cross-slab.

KIRRIEMUIR 2 114 x 59 x 11cm **O**

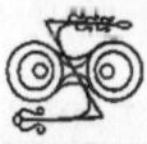

ECMS III, 227–228

This is a larger almost intact slab. Its cross, which is decorated with key-pattern, has two intertwined beasts in the bottom panel of its shaft. Angels are in the upper quadrants, to the shaft's right a stag is being attacked by a bird, beneath them run a hind and two hounds, and to the shaft's left is the figure of a man in a plaid and tunic or kilt. He strides out, his right hand holding what may be the mouth of a sack over his shoulder and his left a wallet and staff or very small square shield and spear. He is either a pilgrim or a Pictish-haired and Pictish-dressed David.

The back of the stone is a single framed panel. In its upper part is a bearded rider with an elaborate hairstyle, a horizontally-pleated plaid over a kilt, and a spear. Behind him is a small and very corrupt **double-disc and Z-rod**, the stone's only symbol. Below him gallops another horseman, with a curling queue of hair and wearing a jacket-like upper garment. He has a shorter spear, which he is about to throw or thrust into a stag running beneath him and being savaged by a hound. Both riders sit on saddles which are long-flapped, shaped to lie under their legs and secured by girths.

Wester Denoon 41 x 35 x 12cm **O**

Atkinson 1994

The stone was found during ploughing at NO 350 434. It may have come from the field dyke and before that from an ancient chapel site close to the field.

It is a small sandstone cross-slab, the top of which has been broken off and the base sheared at an angle. The cross, with rectangular arms, shaft of thick interlace and penannular re-entrants, is complete except for the summit arm, and on either side of the shaft are vertical columns of cross-patterns.

On the reverse is a human figure carved full-face and almost certainly female. The upper part of her head is missing, but the pointed chin is very like the lady's on Kirriemuir 1 and there are traces of a hairstyle on at least one side of her head. More apparent is her dress, a gown with considerably decorated high shoulders and a deep hem of heavy interlace. The gown is wide and conceals her arms and hands, but beneath it her feet can be seen in profile. In its very centre is a huge and long-pinned penannular brooch which closely resembles a seventh-century bronze brooch from Mull. To the left of the figure is a **mirror-and-comb**. The mirror, which is upside-down, is rimmed, has a convex face and has the remains of a boss at the handle-end. The comb, carved vertically below the mirror, is double-sided and wide-toothed. On the other side is a column of interlace, but no other symbols. These may have been on the lost base. This stone brings the total of Class II stones with a mirror-and-comb and a human figure or figures to seven – five with a female figure.

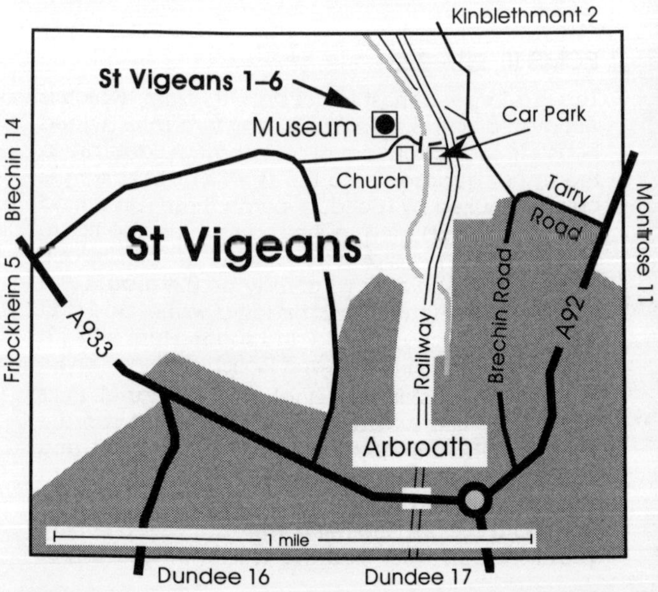

ST VIGEANS MUSEUM

Kirkstyle, St Vigeans, By Arbroath, DD11 4RB **A**
Tel: 01786 450000

Apr–Sep	Mon–Sat	0930–1830
	Sun	1400–1830
	Free	

This small Historic Scotland museum (see map p.68) contains an important collection of carved stones which were found in the 12th-century church and among which are six Class II symbol stones or fragments. It is a mile up the Brechin Road from the A92 in Arbroath. There is a Historic Scotland sign at the junction of the road leading to the carpark. A key is available from the nearby keyholder's cottage.

ST VIGEANS 1 (*The Drosten Stone*)

inscription

ECMS III, 234–239 182 x 53 x 18cm **O**

Only two pieces of this cross-slab were found, both at the foot of a stairway in the church, and the stone has been re-erected with the missing segment replaced by concrete. On the cross-face is a long-shafted cross filled with thick interlace, and about it are various figures, including an angel, a bird, beasts and serpents. The left-hand side of the slab is carved with vine-scroll, the right-hand with thick interlace, and at the foot of one is a panel with an inscription incised in Hiberno-Saxon script. This reads DROSTEN IPE UORET ETT FORCUS, which may mean 'Drosten, Descendant of Uoret and Fergus'.)'IPE' may be a form of the British/Welsh 'ap' and 'ETT' the Latin 'et'.)

On the reverse is a host of carvings – two hounds pursuing a stag, a hooded cross-bowman facing a charging boar, a three-toed unicorn, a bird pecking at a fish, a strange beast, a large bear and a hind suckling a fawn. Immediately under the fracture, is a large **double-disc and Z-rod**, and under it are a **crescent** and a **mirror-and-comb**, the comb double-sided and the long-handled mirror rimmed and convex-faced. The crescent, decorated with interlocking spirals, is rather squat in shape, and the interlace-filled discs of the double-disc and Z-rod are joined by a straight and very narrow bar. In addition the Z-rod, a true Z, is spear-pointed at both ends and has floriations on both arms. These are late symbols.

Although there is a mirror-and-comb among the symbols the inscription may mean that the stone commemorates a man called Drosten The stone could however have been raised to mark a woman's grave and the inscription carved at the same time for some additional purpose.

Symbol stones in Historic Scotland's museum of early carved stones at Meigle, Perthshire, are described on pages 51–53

ST VIGEANS 2 103 x 49 x 8cm **O**

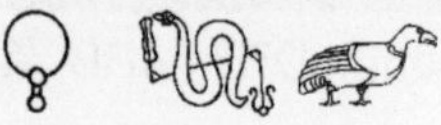

ECMS III, 239–240

This stone, the lower part of a cross-slab, was also found at the foot of the church stairway. Carved on one face only, it has a cross-shaft divided into three decorated panels, the first interlace, the second key-pattern and the lowest spirals. To the left of the shaft is a rimmed **mirror** with a wide handle and to the right an upward-looping **serpent and Z-rod** over an **eagle**. The rod is a true Z with a vertical central arm and spearheaded ends.

ST VIGEANS 3 18 x 20 x 5cm **O**

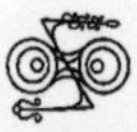

ECMS III, 240

This fragment, which was found in the churchyard, is carved on one face only. On it is part of a **double-disc and Z-rod**.

ST VIGEANS 4 20 x 28 x 7cm **O**

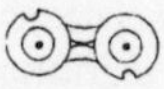

ECMS III, 240–241

Found in the church, this is the top-left corner of a small cross-slab. On one face are most of the upper arm of the cross, part of a broad ring of glory, and a triquetra. On the other face are from left to right the upper part of a gowned and hooded figure, part of a crozier, and a small vertical **double-disc**.

ST VIGEANS 5 30 x 27 x 3cm **O**

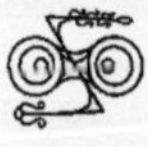

ECMS III, 241

Like No. 3 this fragment has only one carved face and was found in the churchyard. It is part of a narrow slab with a raised rim down each side of the face and has on it what may be part of the base of a cross. Below this is a **double-disc and Z-rod**. Both ends of the rod are spear-pointed.

ST VIGEANS 6 13 x 25 x 7cm **O**

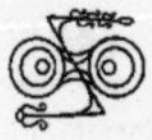

ECMS III, 241–242

This fragment, found in foundation rubbish, has interlace on one face and a late **double-disc and Z-rod** on the other. All that remains of the rod is some of the slanting arm.

Ardlair

Δ **D**

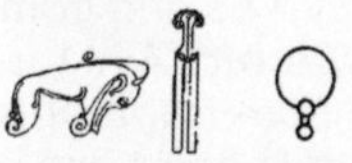

120 x 104 x 30cm **E** NJ 555 278
ECMS III, 505–506

Kennethmont is on the B9002 seven miles south of Huntly, and just past the church on its east side a minor road runs south-east. A mile down this is Ardlair farmhouse, where permission should be sought. The stone, one of two standing stones, is three hundred metres south-south-west of the farmhouse.

On the south-east face is an **elephant** incised facing right with a vertical **tuning-fork** in front of it. Below the pair is a **mirror**. The symbols are very faint.

Birse

ΔΔ **A**

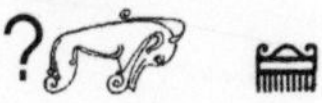

25 x 27cm **E** NO 555 973
DES 1995, 34

Birse Church is off the South Deeside road (B976) about two miles east of Aboyne. Beside it is the former manse, now a private house. There is a symbol stone fragment built into the inner face of its garden's front wall between the garden gate and the house.

The fragment, which faces north, is carved in low relief with a double-sided **comb** and what may be part of the hind leg of an **elephant**.

Bourtie

Δ **C**

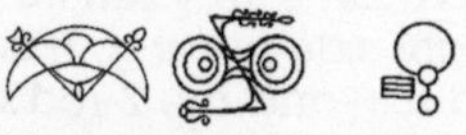

70 x 35cm **E** NJ 805 249
ECMS III, 157

Between the B9170 and A947 south of Old Meldrum runs a minor road. A mile east of where it leaves the B9170 is Kirkton of Bourtie, and the stone is built into the outside of the south wall of the church. It is near the wall's east end about six metres from the ground and is on its side, the original top to the right.

As the stone has been trimmed the left sides of two of its symbols, a **crescent and V-rod** over a **double-disc and Z-rod**, are missing. Below them is a **mirror-and-comb**. The crescent, its V-rod ending with a curlicued arrowhead, is almost without decoration. Little can be made out of the double-disc, and its Z-rod is not now visible. The mirror, which is rimmed and has a twin-bossed bar handle, is also very indistinct, as is the vertical double-sided comb.

Brandsbutt ΔΔΔ **A**

140 x 150 x 106cm **E** NJ 760 224
ECMS III, 506–507

The Brandsbutt stone is beside Gordon Terrace on the north side of Inverurie. It is signed both from the Blackhall junction on the Inverurie Bypass and from the north end of North Street (the old A96) in Inverurie. The stone, reassembled from fragments found in a dyke within the area of what had been a stone circle, is not complete and some of the missing parts have been replaced with cement.

Incised on the south-east face is a **crescent and V-rod** over a **serpent and Z-rod**. The crescent has a central pelta and a spiral in each wing, and the right end of the V-rod is arrow-pointed, but the left is a quite unique egg-shape. The serpent, which loops from right to left, is one of the three scaled serpents. Both Z-rod ends are curlicued half-circles.

To the left of the symbols is a line of Ogam which runs up the stone. It reads IRATADDOARENS, some of which may be a version of Etherman.

Clatt 1 Δ **A**

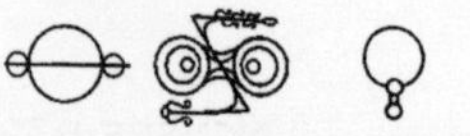

144 x 63 x 13cm **O** NJ 544 241
ECMS III, 157–158

The stone is at Knockespock House, the entrance to which is a mile south of Clatt, a village three miles east of Rhynie. Permission should be sought at the house. This natural slab, some of its right side broken away and some of the face flaked, is beside the front door steps and faces north-north-east. It was found in a wall of Clatt Churchyard

On it is a **triple-disc** over the remains of a vertical **double-disc and Z-rod** and to their right part of a **mirror**. The triple-disc, one with a bar, is very simple. The double-disc, some of its right side missing, has dot-centred discs within the discs, and the Z-rod's upper arm is spear-pointed and floriated, the lower ball-ended and curlicued. To the right is what remains of the mirror, which is the left side of its rimmed head and part of the handle's upper boss.

Clatt 3 ΔΔ **A**

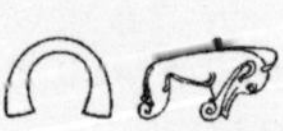

76 x 38cm **E** NJ 538 260
Ritchie, J 1910, 208–209

This stone is built into the base of the outer face of the west (rear) wall of Clatt Churchyard at a point ten metres south of the rear gate. A photograph taken by Ritchie shows the lost Clatt 2 fragment beside it *(see p.138).*

It is part of an irregularly-shaped slab and is on its side, the original top to the right. The symbols are a **horseshoe** over an **elephant**. The horseshoe, some of its left side missing, has a long arc in each arm, and the elephant, only the front half of which remains, is well shaped but very simply drawn. There is a single shoulder scroll within its body.

Crichie ΔΔΔ D

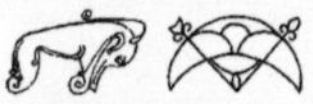

142 x 104 x 36cm **E** NJ 779 197
ECMS III, 160–161

This stone stands a mile south of Inverurie in the centre of a henge. It can be reached from the bypass roundabout south of Inverurie by taking the road to Inverurie but almost immediately turning right down Mill Road. The henge is fifty metres east of a continuation of Mill Road. The stone originally stood to the east of the henge.

On the south face is an **elephant** over a **crescent and V-rod**, both very clear. The elephant, which looks right, has the almost standard long scroll within its body and an additional 'paw' behind each leg. The crescent and V-rod contains dome-and-wing decoration, one end of the V-rod is flighted and the other is arrow-headed. Behind both are curlicues.

Craigmyle MAP below ΔΔ D

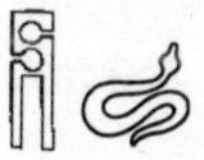

198 x 137 x 60cm **E** NJ 640 024
ECMS III, 159–160

This stone is best reached by taking the B993 north-east from Torphins and, within a mile, turning right at the first crossroads. On the east side of 'Sunnybank', is a broken iron gate into a fenced and walled strip leading uphill to a vague path through bracken and rough grass to the stone. The stone is about 400 metres from the road and 100 metres south of Cothill. The path will no doubt improve with use.

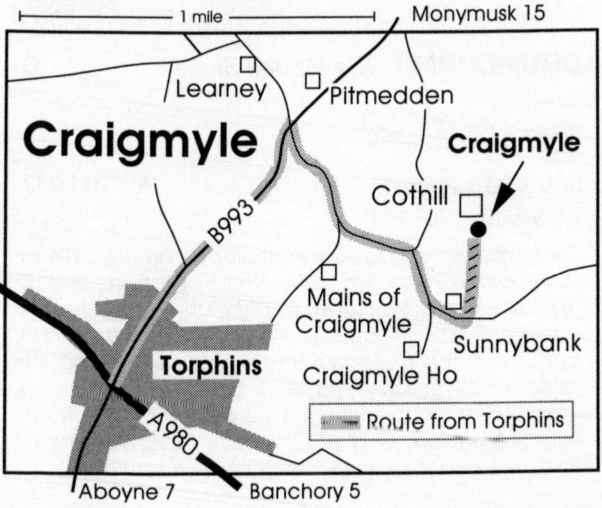

The stone is a huge granite slab with symbols incised on its south-south-west face. The symbols, which are worn, flaked and lichen-covered, are a peculiar **divided rectangle** and a **serpent**. The serpent, which is easier to make out, is just over halfway up the slab. It seems a primitive example. Above it is the divided rectangle.

Daviot ΔΔ A

78 x 66 x 20cm **E** NJ 767 286
ECMS III, 161–162

Once at a roadside (at NJ 760 288) this stone stands close beside Mounie Castle, the entrance to which is on the south side of the A920 two and a half miles west of Old Meldrum. The stone is under a yew tree twenty metres south of the castle.

The stone, which was broken in two pieces when moved, has on its north-east face a **crescent and V-rod**, a **crescent** below this, and a **mirror-and-comb**. Both crescents are decorated with twin domes, and the twin-lined rod is flighted and arrow-headed (but not now clear). The mirror is rimmed and has a twin-bossed bar handle; the comb is single-sided.

Drimmies ΔΔΔ A

101 x 63 x 33cm **E** NJ 743 235
ECMS III, 162–163

On the east side of the A96 just over two miles north-west of Inverurie is the Brandsbutt road. From it a slip road leads north to Drimmies Farm. Set in concrete on the near side of the second entrance to the farm buildings is part of a Class I stone facing north-west. Permission should be asked at the house.

Incised on the stone, the top of which has been trimmed off, are the ends of a **horseshoe**, most of an **ogee**, and a **mirror-and-comb**. The ogee is decorated with a central collar and an arc in each arm. The mirror is plain, its handle a single line between two bosses and the comb is double-sided. (See p.5, fig.1)

DRUMDURNO (*The Maiden Stone*) ΔΔ C

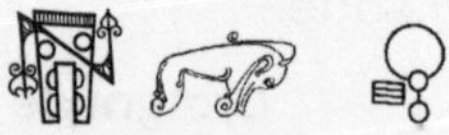

320 x 86 x 25cm **E** NJ 704 247
ECMS III, 190–191

There are signs to the Maiden Stone from the A96 at three points, one two miles north of Inverurie (just after the Brandsbutt road) and the others, at Pitcaple and near Mill of Carden. The distance to the stone from the first is some two and a half miles along the minor road through Chapel of Garioch. The stone is a mile beyond the village and stands on the south side of the road. Its symbolled face faces east south-east. A protective shelter is to be built round it.

The cross-face is very worn and defaced, but on the also damaged reverse are four clearer panels. In the worn top panel are beasts and a Pict-headed centaur, and in the next, which is less worn, is a **divided rectangle and Z-rod**. Less worn still are the other two panels, one containing an **elephant** and the lowest a **mirror-and-comb**. The divided rectangle and Z-rod, one of the only two Class II examples, has semicircular 'chariot wheel' re-entrants, but each rod-end is no more than a twin curlicue. The elephant, which is angled upwards from left to right, is closer to its Class I counterparts, being of standard shape. There are scrolls or spirals within the body, which although rimmed, is not decorated. The Maiden Stone's symbols may demonstrate that it is not a late Class II stone.

East Balhalgardy ΔΔ A

173 x 25cm **E** NJ 761 238

Ritchie, J 1915, 33–34

The East Balhalgardy steading is a mile north of Inverurie by the B9001 and not far west of the road.

The lintel above a ground floor window on the north side of the main building may have been part of a Class I stone incised with most of a **disc.**

Fetterangus A

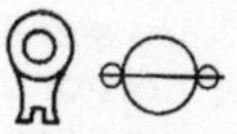

110 x 79 x 10cm **O** NJ 981 506

ECMS III, 164

This stone, the symbols on which are virtually invisible, is inside the old churchyard on the west side of Fetterangus, which is west of the A92. It is against the wall to the right of the entrance.

Near the top was a figure composed of a horizontal line and two curved lines, one with a spiral end, below this was a rimmed **mirror-case**, its base containing opposed arcs, and near the bottom was a simple **triple-disc** and bar.

FORDOUN (*St Palladius Stone*) ΔΔ B

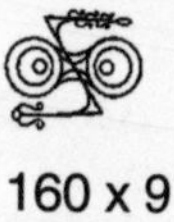 inscription

160 x 91 x 10cm **O** NO 726 784

ECMS III, 201–203

This cross-slab was found beneath the pulpit of the old Fordoun Parish Church when the church was being demolished prior to its re-building in the 1780s. It was then transferred to the old St Palladius Chapel nearby but is now in the rebuilt church.

The stone is carved only on one face, the top is missing and some of the face has flaked away. On it is most of an equal-armed cross with re-entrants bored right through the stone. In the remains of the summit arm are parts of fish-bodied creatures, in the left arm and in the square centre is interlace, and in the lower arm a mounted Pict rides from right to left. Behind him is another rider, and in front of him is a third. They all carry spears and are hunting, with two hounds. Just below the cross is a **double-disc and Z-rod.** Although decorated with peltae and interlocking spirals it is of standard shape, but the Z-rod has spear-points at both ends and floriations along both arms.

Above the cross's left arm is an inscription in Hiberno-Saxon script, which reads PIDARNOIN. 'IDARNOIN', like EDDARRNON(N) in Ogham, may be the Pictish name Ethernan or Ithernan, and the 'P' before it a short version of 'ap' or 'map', the P-Celtic for 'son of'.

Fyvie Parish Church — NJ 769 378

ECMS III, 164–166, 184–185

Fyvie Parish Church is at the east end of Fyvie, on the south side of the B9005. Set in triangular formation in the outside of the east wall of the church are three rather worn symbol stones, all of which have been trimmed.

Fyvie 1 — 71 x 53cm E ΔΔ A

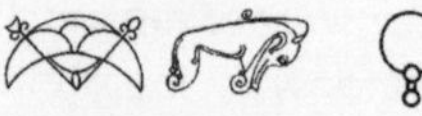

This trimmed and cracked or broken left-hand stone, was once built into the wall of the schoolhouse.

On it is only one complete symbol, an **elephant** incised from right to left. Not a graceful creature it has a shoulder scroll which is linked to a reverse scroll above the hind leg. Above it is the lower part of a **crescent and V-rod**, and to the left is most of a plain **mirror** with a small head and long handle. The mirror's crescent-like handle-end is not unlike that on Inveraven 1 (MOR) (see p.100).

Fyvie 2 — 68 x 30cm E ΔΔ A

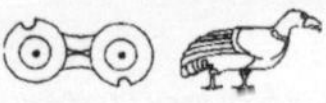

The right-hand stone was found built into a wall of the church.

It has on it the right-hand disc of a **double-disc** and below this the centre part of an **eagle** incised from left to right. The disc is rimmed, and the joining bar contains a vertical arc, a feature found only on Huntly 2 (see p.35).

Rothiebrisbane — 73 x 51cm E ΔΔ C

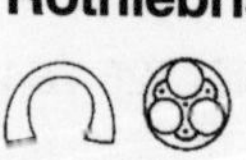

The top stone will require a pair of stepladders if it is to be photographed or examined closely. It was found in use as a drain cover on a road (now the B992) running south from Kirkton of Auchterless.

Although rather more worn than the others it is the most complete, and its symbols, a **horseshoe** over a **disc**, are intact. The horseshoe is one of the rare 'hinged' variety, the 'hinge' being a scroll projecting down from the centre of the arch, and in the arms of the horseshoe are two curving columns of short parallel arcs. The disc comprises three small discs in triangular formation within a rimmed disc. The small discs vary in size, and the rimmed disc is misshapen.

Huntly 1 — A

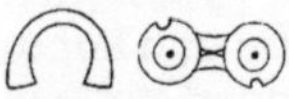

100 x 75 x 45cm **E** — NJ 529 400
ECMS III, 166

The two 'Standing Stones of Strathbogie' are in Huntly's market place. On one of them most of a **horseshoe** could at one time be distinguished with below it traces of a **double-disc**, but in 1903 Allen wrote, "In a few years all traces of the symbols will have disappeared." They almost have. Even the horseshoe is, to quote from the 1994 RCAHMS Handlist, "all but invisible."

Inverurie — NJ 780 206 A

ECMS III, 168–170

The four stones, three of which are fragments, were built into the churchyard walls. They are now in the cemetery at the Bass of Inverurie, on the east side of the town not far along the Keith Hall/Whiterashes road (B993). The stones are in a line about forty metres left from the gate, at the end of the nearest line of trees.

Inverurie 1 — 180 x 48 x 35cm **O** ΔΔ

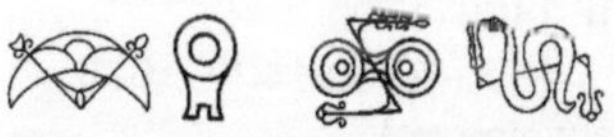

No.1 is a long slab with some of each side trimmed or broken off. It lies prone north to south supported by other stones. On it are four worn symbols only one of which is complete. As one pair is upside down in relation to the other this is a reused symbol stone.

At one end is most of a **crescent and V-rod** over a **mirror-case**. The crescent is decorated with dome-and-wing pattern and the rod has flights at its left end (the right is missing). The mirror-case is without decoration other than an internal disc.

At the other end are parts of a **double-disc and Z-rod** above a **serpent and Z-rod**. The one remaining disc is of three concentric rings with a central dot, and little more is left of the Z-rod than the middle arm and some of the lower. The serpent, its head missing, loops from left to right. At one time the middle arm of its rod could be seen, apparently imposed on the serpent and not running through its coils. The rod's outer arms, if any, were lost when the stone was trimmed.

Inverurie 2 — 32 x 40 x 21cm **E** ΔΔ

No.2, the left-hand stone, is a very small fragment that stands facing east. Incised on it is part of a **mirror** with an ornately-patterned head and a short handle that ends in a large boss.

Inverurie 3 — 77 x 60 x 30cm **E** ΔΔΔ

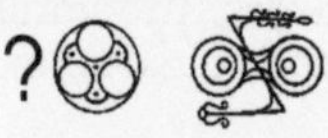

No.3, the second from the left, is the lower part of a slab trimmed down the right side. It faces east. Incised on it is almost all of a **double-disc and Z-rod**, each disc rimmed and with a small dotted circle in the centre. Within the concave-sided joining bar is a bar with its arcs touching and a small dotted circle at each end. The rod's upper arm is floriated and spear-pointed, but its other end has disappeared as the result of flaking. Above the double-disc and Z-rod is what may be the lower part of a **disc**.

Inverurie 4 — 127 x 65 x 30cm **E** ΔΔΔ

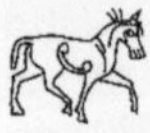

On this irregularly-shaped slab, which is the right hand of the group and faces west, is a horse cantering from left to right. Although there are no other examples it is a symbol. There is no other carving on the stone, and within the horse's body is a curling bar with scroll ends.

INVERURIE MUSEUM

Inverurie Library **D**
Market Place, Inverurie AB51 3SN
Tel: 01467 621619; 01779 477778 Museum Service

Mon/Tue/Thu/Fri	1400–1700
Saturday	1000–1300/1400–1600

Free (Donations welcome)

FORMASTON — 86 x 43 x 13cm **E**

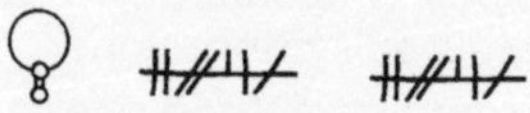

ECMS III, 188-189 (1993 edn fig.205 faces p.183)

This fragment is near the foot of the stairs up to the museum. It is carved on one face only with a small rimmed **mirror** and part of an interlace-filled cross-shaft. The mirror has a long handle with a boss at the end. Beside it are two vertical Ogams, MAQQoi TALLUORRH and NAHHTVROBBACCAANNEVV. 'MAQQ' may mean 'son of' or 'descendant of'. (The 'oi' which follows it is expressed as a small circle.)

It was found in Formaston Churchyard (NJ 541 001).

Kintore 4 — 68 x 50 x 17cm **O**

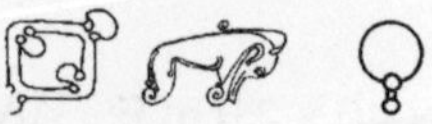

Woodham 1974

This fragment was found in a local garden (NJ 790 162).

On it are the unique **square**, most of a well-shaped **elephant** and some of a plain **mirror**. The elephant has linked scrolls within its body, a 'chin' scroll and additional fore and rear 'paws'. Only the upper left segment of the mirror remains on the stone.

Keith Hall ΔΔ D

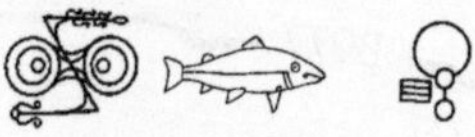

120 x 60 x 38cm **E** NJ 788 214

ECMS III, 170 (1993 edn fig.183 faces p.169)

This stone, which stands on a ditched mound called Caskieben in the grounds of Keith Hall near Inverurie, was found in the River Don at NJ 780 202. To get to it leave Inverurie by the B9170 to Old Meldrum, once over the Urie turn right along the minor road to Kingoodie and almost immediately turn right again through estate gates where there is a sign to Keith Hall Gardens. Follow the metalled estate road for about three-quarters of a mile, disregarding a track that turns east from it to the gardens. The metalled road bends left at a cross-roads, but here go straight ahead, up a rough drive towards the Hall. 100 metres on, after passing two large stone balls, walk to the right for another 100 metres to find the mound, which is among trees. The top of the mound is encircled by head-high weeds, but there is a clearing in the centre where the stone stands.

The stone faces south-south-west. On it is a **double-disc and Z-rod** over a **salmon** and below that a **mirror-and-comb**. The discs and bar are of standard pattern. The discs are wido-rimmed and dot-centred, and the concave-sided bar contains another bar. The Z-rod is less typical. It is almost right-angled and has a very large ball-butt but no spearhead, only a vertical egg-shape near the end of the upper arm. The salmon, which like the majority swims to the right, is rather clumsy in appearance. Those two symbols are worn, and some of their details are not very clear because of the stone's irregular surface. The mirror-and-comb is less distinct. The mirror is rimmed and has a twin-bossed bar handle. The comb is a plain divided oblong.

Kinellar MAP p80 ΔΔΔ B

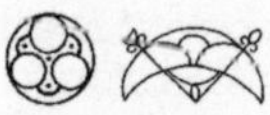

99 x 56cm **E** NJ 821 144

ECMS III, 170–171

Kinellar Church can be reached from the B979, which runs north from Blackburn on the A96 eight miles from Aberdeen. This trimmed stone, now built into an inside wall of the porch, was found in the church foundations. The church is locked, and the keys are held at the manse in Keithhall, east of Inverurie by the B993. (Tel: 01467 620435)

The stone has a **disc** above a **crescent and V-rod**. The disc, like most others, contains three smaller discs in triangular formation. These are dot-centred, and there are also three small triangles in the spaces between the discs. The crescent, with two linked spirals in the centre and a curved line in each wing, is clumsily incised as is the V-rod, the arms of which are not straight. Allen's figure no.184 shows the left rod-end to be flighted and the right pointed, both with a pair of curlicues, but only the curlicues are now distinct.

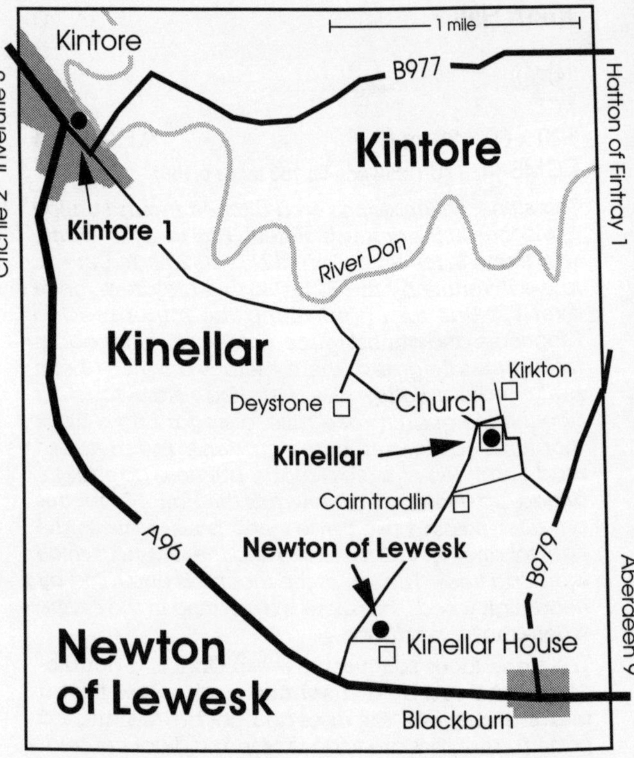

Kintore 1 MAP above ΔΔΔ **A**

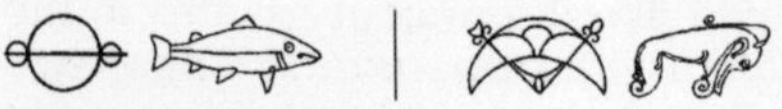

112 x 51 x 25cm **E** NJ 793 163
ECMS III, 171–172

Kintore Church is in the centre of Kintore, at the junction of the A96 and B977, and the stone, which was discovered underground in the churchyard, stands near the inner face of the churchyard wall in a recess to the right of the entrance. Beside it is an explanatory board illustrating all the Kintore stones.

It is a reused stone with on the south face a horizontal **triple-disc** over a **salmon** and on the north a **crescent and V-rod** over an **elephant**.

The south face symbols are beautifully shaped. The triple-disc, its large disc single-lined and the side rings rimmed, has a twin-lined bar across it. As the bar lies over the large disc but passes through each ring this symbol does seem to represent something like a cauldron suspended from a crossbar.

On the north face the crescent is filled with clumsy dome-and-wing decoration, and the V-rod ends are similar to each other in shape, being broad-headed and curlicued. The elephant is a graceless creature, and any carving within it other than the eye is uncertain. Although these north face symbols are fainter than the south they appear to be later in style.

Leith Hall — NJ 540 300 **B**

Leith Hall, a National Trust property, is seven miles west of Insch by the B9002, and is well signposted. Its entrance is on the right of the road just beyond the bridge over the railway north of Kennethmont. The stones are north-west of the Hall. They stand in an open-fronted shelter against the north wall of the walled 'East Garden'. The way into this is on the left before the car-park, via a gate into an open garden and then up the west wall of the walled garden, through which are two gates, one halfway up, the other near the top. The stones, which face south, are admirably displayed, Newbigging Leslie at the left end of the shed and Percylieu at the right. Beside each is an explanatory board. The grounds are open daily from 0930 till sunset all year. Admission charges: adult–£1.60; conc–£1. (When the ticket kiosk is closed the respective charges are £1 and 50p – to be put in the 'honesty box'.)

Newbigging Leslie — 68 x 71 x 15cm **O** ΔΔΔ

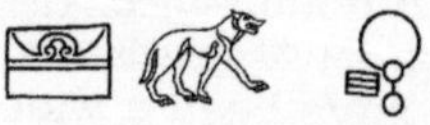

ECMS III, 177–178

One stone was found below ground on the farm of Newbigging Leslie (NJ 603 258), five miles south-east of Kennethmont.

On one face of the stone, which has lost some of its base and right side, is a **wolf** with a small **rectangle** over it and a **mirror-and-comb** to the right. In the wolf's body are curved lines and a shoulder scroll, and it pads from left to right, very like the Ardross wolf in Inverness Museum. Below it the stone is flaked, and parts of the wolf's legs and feet have been re-incised. The rectangle has two decorative spirals inside it. The mirror is rimmed and has a twist-handle between two bosses, not unlike the Picardy Stone's mirror. The comb is single-sided with a three-pointed handle and is clearly toothed. Some of the mirror-and-comb is missing.

Percylieu — 90 x 45 x 10cm **O** ΔΔΔ

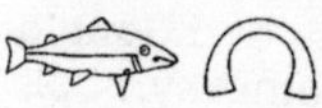

ECMS III, 181–182

The Percylieu stone was found deep underground near the farm of Hillhead of Clatt (NJ 523 265), not far south of Kennethmont. Close to the site were cairns and a stone circle (Stuart 1856, 4). It then measured about 120 by 60 centimetres but was later trimmed to be used as a flagstone.

All that is on it now are the lower fins of a **salmon** and most of a **horseshoe**. The horseshoe which has a central collar, has a long arc in each arm, and stretching outwards from these are short arcs.

The salmon must have been complete when the stone was found. After its discovery the stone was erected beside a nearby well which became known as the 'Salmon Well'.

Logie Elphinstone — NJ 703 259 **B**

ECMS III, 175–177 (1993 edn fig.189 faces p.173)

Logie House, which is largely a ruin, is just over six miles north-west of Inverurie by the A96 and on the other side of the Urie. In its grounds are three symbol stones from the nearby Moor of Carden (where they either stood in or lay beside a stone circle). The three now stand among trees two hundred metres west of the house and forty metres north of the drive to it. Each one is incised with two symbols one of which is a crescent and V-rod. All three stones are lichened. The entrance gates are at NJ 699 257 on the A96, just before a picnic area.

Logie Elphinstone 1   100 x 74 x 30cm E   ΔΔΔ

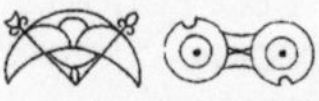

Viewed from the north, No.1 is the left in the group. It faces west.

Its **crescent and V-rod** is over a **double-disc**. The crescent has a central decoration of two spirals, and the V-rod ends are what may have been a wide arrow-flight and a leaf-shaped head. The discs have small interior concentric circles, and between them is a wide joining bar with convex sides. Inside it is a concave-sided bar.

Logie Elphinstone 2   137 x 76 x 28cm E   ΔΔ

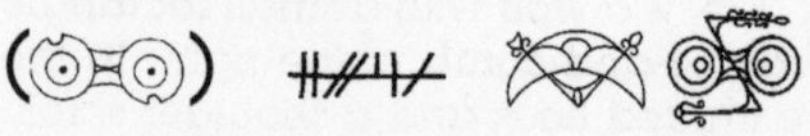

No.2 is on the right and faces east.

The **crescent and V-rod** on it is over a **double-disc and Z-rod**. The crescent contains two spirals, and in each wing is a triangular shape. The V-rod's left end is very clearly flighted; the right is curlicued and arrow-headed. The discs are plain and linked by a wide straight-sided bar with an internal concave-sided bar. The Z-rod's upper arm is spear-headed; the lower ends with a pair of long curlicues. Above the symbols is an Ogam on a circular stem-line. Read clockwise from the bottom the letters are QUDDALT. Also on the stone are the erased traces of a **double-disc** between and overlapped by the other symbols.

Logie Elphinstone 3   104 x 74 x 20cm E   ΔΔΔ

No.3 is the centre stone, its symbols on the north face.

The **crescent and V-rod**, which is the lower symbol, is very simple, with no decoration other than two spirals rising from a central arc-sided triangle. The V-rod ends are faint, the left composed of two convex arcs and the right of two angled lines or arcs with only the upper arc of the crescent for a base. Above it is a very poor **elephant** which faces right and is, except for a shoulder scroll, little more than an outline.

MIGVIE

MAP below ΔΔ **B**

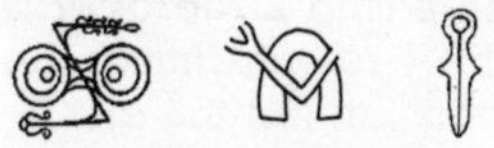

180 x 70 x 38cm **E** NJ 437 068

ECMS III, 191–192

Migvie, which is two miles north of Logie Coldstone, is on a minor road east of the A97. A roughly-shaped granite cross-slab stands in the churchyard.

The cross, which is carved in low relief on the stone's east face, is composed of coarse double-interlace. From the intersections of the arms and from the top corners of the summit are short projections ending in rings, which may represent hanging or securing rings. In each quadrant is a symbol or figure in very low relief. In the upper left is a small and clumsy **double-disc and Z-rod**, the rod's arms both floriated, the lower ending in a curlicued spear-point and the upper either forked or flighted. In the upper right is an even smaller **horseshoe and V-rod**. The left end of the rod is forked, perhaps representing an arrow-flight. The right end is indistinct. Below the cross's right arm are the remains of a mounted figure, and in the lower left quadrant is an additional symbol, a pair of **shears**, the only example of this symbol.

On the natural reverse of the stone is a long-haired horseman in low relief.

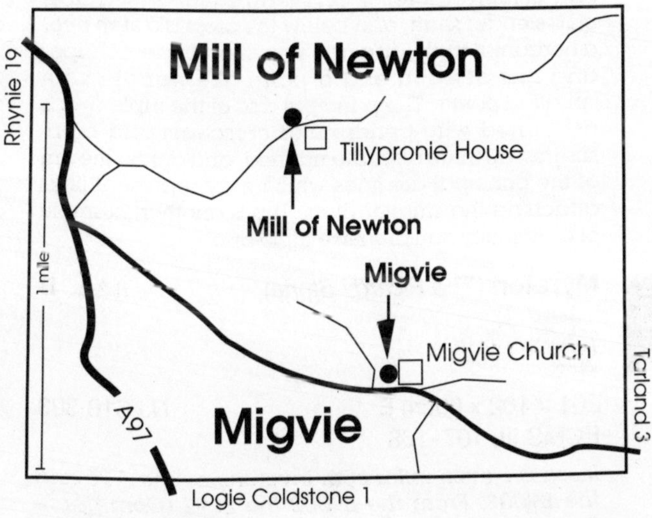

Mill of Newton

MAP above ΔΔ **A**

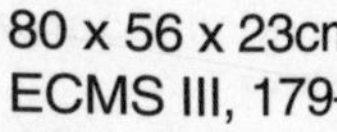

80 x 56 x 23cm **E** NJ 432 080

ECMS III, 179–180

This stone once stood on a mound called Tom a Char at NJ 432 046 and is now outside Tillypronie House, a mile north of Migvie. It stands on the north edge of the drive one hundred metres west of the house. Permission should be asked at the house.

The symbols, which are incised on the south-east face, are a **divided rectangle and Z-rod** over a **crescent and V-rod**. The 'wheel' re-entrants of the divided rectangle are semicircular, not the classic circular kind – but it has small 'horse' arcs in the projections. The Z-rod is a true but right-angled Z, and the upper end looks like an arrow-flight. As the left side of the stone is broken the other end is not clear.

The breakage has removed the left side of the crescent and V-rod. This is decorated with a dome in the centre and a wing on either side. The right-hand end of the rod is a curlicued arrowhead.

MONYMUSK ΔΔΔ C

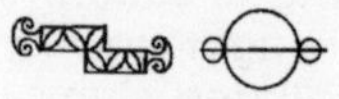

217 x 76 x 51cm **O** NJ 685 152
ECMS III, 192–194

The village of Monymusk, which is on the B993 about seventeen miles west of Aberdeen, can be reached from the A96 by taking either the B994 a mile before Kintore or the B993 just before Inverurie. The cross-slab, now in Monymusk Parish Church, once stood a mile east of Monymusk at about NJ 703 151, in a field "where it had been from time immemorial". The switch for a spotlight is behind the left-hand rear pew.

It is an irregular pillar of granite carved on one face only in fairly low relief. On it is an equal-armed cross on a slender shaft, and below the cross is a **step** over a horizontal **triple-disc**. The step contains leaf-shapes and has at each end a pelta-like handle with spiralled points. The principal disc of the triple-disc is decorated with penannular crescents and bulb-shapes, all three discs are rimmed, and across the rim of the principal are lines which may represent links attaching the smaller discs. This is another example of a distinctly cauldron-like triple-disc.

Myreton (*The Picardy Stone*) ΔΔΔ B

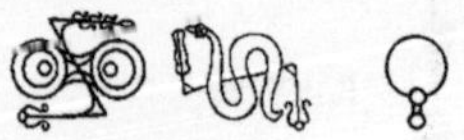

201 x 102 x 60cm **E** NJ 610 303
ECMS III, 167–168

Insch is eleven miles from Inverurie by the A96 and the B9002. From the B9002 the B992 (Commerce Street) runs northwards through the village, and at the cross-roads with High Street on the right and Market Street on the left is a Historic Scotland sign to the 'Picardy Stone' pointing up Market Street. The stone is two miles up this minor road, standing on its original site, a low cairn, which is in a fenced enclosure close to the left side of the road. In front of the stone was a grave (Stuart 1856, xxiv).

The stone's symbols are incised on the south face, a **double-disc and Z-rod** near the top of the stone, a **serpent and Z-rod** below it and a **mirror** below that. In each disc of the double-disc is a small concentric circle with centre dot, the joining bar has a narrower bar within it, and the Z-rod, which is floriated along the upper arm, is spear-pointed and ball-ended. The double-disc and Z-rod is of standard pattern – but the worn serpent and Z-rod is not. Although its rod is conventionally laid out both rod-ends are curlicued balls and the upwards-pointing arm has a pair of floriations. The mirror is also unusual, having a double-twist handle between its two bosses.

Nether Corskie Δ D

275 x 150 x 70cm **E** NJ 748 096

Ritchie, J 1915, 37–39

The farmhouse of Nether Corskie is beside the B977 just north of Dunecht, which is twelve miles due west of Aberdeen by the A944. A quarter mile to its north-west are two standing stones, and on the south-east face of the western one is a very faint yet very interesting pair of symbols. Permission to look at the stone should be asked at the house.

Not only is the stone a reused standing stone (and cup-marked), but the symbols are not a conventional pair. Only one is a 'family' symbol, a simple rimmed **mirror-case**; the other is the 'additional' **mirror-and-comb.** The mirror-case is to the left, beside it is a rimmed mirror with a twin-bossed bar handle, and beside the mirror is a single-sided comb.

Newton House 1 ΔΔΔ B

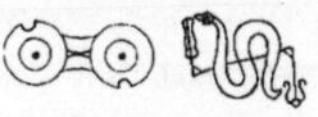

206 x 61 x 40cm **E** NJ 662 297

ECMS III, 178–179

The entrance road to Newton House is on the east side of the A96 a short distance before its junction with the B992. A magnificent blue gneiss pillar that once stood in a plantation about a mile south of Newton House now stands amid trees less than a hundred metres east of the house. Permission to see the stone should be sought in advance by telephoning 01464 5 346.

Figure 21

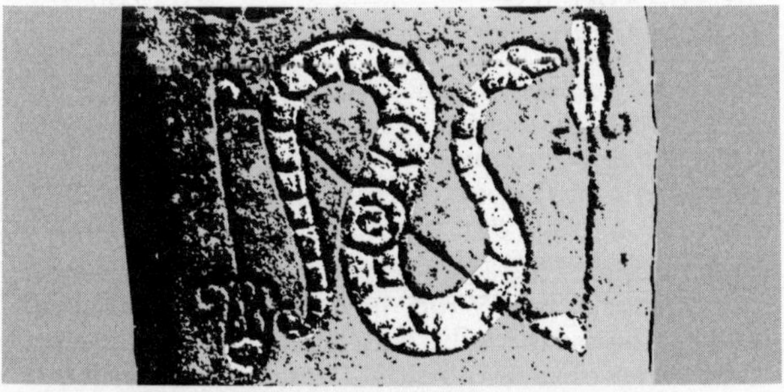

Serpent and Z-rod: Newton House 1 (ABE), for its double-disc see p.7, fig.2

On the south face is a **double-disc** over a **serpent and Z-rod**. The double-disc, rimmed and with a narrow joining bar, is one of the three notched examples. The serpent is one of the three that loop from left to right and one of the three with scales. The upper end of the Z-rod, a true Z, is a 'flamboyant' spearhead, the lower is rounded and curlicued.

There are very obvious pockmarks in the incisions. Pocking, followed by rubbing with an abrasive material, was a common method of incising symbols.

Beside this symbol stone is another blue gneiss pillar without symbols but with two inscriptions. One, which has not been satisfactorily translated, is apparently in Roman letters, and the other is an Ogam. It begins with 'IDDARQNNN', which may be a version of Ethernan or Ithernan.

The inscribed stone stood in the same plantation as the symbolled pillar. Graves were found near the two stones (Stuart 1856, 1).

Newton of Lewesk MAP p.80 ΔΔ A

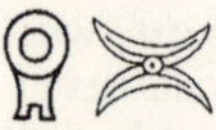

86 x 40 x 18cm **O** NJ 815 129

Ritchie, J 1916, 279–285

A mile west of Blackburn by the A96 the road to Cairntradlin runs northwards. Two hundred metres up it on the right hand side is the entrance to Kinellar House. The stone stands facing south set into the bank on the north side of the drive, opposite the near end of the house. It was found at NJ c692 276 face down in a field on Newton of Lewesk farm, which is to the east of Old Rayne. It may have been over a grave.

As well as other damage some of the stone's base and left side is missing. Near the top is a simple **mirror-case** with a pattern of arcs in the disc, and near the base is a complex **double-crescent** not all of which is exposed and the left side of which is incomplete. In the space between them and overlapping part of the mirror-case is a crudely-drawn oblong shield on a simple cross-hilted sword. This is thought to be a later addition.

Park House Δ B

?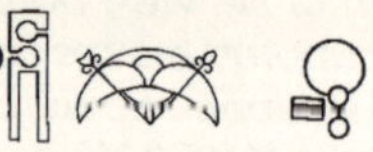

74 x 35 x 32cm **O** NO 780 977

ECMS III, 180–181

This worn fragment, found at about NO 794 984 at the west end of Keith's Muir, is set up on a pedestal about 150 metres to the north of Park House, which is south of the A93 between Banchory and Peterculter. Permission to see the stone should be asked there.

In the centre of the south-east face of the stone is most of a **crescent and V-rod**, its left wing and rod-end missing, below this is the right half of a rimmed **mirror** and some of a single-sided **comb**, and above is what may be some of the lower part of a **divided rectangle**. To the right of this is the lower half of a shape like a straight-chorded half moon. The crescent and V-rod, which is decorated with arcs, has a curlicued arrowhead at the visible rod-end, and the mirror has an upper handle-boss. Something like the stone's carvings have been incised on the pedestal, but there only the crescent and V-rod and comb are similar in appearance to the originals.

Logan 1829, 55–56; ECMS III, 182–184; Shepherd and Shepherd 1978, 217–219

Rhynie is eight miles south of Huntly at the junction of the A97 and the A941. Seven symbol stones have been found there, No.1 still stands on its original site, in a field not far from the old churchyard, No.4, which also stood south of the village, was broken up and lost, and the others are now in various places. Nos 2 and 3 now stand in the Square, and Nos 5 and 6, both from the foundations of the old kirk at NJ 499 265, which was demolished in 1878, and No.8, which was picked up at NJ c497 262 (close to the Craw Stane) are in a shelter in the carpark north of the old churchyard. It is possible that 5 and 6 also came from the Craw Stane area and were used in building the kirk after they had perhaps already 'slipped' some way downhill towards the kirk site.

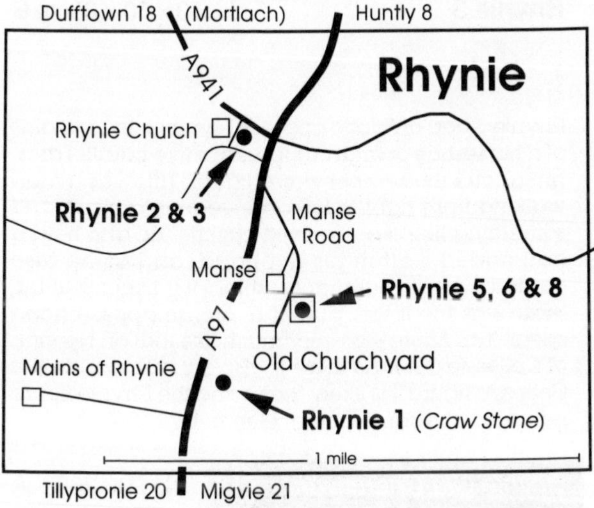

Rhynie 1 (*The Craw Stane*) ΔΔΔ D

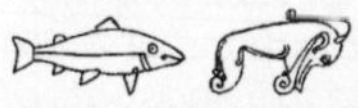

180 x 102 x 43cm **E** NJ 497 263

The farm track to Mains of Rhynie, is to the west side of the A97 not far south of Rhynie. The Craw Stane is in a field opposite the junction, standing about one hundred metres east of the road and slightly nearer to Rhynie. It stands at one side of the inner entrance to an almost imperceptible multi-vallate circular enclosure which crowns the end of a low spur. It may have been an entrance jamb or other structural feature which was later re-used in situ as a symbol stone. Depending on the time of year and the crop it is not always visible from the road. Permission to view it should be asked at the Mains.

The stone faces south. Near the top is a large **salmon**, and below it is an even larger **elephant.** There are no scrolls within the elephant's body, only a loop where the front leg joins.

Rhynie Square NJ 498 272 **A**

Little or nothing can now be seen of the carvings on the two stones which stand inside the fence on the north-west side of the Square. No.2 is on the east side of the gate and No.3 on the west, both facing south-east. They are illustrated, with Nos 1 and 4, in RCAHMS 1994, 11.

Rhynie 2 59 x 48 x 19cm **E**

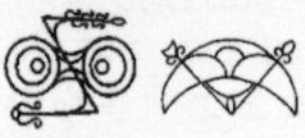

On Rhynie 2 was a very plain vertical **double-disc and Z-rod** above an equally plain **crescent and V-rod**. The Z-rod was a true Z, its lower end heart-shaped. The top of the stone appears to have been sheared off and so the end of the upper arm was missing, but this would have been the pointed end; on the upper arm were five staggered floriations. Of the V-rod's ends only the right-hand, a diamond-shaped arrowhead was still visible.

Rhynie 3 70 x 50 x 30cm **E**

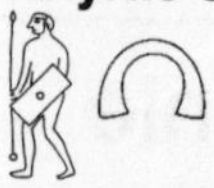

Rhynie 3 had only one apparent symbol, the remains of a **horseshoe** or arch composed of five parallel arcs, but above the symbol was a figure. This was a man walking from right to left and wearing a cloak and something like a ball-ended necktie. He also held a ball-ended staff in his left hand, and as he also carried a small rectangular shield it is likely that the 'staff' was the lower part of a 'bronze apple'-ended spear. This figure was very much like that on Newton of Collessie (FIF). As there is also an arch beside the Collessie figure it is likely that it and the Rhynie figure represent the same being. (See p.43)

Rhynie Old Churchyard NJ 500 265 **A**

The car-park shelter housing Rhynie 5, 6 and 8 is near the end of Manse Road. From the left they are 6, 8 and 5, facing south, south-west and west respectively. Beside the shelter is a board with illustrations of them and the Craw Stane, information as to the findspots of all four, and a mention of the lost Rhynie 4 *(see p.138)**.*

Rhynie 5 129 x 80 x 23cm **E** ΔΔ

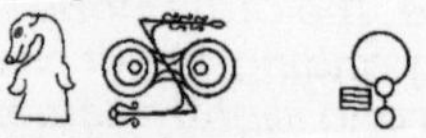

As its top is slightly broken part of one of the upper symbols is missing. This is a rimmed but otherwise plain vertical **double-disc and Z-rod**. Little of the Z-rod's upper arm survives, and it is without floriations, but the lower arm ends in a heart-shape – as did No.2's. To the left is a **dog's head**, the only example of this symbol on a stone. Further down the stone is a **mirror-and-comb**. The mirror is plain-headed with a twin-bossed bar handle. The comb, which is very faint, is single-sided, without apparent teeth and with a four-pointed handle.

There are cup-marks on the back of the stone.

Rhynie 6 75 x 42 x 27cm **E** ΔΔ

On this fragment are one end of a rimmed and vertical **double-disc and Z-rod**, a plain **crescent and V-rod** and a **mirror**. The left rod-end is flighted, the right has a leaf-shaped head with forward-facing curlicues. The mirror has a twin-bossed bar handle and is rimmed. What is left of the double-disc and Z-rod is like No.5's, except that the lower end of the rod is a curlicued ball.

Rhynie 8 43 x 39 x 16cm **O** ΔΔ

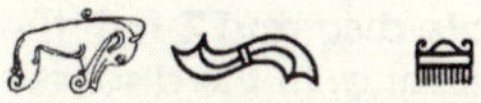

This stone, picked up close to the Craw Stane, had at some time been trimmed. What is left is incised with an almost complete **elephant**, part of an **ogee**, and a small **comb**. The elephant has some features in common with the one on the Craw Stane. At the top of its foreleg is a similar loop, it is without scrolls, and it is much the same shape – but it has a second 'forepaw'. The ogee, only the upper part of which survives, seems to have been plain and vertical. The comb is single-sided and has a three-pointed handle, no internal division and no apparent teeth.

The similarity of the symbols shared by the Rhynie stones other than No.3 may show that the people for whom they were carved were from related families. The similarity of No.3 to the Newton of Collessie stone may demonstrate a relationship too between Rhynie and distant Fife, one which may also be shown by the shared symbols on both Rhynie 5 and the Norrie's Law silver plates, and also found in the Doo Cave at East Wemyss. The relationship may also have included Angus, through the lost bronze plate from Laws, Monifieth, and the Westerton stone (see p.43).

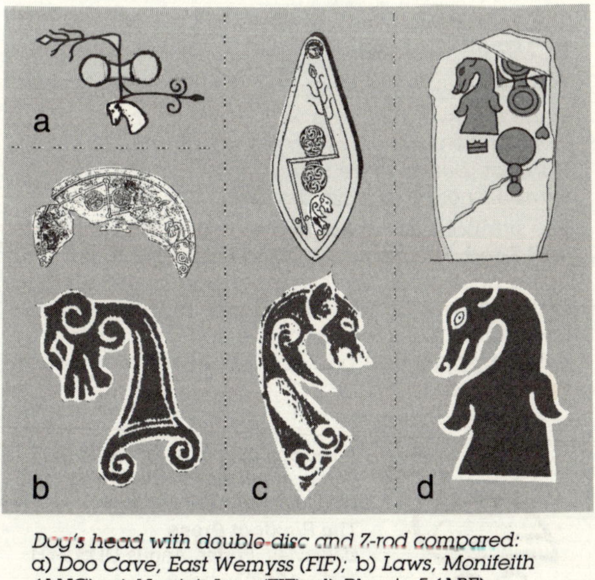

Figure 22

Dog's head with double-disc and Z-rod compared: a) *Doo Cave, East Wemyss (FIF);* b) *Laws, Monifieth (ANG);* c) *Norrie's Law (FIF);* d) *Rhynie 5 (ABE)*

Tullich 1 ΔΔ B

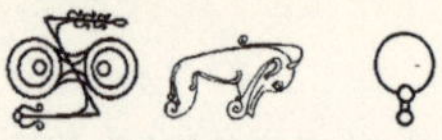

174 x 53 x 10cm **O** NO 391 975
ECMS III, 186–187

On the south side of the A93 about nine miles west of Aboyne is a ruined church, which is between the farms of Newton of Tullich and Milton of Tullich. Standing behind railings amongst other stones against the outside of its north wall is a trimmed and shortened slab incised with faint symbols. It was found in use as a window lintel in the church.

Near the stone's top is a **double-disc and Z-rod**, the outer edges and Z-rod ends missing. In the discs are small dotted discs, the joining bar is plain and the rod's upper arm is floriated. Below is some of a fine **elephant** facing right within which is a long scroll. Below the elephant is a rimmed **mirror** with twin-bossed handle. All that can be readily made out is the mirror, but this is not a stone to disregard.

Turriff Δ A

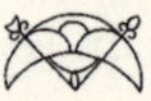

50 x 25cm **E** NJ 723 499
ECMS III, 187

This rectangular fragment is built into the inner face of the north garden wall of the manse, which is on the south side of Manse Terrace in Turriff. It is to the right of the gate and a few feet from the ground.

On it is the left part of a **crescent and V-rod** which is very faint. The left end of the rod is not visible.

Tyrie (*The Raven Stone*) ΔΔΔ C

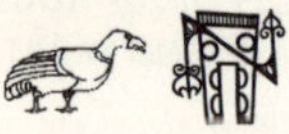

112 x 71cm **E** NJ 930 631
ECMS III, 187–188

Found in the foundations of the old parish church the stone is now built into a wall at the top of a flight of steps in the vestibule of the present church. The stone is intact, but as there is a wooden frame about the symbols not all of it can be seen.

The symbols are an **eagle** over a **divided rectangle and Z-rod**. The eagle is incised from right to left and has a neck scroll. In the upper part of the divided rectangle are circular re-entrants, but the symbol's lower projections are plain. The upper end of the rod is a long-curlicued ball and the lower a curlicued vase-shape.

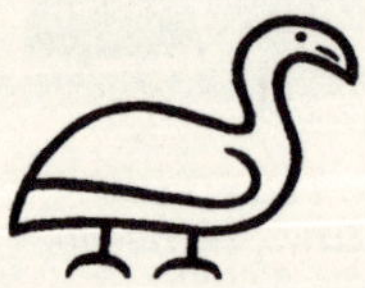

If you can correct or up-date any of the information in this Guide, please contact the publishers:

The Pinkfoot Press
Balgavies, Forfar, Angus DD8 2TH
Tel/Fax: 01307 818669

Beannachar | NJ 913 023 **B**

ECMS III, 200–201

These stones are set into the south-west face of an orchard wall about 250 metres south-west of Beannachar (formerly Banchory House), where permission to see them should be asked at. The entrance to the house is on the south side of the B9077 a mile west of its junction with the A90.

No.1 was found built into the remains of a low wall on the top of a rock stack called Dunnicaer, which is at NO 884 847 on the coast a mile south of Stonehaven. The others lay on the shore below. All are small stones and two at least, Nos 2 and 5, are not fragments. They appear to have been waterworn and rounded before they were incised. None of the four are typical symbol stones.

Dunnicaer 1 ABE — 52 x 65cm **E** ΔΔΔ

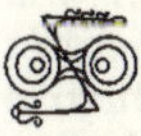

No.1, the centre stone, is incised with something like a **double-disc and Z-rod**. The discs are small, and the 'Z-rod' is a true Z but of many complex lines.

Dunnicaer 2 ABE — 38 x 68cm **E** ΔΔ

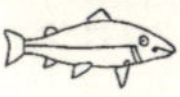

On No.2, which is the stone above No.1, is a faint **fish** with a small triangle above its head.

Dunnicaer 3 ABE — 24 x 43cm **E** ΔΔ

On No.3, the left-hand stone, is a small equilateral triangle pointing up into a plain **crescent**.

Dunnicaer 5 ABE — 21 x 39cm **E** ΔΔ

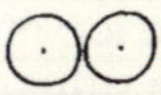

On No.5 are two small adjacent **discs**, which are plain except for a central dot in each.

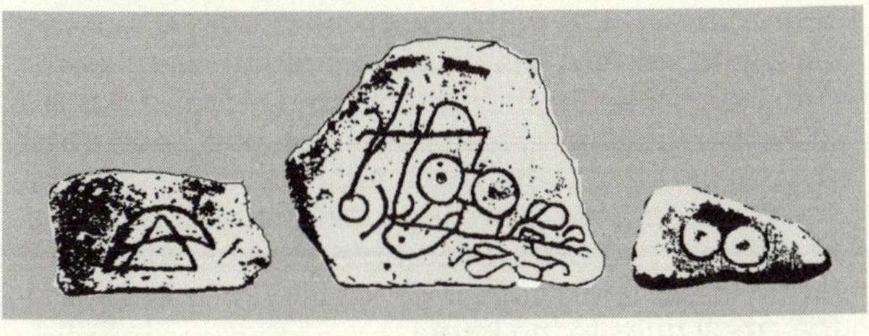

Figure 23

Dunnicaer (ABE): from left to right, Nos 3, 1 and 5

Dyce — NJ 875 154 A

Dyce, which is on the A947, is about six miles north-west of Aberdeen. Not far past the sign to Dyce Station are traffic lights where Pitmedden Road, signed to 'Industrial Estate and Kinaldie', runs north-west (to the left). Just over a mile up this, the road curves left over a new railway bridge. Turn right at the first side road after the bridge (within 200 metres), then less than a quarter mile up it turn right again at the sign 'Dyce Symbol Stones'. Thereafter follow the signs to arrive at the ruins of Dyce Old Kirk. The two stones are set into a transverse wall built inside the kirk doorway, which is in the east gable. No.1 was said to have been found in the kirkyard wall (Stuart 1856, 5), No.2 in the nearby glebe.

Dyce 1 — 168 x 68cm E ΔΔΔ

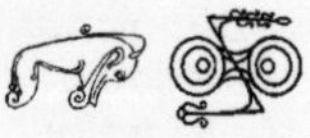

ECMS III, 163–164 (1993 edn fig.172 faces p.161)

The Class I stone, an irregular slab with a trimmed base, is the left-hand of the two. Incised on it is an **elephant** over a **double-disc and Z-rod**. The elephant, which faces right, has a long curving scroll within its body, and it has another at its 'chin', the junction of its body and head. The line of the latter scroll runs down the foreleg. Its antenna, which is double-lined, also ends with a scroll-like shape. The discs of the double-disc and Z-rod are wide-rimmed and dot-centred, and the short joining bar is concave-sided with another inside. It is one of the non-standard joining bars. The Z-rod, like the Congash 2 (HIG BAD) Z-rod, emanates from it. The upper arm is floriated and spear-pointed, and the lower ends with long curlicues.

DYCE 2 — 137 x 60cm E ΔΔΔ

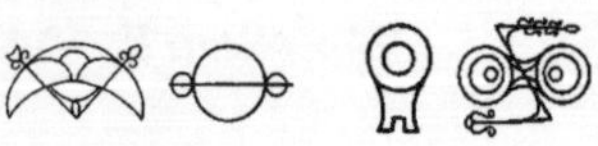

ECMS III, 189–190

The cross-slab is irregular in shape, is carved only on one face and lacks some of its base. Part of the left side too has been broken off and only some refitted. The cross, which is filled with thick interlace, has a circular centre and spirals projecting from the top of the summit and the ends of the transverse arms. To the left of the shaft is a **crescent and V-rod** over a vertical **triple-disc**, and to the right is a **mirror-case** over a **double-disc and Z-rod**. The symbols are ornamented, the mirror-case head with the same bulb pattern that fills both discs of the double-disc and Z-rod. This, like the crescent and V-rod, is clumsy in shape, and there are floriations on both Z-rod arms and on the arms of the V-rod. Although these symbols seem late in style and shape the mirror-case is one of the only two Class II examples and the triple-disc is one of the few which have additional links joining the small rings to the larger.

MARISCHAL MUSEUM

Marischal College **D**
University of Aberdeen, Aberdeen AB9 1AS
Tel: 01224 273131

Mon–Fri	1000–1700
Sun	1400–1700
Free	

Only one of the stones in the collection is on display at present, the Collace (PER) stone but there are plans to have all of them on permanent exhibition. Any not on display can be viewed in the store by prior arrangement.

Collace PER 60 x 40 x 8cm **O**

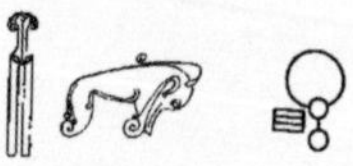

Small 1962

This stone, its top and base missing and its right side damaged, was found during ploughing at NO 207 332.

Its smooth face is incised with a pair of symbols and a **mirror-and-comb**. Only part of the upper of the pair survives, the prongs of a **tuning-fork** decorated with leaf-shapes, but the other is almost complete. It is an **elephant**, one without internal scrolls but with a spiral at the shoulder and a second rear 'paw'. The mirror below it is plain-headed and has no upper handle-boss. Instead the handle, the lower end of which is missing, flares wide to meet the head. The comb is single-sided and toothed and the line of its handle, which has two spiral projections, is parallel to the bottom edge of the teeth, but the line between the handle and teeth is angled – a possible carving error. Another may be the mirror's handle which is off-centre in relation to the head. The elephant's hind leg has been revised, having first been carved angled further backwards.

Dunnicaer 4 ABE 67 x 39 x 10cm **O**

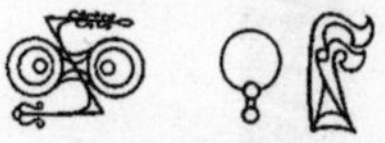

ECMS III, 201; Ritchie, J 1915 36–37

This Class I fragment was found on the shore below Dunnicaer, the rock stack at NO 884 487. It is unlike the small stones built into the orchard wall at Beannachar, being part of a conventional (and reused) symbol stone.

The fragment is the upper part of a regularly-shaped slab with a prepared face. Up the right side of the face is a raised rim, and partly incised, partly in low relief within the rim is a **double-disc and Z-rod**. It is of standard design but with a plain joining bar and is angled up from left to right. The end of the Z-rod's upper arm is indistinct, but the arm itself is floriated. There are forward-facing curlicues at the end of the lower arm also. The rod-end beyond these is missing.

Although simple in style the double-disc and Z-rod was not the first of the symbols on it. On the other face are the remains of others which rise upwards from one side of the slab. At the regular end is more than half of a plain **mirror** the left side of which is missing, apparently lost when the stone was trimmed into a slab. The upper boss of the handle can just be distinguished. Next is a very faint double-sided **comb**, and near the broken end of the slab is the upper part of a **flower** its single head drooping to the right and its base missing. These seem to be the remains of the first symbol set, which was carved when the stone was of a different shape. Between the mirror and the flower is also a cup-mark.

Tillytarmont 1 ABE 89 x 51 x 24cm O

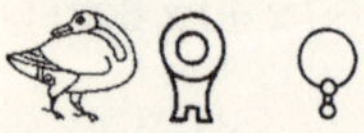

ECMS III, 185–186

This stone was the first of five Class I stones found below ground on Donald's Stone Haugh (NJ 533 473), a narrow spit of land between the Rivers Isla and Deveron. It was then built into an outhouse wall beside the farmhouse of North Tillytarmont, which is now demolished. It is an irregular and rough-surfaced slab and appears to be intact.

On it is a **goose** above a **mirror** and a **mirror-case**. Like the other two examples the goose is carved from left to right, but this one does not peer backwards. The mirror-case is very simple, its head disc-centred and its base plain. The equally simple mirror is plain-headed, and its handle is a single line between two circular bosses.

Figure 24

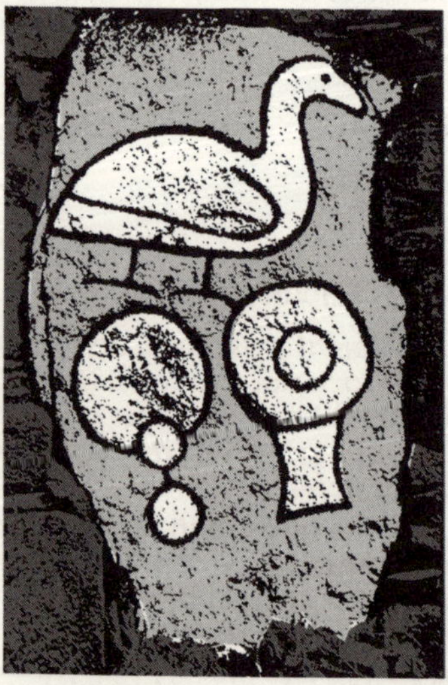

Tillytarmont 1 (ABE): when built into an outhouse wall at North Tillytarmont (also see p.151 fig.51)

Tillytarmont 4 ABE 125 x 140 x 18cm **E**

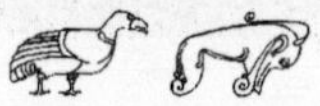

Trewin 1972

Incised on this irregularly-shaped stone, which was the fourth found at Donald's Stone Haugh (at NJ 533 472), are two large and superb symbols. A beautiful **eagle** walks from left to right, and below it is a slender and perfect **elephant**. The eagle's body has two rare features, a scroll behind the rear leg and another at the base of the neck. The elephant's body contains the standard long curving scroll and there is a scroll-line around the 'chin'. Its antenna and tail, both single-lined and spiral-ended, begin with teardrop-like loops, and it has additional 'paws'.

Tillytarmont 5 ABE 133 x 63 x 31cm **E**

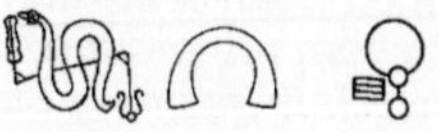

Trewin 1974

This pillar slab was found in Donald's Stone Haugh in the area of a disturbed stone spread (Ashmore 1980, 349–350). Its symbols are incised at the top of one face. The first is a very faint **serpent and Z-rod**. The serpent loops from left to right, but the Z-rod is laid out as for one going the other way. The spear-pointed arm is on the left, the other, which has an indistinct end, points downwards on the right. The rod is also unlike that of any other serpent in that the upper arm is floriated and the lower has two sets of curlicues. Below is a **horseshoe**, containing linked spirals and with a small arc at the foot of each arm, and to its right is a **mirror-and-comb**. The rimmed mirror has a twin-bossed and wide bar handle, the bosses also rimmed. The single-sided comb has a rectangular handle and is toothed, with no transverse line at the ends of the teeth.

Wantonwells ABE 116 x 78 x 18cm **O**

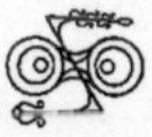

Inglis 1983 and 1987

This fragment, which was ploughed up at NJ 614 274 and may have slipped downhill from 'the tattered remains of a stone circle' (Inglis 1987, 75), is incised with most of a large and very faint **double-disc and Z-rod** of considerable interest. From the small dot-centred discs in the centre of each large disc rise radial lines which curve clockwise, a decoration reminiscent of the whorls on Dunnichen (ANG). In addition, the Wantonwells joining bar is not only proportionally shorter and thicker than that of any other Class I example but contains a quite unique decoration. A line runs from the upper right junction of bar and disc to just above the centre point of the Z-rod, and another runs from below that to the lower left junction. This symbol is one of the five double-discs and Z-rods with decorated discs and one of the seven with non-standard joining bars.

Arndilly MAP below ΔΔΔ **A**

79 x 81cm **E** NJ 291 471

ECMS III, 151–152

From Craigellachie cross the bridge over the Fiddich and immediately turn left for Arndilly House, which is a mile and a half along the 'Speyside Way'. The stone is built into a side wall of the house 12 metres left of the front entrance. It is less than a metre from the ground, is upside down and faces south-west. It was found in the wall of an old church on the same site. Permission should be sought at the house.

On the stone, which has been trimmed, are a **mirror-case** and a **divided rectangle and Z-rod**. The mirror-case head is rimmed and has a cross-filled star in its centre surrounded by small arcs, and the concave-sided base is decorated with a triangle and two curves, all containing small parallel arcs. The divided rectangle and Z-rod is a superb example. In it are two circular 'chariot wheel' re-entrants and four arc-like 'horse body' re-entrants, and the Z-rod, a true Z, is flighted and arrow-headed.

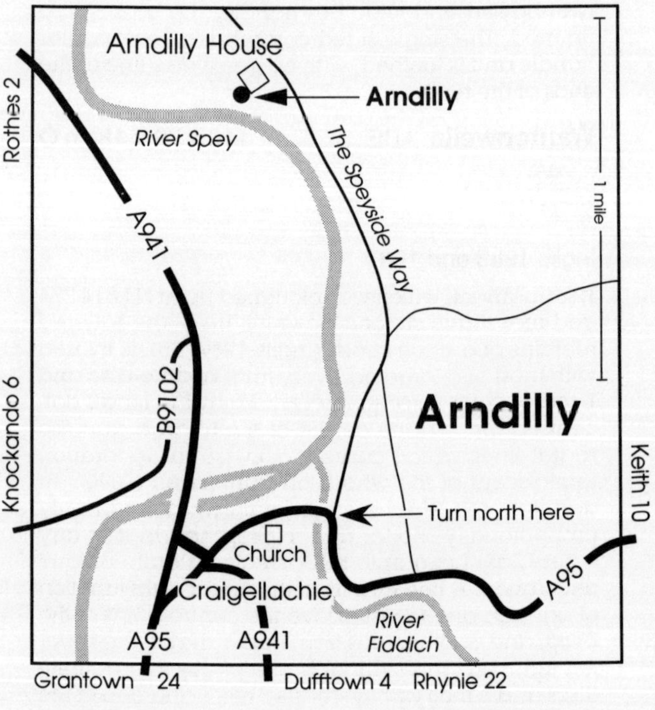

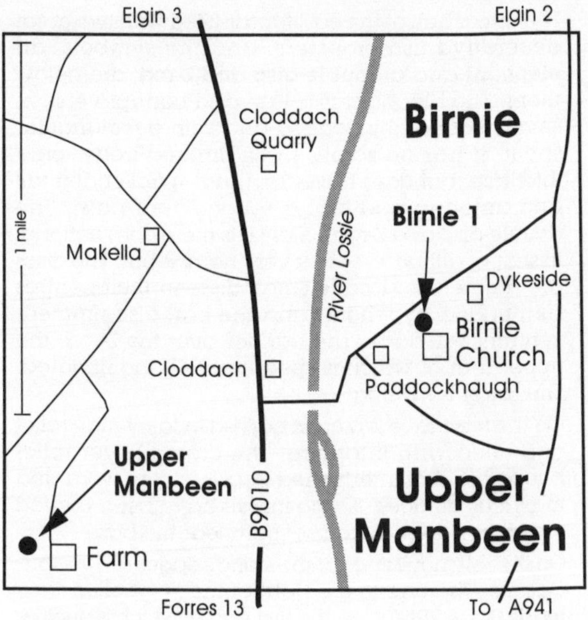

Birnie 1

MAP above Δ **A**

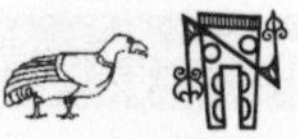

107 x 69 x 53cm **E** NJ 206 587

ECMS III, 118–119

Birnie Church is on a minor road that runs south-west from the A941 at New Elgin. It can also be reached from the B9010 from Elgin. The stone, which faces north, stands in the churchyard close to its west wall and beside a small gate. It was found built into a wall of the churchyard.

On it is an **eagle** incised facing right over a **divided rectangle and Z-rod**, the same symbol pair that is on the Tyrie (ABE) stone. Birnie's are very worn and heavily lichened, but the divided rectangle and Z-rod was a virtual replica of Tyrie's.

BRODIE (*The Rodney Stone*)

ΔΔΔ **A**

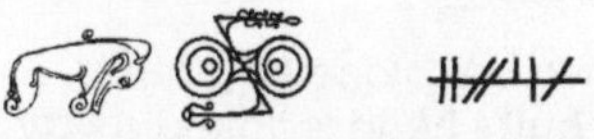

193 x 104 x 13cm **O** NH 984 577

ECMS III, 132–135 (1993 edn figs 136 and 136a face p.127)

This cross-slab is on the left side of the east drive into the grounds of Brodie Castle and about fifty metres inside the entrance gate. The entrance is a quarter of a mile north of a minor cross-roads on the A96 seven miles from Nairn and three miles west of Forres. The stone, its base missing, stands in a roofed shelter and is held up by metal supports. It was found while digging the foundations for the church in nearby Dyke (NH 990 584) and was then re-erected in the village in honour of Admiral Rodney's victory over the French in 1782. It was moved to the driveway in about 1842.

The upper half of the east face is filled with two great decorative fish-monsters, and the symbols, an **elephant** and a **double-disc and Z-rod**, are below them. The elephant is a late and corrupt version, small-headed, thin-legged and with a rectangular snout. It has no scrolls in its rimmed body, only interlace, but does have the usual spiral-ended tail and antenna and also a second 'rear paw'. The double-disc and Z-rod below it is more conventional in shape, although with a very narrow bar. The discs are rimmed and have small discs in their centres surrounded by whorls, and the bar, also rimmed, contains interlace. The bar lies over the Z-rod, the upper arm of which is spearheaded and floriated. The lower is missing.

On the west face is a cross carved in fairly high relief and filled with interlace. The cross's lower relief background of intertwined beasts is very worn and in places defaced. Large initials have been carved on either side of the cross-shaft near the base.

On the roll mouldings at the stone's edges are various Ogams. The one to the right of the symbolled face reads EDDARRNON Q, the first part of which is another Ogam example of the name Itheman or Etheman.

BURGHEAD MUSEUM

Burghead Library, Grant Street **A**
Burghead IV30 2UE
Tel: 01343 830186 (or 01309 673701)

The stones and a cast of No.5 (in the British Museum) are displayed in a window of the library, which is on the south side of the street, and can be viewed at any time.

The great Pictish fortress from or from near which the bull stones came is at the end of Grant Street. Much of it was destroyed by the building of the harbour and town in the early nineteenth century.

Burghead 2 — 30 x 48 x 10cm **O**

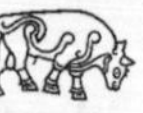

ECMS III, 119–121

This is the larger of the two bull stone fragments. Its base is missing, and the **bull**'s head is flaked away, but most of the body remains, including the great scrolls in front of the hind leg and at the shoulder. It was found in 1862 during improvement work at the harbour.

Burghead 4 — 28 x 28 x 10cm **O**

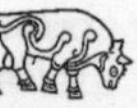

ECMS III, 122

On this fragment, which is the right upper part of a slab, is a **bull**'s head, part of its body (with a shoulder scroll) and its left foreleg. It was found in 1867 during the demolition of a house on the south quay.

ELGIN CATHEDRAL

Tel: 01343 547171

Apr–Sep	Mon–Sat	0930–1830
	Sunday	1400–1830
Oct–Mar	Mon–Wed	0930–1630
	Thursday	0930–1300
	Saturday	0930–1630
	Sunday	1400–1630
	£1.50; conc £1; child 75p	

ELGIN Δ **A**

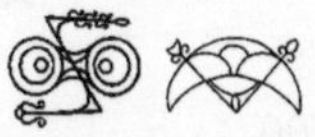

202 x 75 x 18cm **E** NJ 222 631
ECMS III, 134–136

This cross-slab was found underground near St Giles Church in Elgin but now stands in the ruins of the Cathedral.

The top of the slab is broken and the base missing. On the south face is a worn cross with various figures about it. Below the cross are intertwined beasts.

On the other face at the top are the remains of a carving the meaning of which is uncertain. Below this is a **double-disc and Z-rod** over a **crescent and V-rod**. The double-disc and Z-rod is like some other Class II versions in that the discs are joined by two parallel bars and the Z-rod runs between them. The rod's upper end consists of something like two pairs of floriations, and the lower is very similar to the flighted end of the V-rod below it. The crescent and V-rod is, although rimmed and much-decorated, standard in pattern.

Below the symbols is a worn hunting scene with a stag and hounds and four horsemen, the principal one having a hawk on his outstretched arm.

ELGIN MUSEUM

1 High Street, Elgin IV30 1EQ **A**
Tel: 01343 543675

Easter–October

Mon–Fri	1000–1700
Saturday	1100–1600
Sunday	1400–1700
Other times by arrangement	
£1.50; conc 75p; child 50p; family £3.50	

Burghead 3 40 x 53 x 18cm **O**

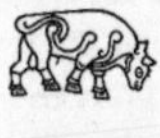

ECMS III, 121

Although this is only a fragment its **bull** is complete, the body containing no less than four scrolls. The fragment was found 'in rubbish' in the town.

Burghead 6

60 x 45 x 15cm **O**

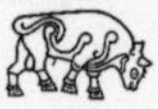

ECMS III, 123–124

This fragment has only the front half of a **bull** with its head up. Behind and in front of the right foreleg are scrolls. It was found in 1854 during alterations to the south quay of Burghead Harbour.

FALCONER MUSEUM

Tolbooth Street, Forres IV36 0PH **A**
Tel: 01309 673701

May–Sep	Mon–Sat	1000–1700
Oct–Apr	Mon–Fri	1000–1700
	Free	

Forres 2

54 x 38 x 16cm **O**

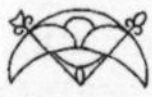

Gray 1992

This stone is a trimmed fragment in two pieces. These are incised with some of the right half of a **crescent and V-rod**. No rod-end is visible, but in the crescent's wing is an unusual shape, a rimmed pointed oval.

The stone was in a garden wall (at NJ 034 587) in Forres. When it was built into the wall it was already in two pieces, but these must have been recognised then as parts of a symbol stone as they were found cemented together.

The stone may not yet be on display in the museum. If not it can be seen by arrangement.

Inveraven Church

NJ 183 376 **B**

The narrow road that winds down to Inveraven Church is signposted on the A95 14 miles north-east of Grantown. The four stones, which are fixed to the church's south wall, are from left to right Nos 2, 3, 1 and 4. The first three were found in the foundations of the old church and the fourth in the churchyard.

Inveraven 1

170 x 86 x 15cm **O** ΔΔΔ

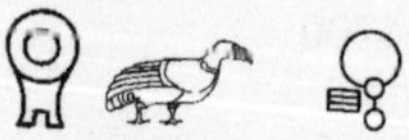

ECMS III, 152–153 (1993 edn fig.158 faces p.151)

This stone was broken but reassembled and is remarkably clearly incised with a **mirror-case** above a large **eagle** with a **mirror-and-comb** in front of it. The eagle, long-necked and facing right, is well-plumaged and has spirals at its leg and neck. The small mirror is almost unique in shape, its long handle ending with a straight-based arc. The mirror-case is one of the more ornate examples. The head contains two concentric discs each with domes about them,

and the almost rectangular base, vertically divided into three parts, rests on a dome-decorated arc. The comb is double-sided and apparently toothed. A few of the details on this excellent stone are lost as a result of its breakage.
The outline of the Inveraven mirror-case is very like the mirror beside it, and together they give some credence to the concept that the so-called 'mirror-case' symbol is indeed a representation of such an object. (Close-Brooks 1989, 15).

Inveraven 2 147 x 58 x 15cm O ΔΔΔ

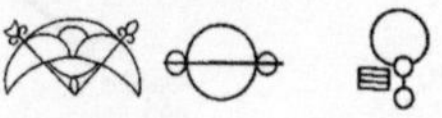

ECMS III, 152–154

Incised on it is a **crescent and V-rod** over a plain **triple-disc** with a bar. Below them is a **mirror-and-comb**. The crescent is decorated with a small dome between two large wings, and the right rod-end is a curlicued diamond-shape, the left curlicued flights. The mirror is rimmed and has a twin-bossed bar handle, the bosses also rimmed. The comb is single-sided, has a two-pointed handle and is very clearly toothed.

Inveraven 3 33 x 20 x 15cm **O** ΔΔΔ

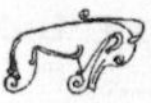

ECMS III, 152, 154

This fragment is incised with part of what was a very fine **elephant** facing right. All that remains is its head and curving snout and some of its foreleg. It has a 'chin' scroll.

Inveraven 4 107 x 53 x 8cm **O** Δ

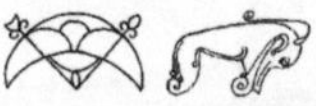

Small 1964

This is a very worn stone and it has been trimmed down some of the left side. It bears a **crescent and V-rod** over an **elephant**. The decoration in the crescent's centre is indeterminate, not much of the V-rod is visible, and the elephant is little more than an incomplete outline. The only detail in the body and head is a shoulder spiral and the eye.

Figure 25

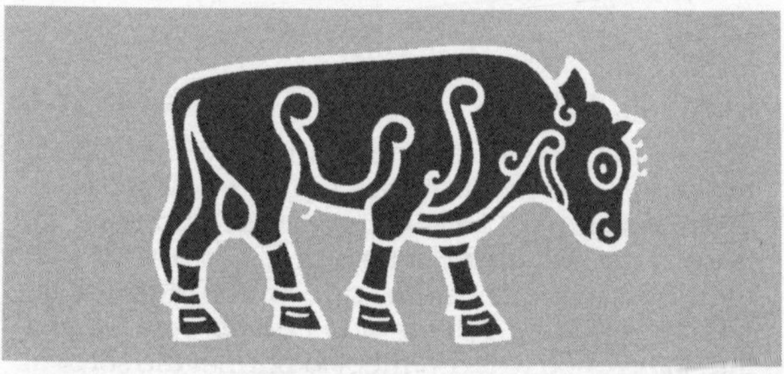

Bull: Burghead 3 (MQR), see p.99 (after ECMS fig.125)

Knockando Church | NJ 187 429 **A**

Knockando Church is not far up the road that runs north-west from the B9102 seven miles west of Craigellachie. Two trimmed symbol stones, which came from Pulvrenan burial-ground (NJ 203 422), are built into the inner face of the churchyard wall between the two gates. No.1 is on the left, No.2 next and an almost featureless stone is on the right. They face west.

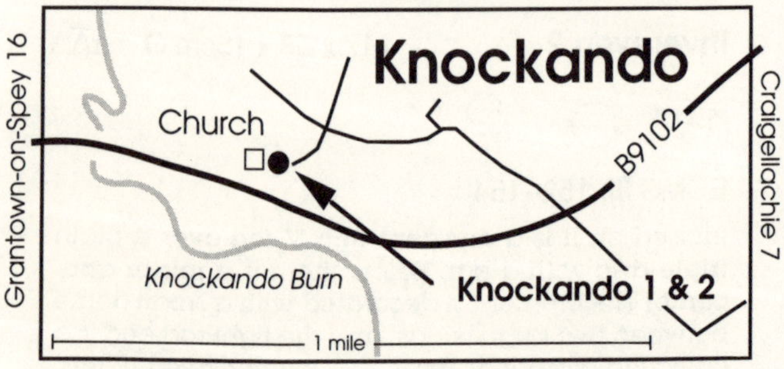

Knockando 1

MAP above ΔΔ

ECMS III, 127–128 — *c*145 x 56cm **O**

Near the top is a **wheel**, and below this are the remains of two **crescents and V-rods** side by side. The wheel, which may be an additional symbol, has a rimmed centre and thirteen spokes. The left crescent contains dome-and-wing pattern, and the right end of its V-rod is arrowheaded and curlicued. Most of the left end is missing. The right wing of the other crescent is also missing, and its left V-rod end is invisible. The only visible decoration is a dome in its left wing.

Figure 26

Crescent and V-rod: the pair on Knockando 1 (MOR) (after ECMS fig.132)

Knockando 2

MAP above Δ

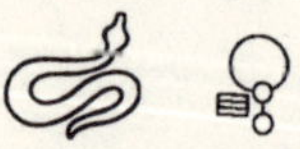

ECMS III, 127–218 — 190 x 46cm **O**

This stone has not only been trimmed but been broken in two parts. At the top is a now-headless S-shaped **serpent** looping upwards, and near the base is a plain **mirror**. The mirror has a very faint twin-bossed bar handle, and to the right of the handle is part of a single-sided **comb**. It is possible that there once was a symbol to partner the serpent, incised in the considerable space between the serpent and the mirror but now erased by wear.

Mortlach Church NJ 324 393 B

Mortlach Church is in the Kirktown of Mortlach, which is half a mile down the minor road running south from the junction in the centre of Dufftown.

MORTLACH 1 180 x 57 x 20cm E Δ

? 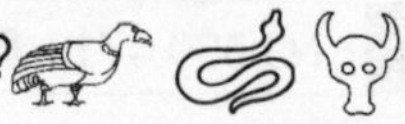

ECMS III, 155–56

This is a primitive cross-slab, a natural pillar which stands in the middle of the lower churchyard.

On the north-east face is a relief-carved cross with two animal-headed fish-monsters above it and a four-legged and claw-footed beast below. On the south-west face the very faint remains of a bird (?**eagle**) are incised almost halfway down the stone, and below it an extended **serpent** wriggles from right to left. A **bull's head** is full-face below this, and nearer the bottom is a mounted man with a hound below him.

Mortlach 2 160 x 25 x 10cm O ΔΔΔ

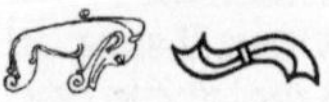

Simpson 1926

This stone, which is in the entrance hall of the church, was found almost two metres below ground not far to the north-west of the cross-slab. It was broken into five pieces to get it to the surface.

At the top is a simple but beautiful **elephant** incised from left to right and unique in Class I in that a line separates snout from head. Below it is a uniquely-shaped **ogee** rather like a double snap-hook.

Upper Manbeen MAP p.97 ΔΔ D

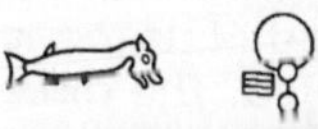

90 x 60 x 35cm **E** NJ 187 576
ECMS III, 128–29

Upper Manbeen Farm is four miles south of Elgin. Take the B9010, fork left at the Pluscarden junction, and after passing Wester Manbeen take the next right but one, which is signed to Manbeen and Milton Duff. Quite soon turn left at 'Makella' (a fairly new house), and in less than half a mile turn left down the Easter Manbeen track. Park at the steading (where permission should be sought), and walk back 100 metres to a gate on the west side of the track. The stone is about one hundred metres downhill.

It is an irregularly-shaped slab with symbols incised on the west face, a horizontal dog-headed **fish-monster** facing right over a **mirror-and-comb**. As they are half way down the stone and have above them a large set of initials it is likely that there was originally a symbol above the fish-monster, one destroyed when the initials were carved. The same carving also caused other parts of the stone's surface to flake, this has removed some of the fish-monster's body. The comb, which is under the monster's tail, is double-sided and faintly toothed, and the mirror, plain-headed with a twin-bossed bar handle, lies on its side to the right of the comb.

There are also carved initials on the east face.

Whitestones House NJ 530 471 **B**

Three stones stand in the garden of Whitestones House, where permission to view them should be sought. The entrance is on the east side of the B9022, just before its junction with the B9118. This is just over five miles north of Huntly and not far beyond the bridge over the Isla.

North Redhill 81 x 58 x 26cm **O** Δ

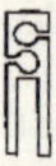

ECMS III, 154–155

The stone was found in the nineteenth century built into a dyke on North Redhill Farm (NJ 560 467).

On this fragment is some of a single symbol, the lower part of a vertical rectangular shape with a U-shaped re-entrant in the base. As the divided rectangle and Z-rod on the Cullaird (HIG INV) fragment has a similar re-entrant this carving may be some of a **divided rectangle** also – but one with no Z-rod.

Tillytarmont 2 ABE 129 x 60 x 15cm **O** Δ

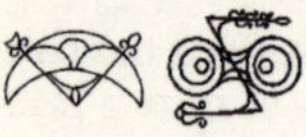

Ferguson 1956

This broken-topped slab was ploughed up in 1944 at NJ 533 472 in Donald's Stone Haugh.

On it is a **crescent and V-rod** over a **double-disc and Z-rod**. The crescent and V-rod contains two arcs in the crescent's centre, and the visible end of its rod is curlicued and apparently flight-ended. The discs have eccentric rings within them and a concave-sided joining bar with an internal bar. The upper arm of the Z-rod is spearheaded with three staggered floriations. The other rod-end is less complete but curlicued. Both symbols are faint and also lichened.

Tillytarmont 3 ABE 114 x 90 x 38cm **O** Δ

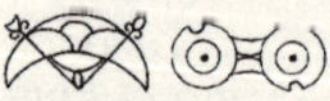

Ferguson 1956

Tillytarmont 3 was found in 1867 in Donald's Stone Haugh. It was not recognised till 1954.

The slab, again broken-topped, is incised with two very faint and lichened symbols. The upper is a plain **crescent and V-rod**, one rod end invisible and the other missing, and the lower is a **double-disc** with wide-rimmed discs and a concave-sided joining bar.

HIGHLAND 10

BADENOCH AND STRATHSPEY

Advie

Δ **A**

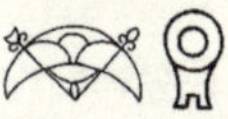

96 x 40cm **E** NJ 127 343
Joass 1906

Advie Church, nine miles north-east of Grantown-on-Spey, is on the north side of the A95 three hundred metres beyond (east of) the turning to Advie itself. Built into the north side of a projection from the rear wall is a symbol stone fragment on its side, the top to the right. It has been trimmed down the right side and has lost some of its base. Found in the cemetery at NJ 142 353 (a mile east of Advie Village) it was used as a window lintel in the old church and then as part of a wall-stile.

On it are parts of a **crescent and V-rod** over a **mirror-case**. In the crescent, the right side of which is missing, is decoration of arcs, curve-sided triangles and a large spiral, all very faint. Little of the V-rod can now be made out, but its left end was a curlicued arrow or spearhead. The mirror-case head is, like Arndilly's (MOR), rimmed and with a four-pointed star in the centre, and the base has a bottom line of small flaps. The impression given is that this is of pleated or gathered material.

Figure 27

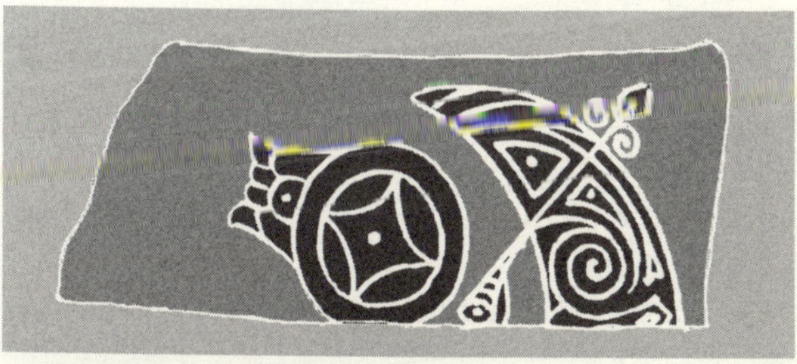

Advie (HIG BAD): set into the wall on its side

Congash NJ 058 262 **D**

ECMS III, 96-97

Congash Farmhouse, where permission should be sought, is on the south of the A95 two miles south-east of Grantown-On-Spey. The stones are best approached by making for a prominent power-line pole on the far side of the field beside the farm buildings and 400 metres east-south-east of them. Beside the pole is a gateway through a double fence, and 200 metres south is a sub-rectangular enclosure, 'Parc-an-Caipel' (the Chapel enclosure), in a field bounded on its far sides by a wood. The enclosure is an overgrown area of stones in scattered piles within a low earthen bank heaped with other stones. The two slabs stand facing one another just over a metre apart at the far south-west end of it.

Whether or not there was once a chapel within the bank it is thought to have enclosed a burial ground (Macdonald and Laing 1968, 33). Perhaps the two symbol stones were found in this and re-erected on the line of the bank.

Congash 1

96 x 66 x 25cm **O** ΔΔ

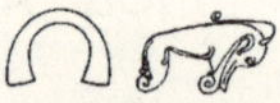

This, the eastern of the pair, faces north-west. Its symbols are incised with wide shallow grooves and are somewhat faint. The upper, which is also lichened, is an almost intact **horseshoe** with curving lines inside it and small arcs at each foot. The lower, not all of which is exposed, is an **elephant** with a twin-lined antenna and a shoulder spiral.

Congash 2

114 x 76 x 13cm **O** ΔΔΔ

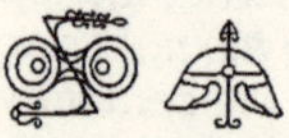

On Congash 2, which faces east, is a **double-disc and Z-rod** over a **helmet**, both deeply incised and rather clearer than the symbols on No.1 – although the double-disc and Z-rod is lichened. The discs are rimmed, and in them are small eccentric discs with dotted centres. The Z-rod's angled arm is not of standard pattern. Like the arm of the Z-rod on Dyce 1 (ABN) it emanates from the outer lines of the joining bar. The upper arm is not floriated and ends with a curlicued flight. The floriations and the spearhead are on the lower arm. This symbol has been incised upside-down. Under it is the only known example of the 'helmet'.

Dunachton

ΔΔΔ **B**

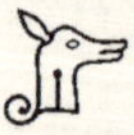

131 x 40 x 11cm **O** NH 821 046
ECMS III, 100

The entrance to Dunachton Lodge, a private house, is from the track to 'Dunachton Farm' leaving the A9 four miles from the east of Kingussie. Once on the track, turn left almost immediately towards 'Dunachtonmore' and turn right at the T-junction slightly further on to get to the Lodge, where permission should be sought.

The stone stands facing north-north-east about 100 metres south-west of the Lodge on the south-east edge of a grassy area among trees outside the end wall of the garden.

Its top right corner has been broken away, but it is otherwise intact. On it is a **deer's head**, some of the nose of which is missing. The head faces right and is ornamented with a spiral behind the neck base and a vertical line up the centre of the neck.

Inverallan

MAP below Δ **A**

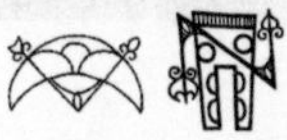

107 x 50 x 14cm **O** NJ 027 260
ECMS III, 101–102

Inverallan Churchyard is south-south-west of Grantown-on-Spey. It can be reached from the parking area on the A95 near the Inverallan roundabout, along a minor road which runs beside the Spey. The stone, which was found during the demolition of the old church, is in a recess halfway along the inner face of the churchyard's west wall (i.e. the furthest from the river).

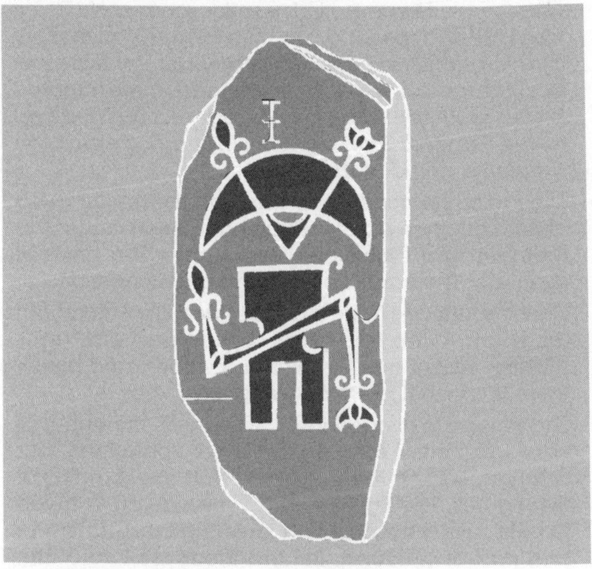

Figure 28

Inverallan (HIG BAD) (after ECMS fig.105)

Very faintly incised on this irregular slab is a **crescent and V-rod** above a **divided-rectangle and Z-rod**. The former is one with the rod's right end flighted and the left arrow-headed. The divided rectangle has semicircular 'chariot wheel' re-entrants. The Z-rod is uniquely double-lined and is apparently arrow-headed and flighted. Both ends are curlicued.

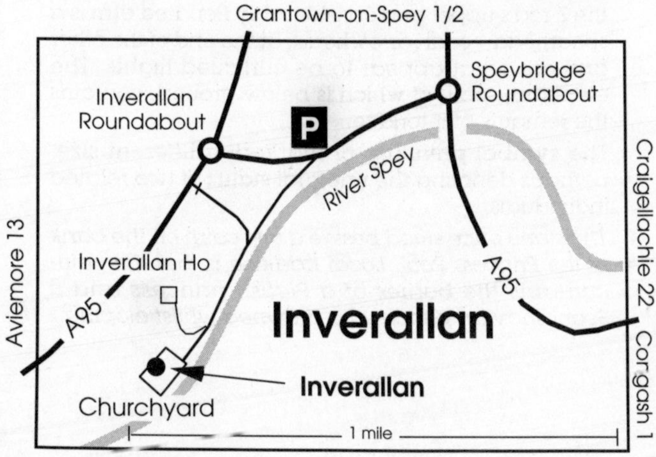

GLENFERNESS (*The Princess Stone*) Δ D

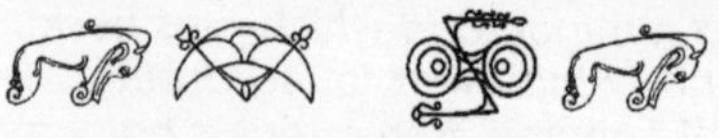

177 x 75 x 11cm **O** NH 937 426

ECMS III, 115–116 (1993 edn figs 119 and 120 face p.97)

Glenferness House is twelve miles south of Nairn by the A939 and the B9007. Its mile-long entrance drive is on the right-hand side of the B9007 almost two miles beyond Ferness. The cross-slab stands three hundred metres south of the house at the side of a path leading to the Princess Pool on the Findhorn. Permission should be asked at the house.

The top of the stone is missing, and the remainder is broken into two pieces which have been cemented together and stand between supporting posts of concrete. The carvings are worn and lichened.

On the south-west face is an interlace-filled cross with the summit arm and parts of the transverse arms missing. About and below it are whorls, and below these is a panel in which two figures wrestle.

The reverse is divided into two panels, the upper of very worn interlace and the lower containing four symbols, something indistinct, and the remains of two figures. The figures, which are carved from left to right, are a hooded and kneeling cross-bowman and part of a hound. Behind them are two of the symbols.

These are a small **elephant** facing left over a small **crescent and V-rod**. What decoration, if any, was in them is no longer clear, but the elephant not only has a second 'forepaw' but scrolls within its body. The crescent is rimmed, and the V-rod ends, both curlicued, are an arrowhead and a set of flights. Below are two large symbols, a **double-disc and Z-rod** over an **elephant**, this one facing right. The discs are rimmed and filled with bosses, and at the end of the Z-rod's upper and considerably floriated arm is a spearhead – or an arrowhead; at the end of the other arm are what appear to be curlicued flights. The elephant, some of which is below ground, contains the remains of interlace.

The symbol pairs are of markedly different size, perhaps denoting the unequal status of two related individuals.

The stone once stood beside a low cairn on the bank of the Princess Pool. Local tradition is that the cairn contains the bodies of a Pictish princess and a Scandinavian prince who drowned whilst eloping.

INVERNESS MUSEUM AND ART GALLERY

Castle Wynd, Inverness IV2 3ED **B**
Tel: 01463 237114
Mon–Sat 0900–1700
Free

As well as the stones listed below, a cast of Brodie (MOR), the 'Rodney Stone', is on display. It is a fine reproduction but rather dimly lit.

Ardross 1 HIG ROS 32 x 51 x 8cm O

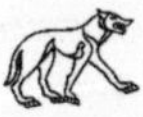

Ardross 2 HIG ROS 22 x 20 x 11cm O

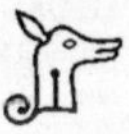

ECMS III, 55–56

These fragments, found built into a wall at Stittenham (NH 65 74), may be from the same stone.
On one is most of a handsome **wolf** with scrolls within its body, and on the other is a horse-like **deer's head**.

Cullaird 35 x 37 x 5cm O

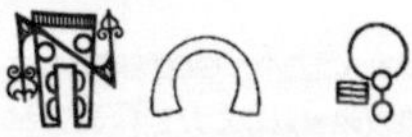

Stevenson 1959, 39–40

On this fragment, which is most of the upper left quarter of a probably rectangular slab, are the remains of a full set of symbols – an intact **mirror-and-comb**, almost half of a **divided rectangle and Z-rod**, and part of a **horseshoe**. Most of the divided rectangle's left-hand 'chariot wheel' re-entrant survives and also half of a smaller semicircle in the base. The left arm of the Z-rod is floriated and spear-headed. Only some of the left half of the horseshoe remains. It is decorated with arcs. The small mirror is plain and long-handled, and the comb is vertical, double-sided and toothed.

This fragment was ploughed up at NH 634 404 on Cullaird Farm, Scaniport, which is four miles south-west of Inverness. Its divided rectangle and Z-rod may show that the symbol on the North Redhill (MOR) fragment is a divided rectangle. Both have the same semicircular base re-entrant.

Garbeg 50 x 50 x 5cm **O**

Wedderburn and Grime 1984, 151, 160–161

On these fragments is part of a **crescent and V-rod** decorated with comma-like scrolls. The visible (left) end of the V-rod is flighted. To the lower right is what may be the end of an elephant's antenna.

The fragments were found at NH 511 323 on Garbeg Farm near Drumnadrochit. They were in the top of a cairn which contained a grave-like pit. The pit was filled with only earth and stones, but in a pit in a nearby cairn were parts of human bones.

Kingsmills 33 x 30 x 6cm **O**

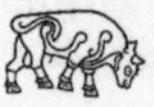

ECMS III, 102–103

This fragment was found in Inverness, at NH 67 44, in use as the step of a cow-byre.

On it is most of a horned **bull** with scrolls above its hind and forelegs. It has more in common with the Lochardill bull (p.111) than with those on the Burghead (MOR) stones.

Figure 29

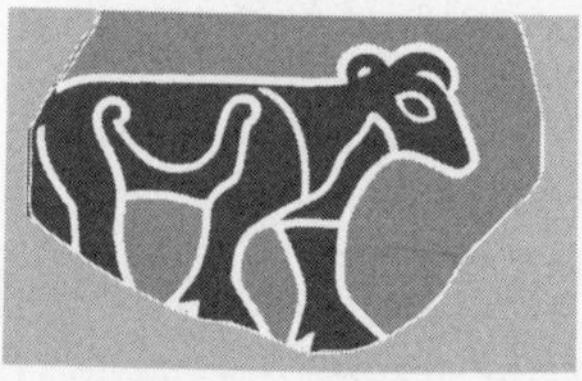

Bull: Kingsmills (HIG INV) (after ECMS fig.106)

Little Ferry Links 4a HIG SUT 46 x 38 x 9cm **O**

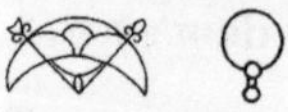

ECMS III, 45-48

With this fragment is the cast of another part of the same stone (No.4), which is in Dunrobin Castle Museum (HIG SUT) (see p.127). The Dunrobin fragment was found at approximately NH 814 966 on Little Ferry Links.

On the pair is most of the left half of a spiral-decorated **crescent and V-rod**, the rod-end ornately flighted and curlicued. Below the crescent and V-rod is what may be part of the head of a rimmed mirror.

Torgorm HIG ROS 50 x 35 x 18cm **O**

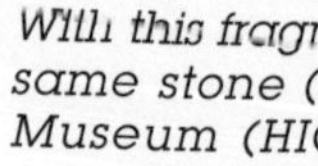

ECMS III, 106–107

This Class I fragment was found at NH c559 549 on Torgorm Farm on the Black Isle.

On it are parts of two differently ornamented **double-discs and Z-rods**, which are one disc of each and some of both Z-rods, including one upper arm. This ends with an ornate spearhead and is floriated – but the floriations, although staggered, are reversed and there is also a pair of curlicues behind the point.

Wester Balblair 71 x 45 x 11cm **O**

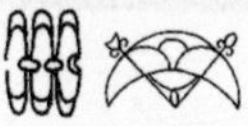

Cameron 1969

The stone was found at NH 510 453 while a new garden was being dug. It had probably been used for the bottoming of an old road that crossed the site.

On this almost intact stone is a **triple-oval** over a **crescent and V-rod**, both very plain. The triple-oval, its ovals pointed and the upper points of two missing, is the simplest known example of this rare symbol. The crescent's V-rod ends are clearly arrow-headed and flighted, neither is curlicued, and both are large in comparison to the size of the crescent.

Knocknagael (*The Boar Stone*) ΔΔΔ **C**

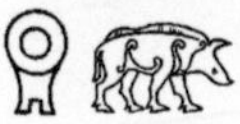

206 x 218 x 34cm **E** NH 662 448
ECMS III, 103–105

This stone is in the foyer at the south end of Highland Council HQ, on the east side of Glenurquhart Road (A82) half a mile south-west of the Ness bridge. It once stood at NH 657 413 in a field of Knocknagael Farm, three miles south of the City. This may have been its original site, but it had been re-erected.

On the stone is a **mirror-case** over a remarkably fine **boar**. The mirror-case is plain except for a dot-centred disc in the centre of the head. The boar has scrolls above the hind and foreleg and forward of the shoulder. Bristles rise from the spine in a crest that runs from behind the ear to above the tail.

Lochardill ΔΔ **D**

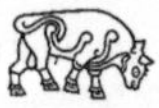

60 x 67 x 7cm NH 690 450
ECMS III, 102–103

This, one of the two Inverness bull stones, is an irregular slab incised with a **bull** facing right. Within its body are scrolls in front of the hind leg, behind the foreleg and at the shoulder, but it does not have the style of the splendid Burghead (MOR) bulls.

"Found in an old dyke close to Provost Ross's house at Inverness" it is now at Stonifield House on the south side of the A96 300 metres east of its junction with theA9. ***NB There is no public access to this stone.***

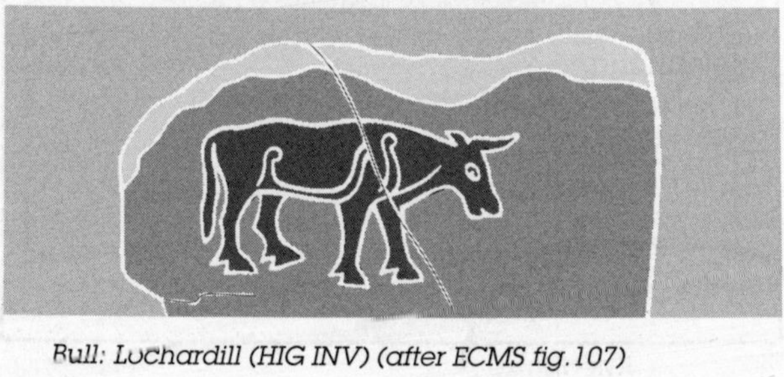

Figure 30

Bull: Lochardill (HIG INV) (after ECMS fig.107)

DUNVEGAN CASTLE MUSEUM

Dunvegan Castle, Isle of Skye IV5 8WF			**D**
Tel: 01470 521206			
Mar–Oct	Daily	1000–1730	
	Entrance to Castle		
	£4.50; conc/group ea £4; child £2.50		

Dun Osdale 75 x 38 x 24cm **E**

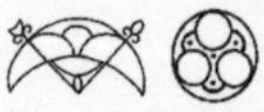

RCAHMS 1928, 165

The stone was found beside a well near Dun Osdale, a broch south-west of the Castle (at NG 242 463).

The symbols are a **crescent and V-rod** over a **disc**. The crescent contains two wings with a dome between them, and the left end of the V-rod is a large open-ended ball-shape, which perhaps represents arrow-flights. The right end is missing. The disc is rimmed and has a small central disc.

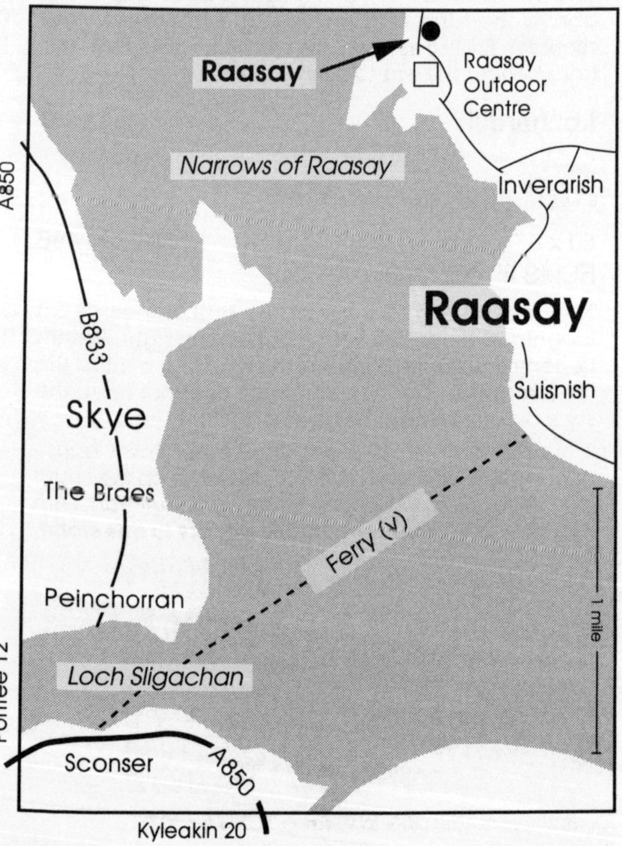

Raasay MAP below opp ΔΔ **A**

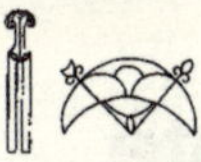

212 x 58 x 14cm **O** NG 547 368

Richardson 1907

This stone is on the Island of Raasay, which can be reached by ferry from Skye (see below).

The stone is two miles north of Suisnish pier, on the east side of the coastal road sixty metres past the northern entrance to Raasay Outdoor Centre. It is behind a gate which is the start of 'Temptation Hill Walk'. The stone, which has been trimmed down the right side, faces west. It was found in the nineteenth century during the making of a road from the pier at Clachan to Raasay House.

There is a contemporary cross above the symbols, but as the cross is incised this natural slab may be regarded as a Class I stone.

The cross is a cross patée in a square frame with a slender shaft below it. The symbols are a **tuning-fork** over a **crescent and V-rod**. The tuning-fork, which is horizontal with its prongs to the left, has a handle similar in shape to those at Abernethy (PER) and Dunrobin (HIG SUT). It is whorl-ended and was probably round-topped but is very plain in comparison to these others. The ends of the prongs are lost because of flaking, and more flaking, wear and trimming have removed some of the crescent and V-rod terminals. The crescent is decorated with dome-and-wing patterns, but as the stone's surface is not only irregular but lichened these are hard to make out.

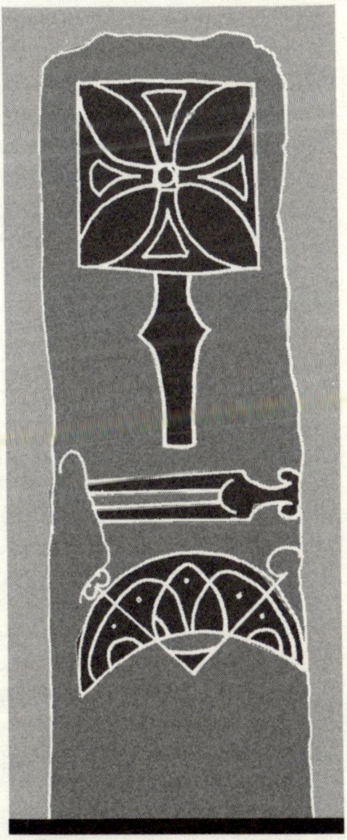

Cross and symbols: Raasay (HIG SKY)

Figure 31

Raasay Ferry Sailings		first	last
Dep Sconser (Skye)	Mon–Sat	0830	1615
Dep Suisnish (Raasay)	Mon–Sat	0800	1645
During summer there are later crossings on Fridays			

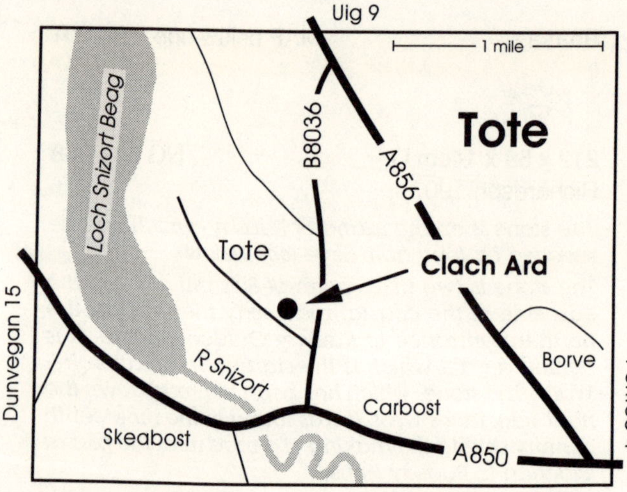

Tote (*Clach Ard*) MAP above ΔΔ **C**

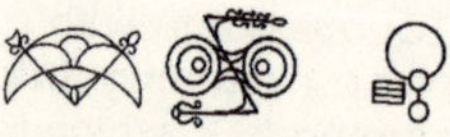

140 x 49 x 37cm **E** NG 421 491

MacLeod 1910, 384–385

Clach Ard, the Tall Stone, is six miles from Portree and can be reached by taking the Dunvegan road (A850) and turning north after Carbost up the B8306 to the minor road to Tote; the stone stands facing south-west two hundred metres up this road. It was found in Tote, NG 418 492, in use as a door-jamb.

As the surface is rough, flaked in parts, and lichened and the incisions shallow and worn the details of the symbols are hard to make out. They are a **crescent and V-rod**, a **double-disc and Z-rod** and a **mirror-and-comb**. The crescent and V-rod stretches across the full width of the stone, but its left end is lost because of flaking and little more than the V-rod arms and the crescent's outline is obvious - except for a small dotted circle in its crest. There is faint hatching in the right-hand point, fainter hatching along the lower arc and two wing shapes. The rod ends can not be made out. Below is the double-disc and Z-rod, which is massive and vertical. The discs, part of the lower missing, are rimmed, and in them are small eccentric circles with dots. The joining bar is of conventional design, concave-sided and with an internal bar, and the Z-rod upper arm appears to be floriated, its end a curlicued spearhead, but the end of the lower is gone. Near the bottom of the stone is the mirror-and comb, which is very faint. The mirror is plain-headed, with a boss-ended bar handle, and the comb is single-sided with a three-pointed handle.

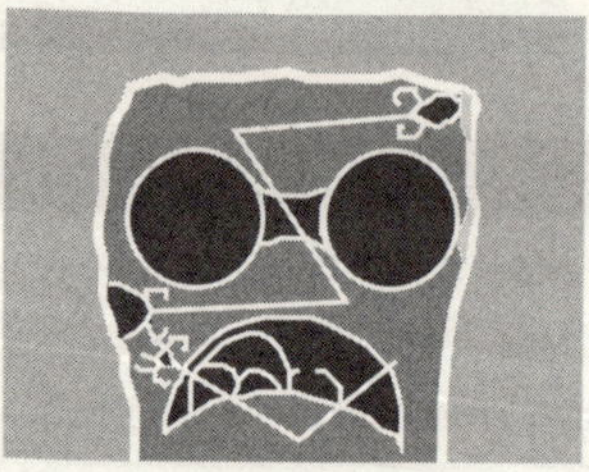

Figure 32

Fiscavaig (HIG SKY): another stone from Skye, in the collection of the Museum of Scotland, but currently on display in the St Mungo Museum, Glasgow, *see p.33*

Dingwall

Δ **A**

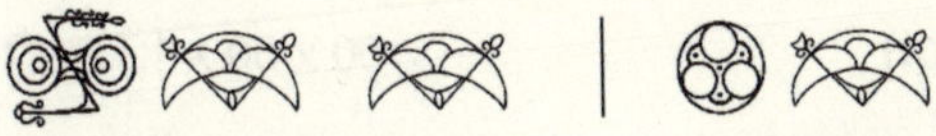

127 x 53 x 20cm **E** NH 549 589
ECMS III, 56–57

This reused Class I stone stands at the south entrance of the churchyard of St Clement's Church, which is in the centre of Dingwall.

On its west face are three faint symbols. At the very top of the stone is a **double-disc and Z-rod**, and in the centre is one of two **crescents and V-rods**, the other being near the base. The discs are rimmed, with smaller eccentric circles within them, the lower arm of the Z-rod ends with a curlicued ball, and the upper is or was floriated. Not much of the very faint upper crescent and V-rod survives, and the lower is little more than an outline. Because the stone has been trimmed some of the left wing of this symbol is missing.

On the reverse are two symbols, the upper a **disc** composed of three small discs in triangular formation but without an encircling disc, and the other another crescent and V-rod. The latter, its right wing lost as a result of the trimming and its left rod end worn away, is large but apparently plain. (See p.120, fig.35)

As the reverse face is also cup-marked this stone was probably an earlier standing stone. It was found in 1880, in use as a lintel in the church.

Edderton 1

ΔΔ **D**

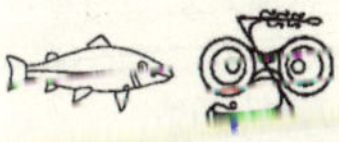

320 x 100 x 43cm **E** NH 708 851
ECMS III, 57–59

This stone, known as Clach Biorach (the Pointed Stone) or Clach Chairidh (the Weir Stone), stands in a field beside the minor road that runs along the west side of Edderton. Near it was a stone circle surrounding a cist-burial (Joass 1868, 269).

Halfway up the east-north-east face of the stone, which is a reused standing stone, is a leaping **salmon** over a vertical **double-disc and Z-rod**.

The salmon, which is long and slender, is fairly typical. The double-disc and Z-rod is also a standard specimen, its discs rimmed and with small dotted circles in their centres, but little of the rod-ends can be made out and no floriations can be seen.

GAIRLOCH HERITAGE MUSEUM

Achtercairn, Gairloch IV21 2BJ **A**
Tel: 01445 712287

Apr–mid-Oct	Mon–Sat	1000–1700
	Other times	by arrangement

£1.50; conc £1.00; group ea 80p; child 50p

Gairloch 90 x 60 x 12cm O

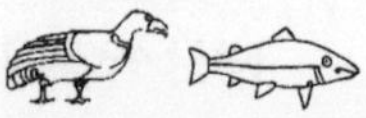

Stevenson 1952, 110–111

This Class I stone was found in former glebe land at NG 799 772 in Gairloch, where bones (and more recently a cist-burial) were found.

As the stone's top is missing and with it some of the upper symbol there is some controversy as to whether this is an eagle or a goose. The feet are as simple as those of the goose symbols and are without apparent talons, but the remaining plumage is very like that of almost every other Pictish eagle. Below the **eagle** swims a fine **salmon**. Both are incised facing left.

GROAM HOUSE MUSEUM

High Street, Rosemarkie IV10 8UF **A**
Tel: 01381 620961

May–Oct	Mon–Sat	1000–1700
	Sunday	1400–1630
Nov–Apr	Sat/Sun only	1400–1600
	Other times	by appointment

£1.50; pen £1.00; conc/child 50p; family £3.50

This small museum houses an important collection of early carved stones from Rosemarkie. Also on display is a cast of the Dunfallandy (PER) cross-slab. There is also a reconstruction of the harp on the Nigg stone.

ROSEMARKIE 1 258 x 77 x 19cm O

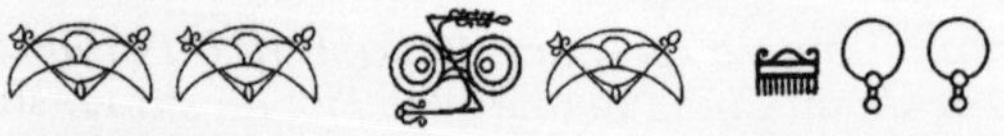

ECMS III, 63–68

The top and some of the base of this great cross-slab are missing, and what remains was found in two pieces under the floor of the old church in Rosemarkie (NH 737 576).

On the front of the stone, which has been strapped together, is a small cross. This is equal-armed, with no shaft or base, and its quadrants are sunk into the stone. About it is continuous interlace that fills all the stone's upper part, and below this are patterns of intertwined creatures within a border.

On the reverse the stone has no less than four 'family' symbols as well as two **mirrors** and one double-sided **comb**. The four are huge, each filling the width of the stone. Three, including the top symbol, most of which is missing, are very complex **crescents and V-rods**, and between the second and third of these is an equally complex **double-disc and Z-rod**. The mirrors, both small, lie on their sides below the lowest crescent and V-rod. The comb is uniquely contained within the double-disc and Z-rod – between the joining bar and the lower arm of the rod.

Both mirrors are rimmed and long-handled, and only one has other decoration, a dotted disc in the centre of the head. The comb is also simple, and the other symbols have not only standard shapes but also some standard features. The ends of the uppermost V-rod are missing, but one end of each of the others is flighted and the other end of one at least is an arrowhead. The upper end of the Z-rod is a spearhead with floriations behind it. The other is oddly- shaped.

NIGG

MAP p.119 ΔΔ **B**

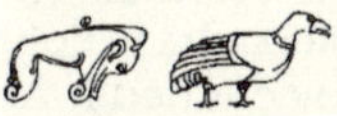

210 x 104 x 13cm **O** NH 805 717
ECMS III, 75–83

Nigg can be reached by the B9175 which leaves the A9 ten miles east-north-east of Alness. Two and a half miles along the B9175 a minor road to Balintore forks left, and less than a mile along this is a right turn to Nigg. The Old Church which houses the stone is two miles from this junction. Alternatively, one can cross from Cromarty by ferry. The church is open from Easter to the end of October between 1000 and 1630 daily except Sundays. The administrators, The Old Nigg Trust, can be contacted at 01862 832214.

The stone once stood in the churchyard but was blown down in a gale in 1729 and later broken. A piece which was carved with an elephant is lost.

This great cross-slab is in a well-lit room at the far end of the church. On the front of the stone is a long-shafted cross with a square centre and square-cut re-entrants. Above it is a scene representing SS Paul and Anthony being brought bread by the raven, and about it is a host of circular bosses. On the reverse, which is bordered by a wide band of interlace and key pattern, are many more figures, most of them worn and badly flaked. At the very bottom a hound pursues a deer, and above them is a mounted Pict with behind him a solitary follower who clashes a pair of cymbals (and who may be a game-beater rather than a musician). Further up the panel a large but now almost vanished figure of David grapples with the lion, with clearer carvings of one of his sheep and his harp in front of him. The figure in the top left of the panel with a spear and a small shield in his left hand could also be David. Above the latter is a plain insert which replaces the missing piece where the **elephant** symbol was. Part of its foreleg can be seen in front of the armed figure and part of its hind leg in front of the uppermost beast. Above the insert is the stone's other symbol, a great **eagle**.

Poolewe ΔΔ **A**

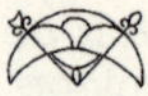

144 x 43 x 11cm **E** NG 861 809
RCAHMS 1994, 16 (Inverewe)

Less than 350 metres along the A832 north-west from the bridge over the Ewe a narrow lane runs uphill to the right for 100 metres to Poolewe Old Burial Ground. On the right inside the gate is a block of walled plots, and seven metres beyond the far end of this a broken-topped natural slab lies embedded in the ground. It may later be displayed in a shelter in the Burial Ground.

There is a **crescent and V-rod** immediately below the break. The crescent is decorated with a series of small circular depressions in the wings and in a line along the top arc; in the centre there is a linked pair of spirals, and two small arcs. Below the crescent the V-rod is double-lined with a dotted boss within the intersection of the arms. Above the crescent the left rod-end is apparently missing, and although the right has at least one curlicue it has no obvious head. As the slab is not only lichened but has a large number of confusing but natural striae or scores other features are hard to make out.

Figure 33

Crescent and V-rod: Poolewe (HIG ROS)

Roskeen Δ **D**

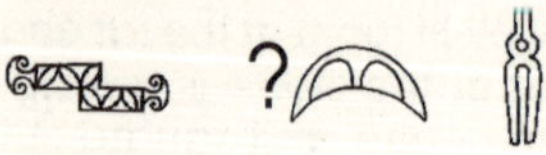

208 x 56 x 45cm **E** NH 681 690
ECMS III, 60–61

The Roskeen stone, known as Clach a' Mheirleach, the Thief's Stone, is probably another reused standing stone. It stands two miles east of Alness in a field on the north side of the B817 to Invergordon.

The stone, which is ten metres from the fence, is a pointed rectangular pillar. Its faces are rough and pitted and covered in lichen. Halfway up the east face a small **step** is incised, and on the south face is a pair of **pincers**, a symbol that appears on only one other stone, Dunfallandy (PER). It is incised vertically not far from the base of the stone. Above the pincers is a faint arc without other visible details which was described by Romilly Allen as "what appears to be traces of the crescent symbol". This '**crescent**' may be one of a pair of symbols, the other being the step and the pincers being additional to the pair.

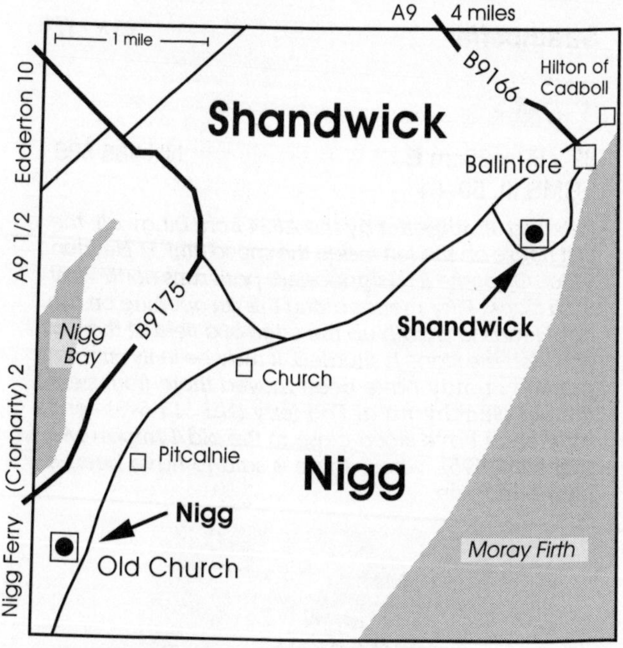

SHANDWICK MAP above ΔΔΔ **D***

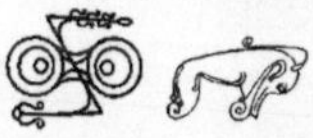

270 x 99 x 21cm NH 856 747

ECMS III, 68–73 (1993 edn figs 66 and 66a face p.65)

Shandwick can be reached from the B9175 or the B9166, both of which leave the A9 north-east of Alness. The stone is in a very prominent position overlooking the sea and the village of Balintore. It is in a glass building in a field about 100 metres from a stile at the side of the road that run south from Balintore. There is also a way in through a field gate downhill from the stile.

* *If contacted in advance (01862 832 525/804), members of the Shandwick Stone Trust will be happy to help any person to the stone. They also hold the keys to the shelter.*

On the eastern face is a long-shafted cross with rectangular arms and semicircular re-entrants. The shaft and arms are each decorated with a double line of small proud bosses, and at the sides of the shaft are angels and beasts and serpents, the serpents and two of the beasts intertwined. Below the cross are two great bosses and the remains of two more.

On the reverse are five horizontal panels, one above the other. The lower two are filled with patterns, the centre panel has a host of figures which include two fighting swordsmen and a hooded crossbow-man, and in the others are the symbols. The panel at the top contains part of a damaged **double-disc** filled with spiralled whorls, and in the panel below this is a now plain **elephant.**

The field where the stone stands has been described as one "where burials took place", but none was found beneath or immediately about the stone when it was removed for conservation.

Strathpeffer

ΔΔΔ **D**

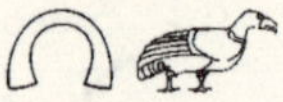

89 x 60 x 25cm **E** NH 485 585
ECMS III, 59–61

Entering Strathpeffer by the A834 from Dingwall, the first house on the left inside the speed limit is 'Newton Villa'. Opposite it a (signposted) path runs north-west up a slope. Fifty metres along this an opening on the right leads to a path up the edge of a field at the top of which the stone is situated. It may be in its original position or may have been moved there from near the old churchyard at Fodderty (NH 513 593) –or it may once have stood close to the old Tympan Mill (NH c489 595), where there is said to have been a clan burial site.

Figure 34

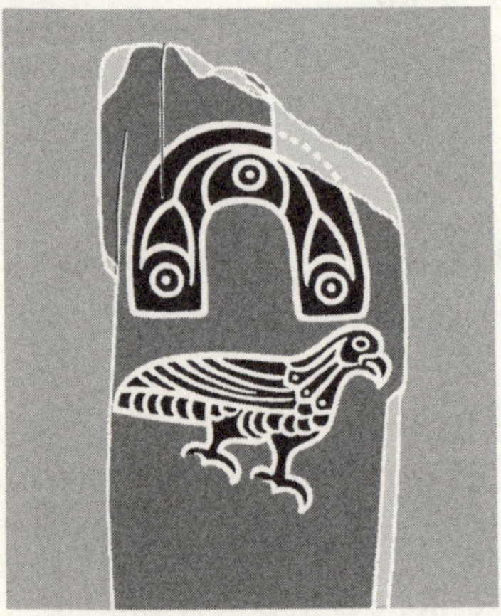

Strathpeffer (HIG ROS)
(after ECMS fig.57)

The stone is known as 'Clach an Tiompain', the Sounding Stone. Incised on its smooth south-east face are two symbols. The upper is a **horseshoe** decorated with a central dome, two hanging bell-shapes joined by an arc and three small discs. Below the horseshoe is an **eagle**, its plumage and talons clear.

Figure 35

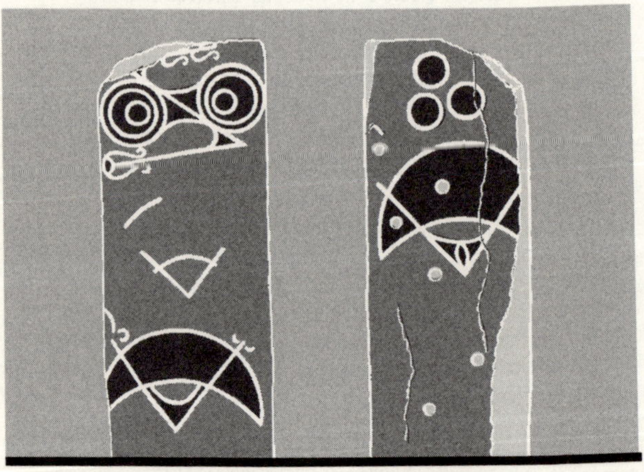

Dingwall (HIG ROS): both sides of the stone, see p,115
(after ECMS fig. 55)

Craigton 1 ΔΔ D

? 

200 x 66 x 45cm **E** NC 851 009
ECMS III, 41

Craigton 1 stands among trees 200 metres east of Dunrobin Castle, which is about a mile beyond Golspie. The best approach is by the path along the edge of the wood above the gardens, via the Castle itself. Although the path near the stone is blocked by a fence and locked gate, one can climb the bank on the right to go round the fence. The stone is best viewed early in the morning. It may be possible by prior arrangement to get to it through the Castle before it opens at 1030. (Tel: 01408 633177)

It is a tall natural pillar incised with three symbols in an unusual and contrasting configuration. A huge vertical **crescent and V-rod** dominates the stone; above it there is a small **divided-rectangle** (described by Romilly Allen as 'resembling a tuning-fork) and below it a small **flower**. All three which are on the south-east face are somewhat obscured by moss and lichen. The crescent, its points to the right, is without decoration except for a triple dumbell shape in the centre. It lies over its V-rod, which is twin-lined and does not have the conventional arrow-like ends. The lower is of two inward-curling spirals with between them a pelta-like shape, and the other is indistinct but may be an arrow-flight. The divided-rectangle, its upper part worn away, is near the top of the stone and is almost horizontal, its shafts to the right. The flower, which is near the base, leans left and is two-headed.

The stone, which may have been an earlier standing stone, either stood or was ploughed up near Craigton (NH 78 98), a now-vanished township some three miles west of Golspie. In about 1840 it was moved to its present site.

Figure 36

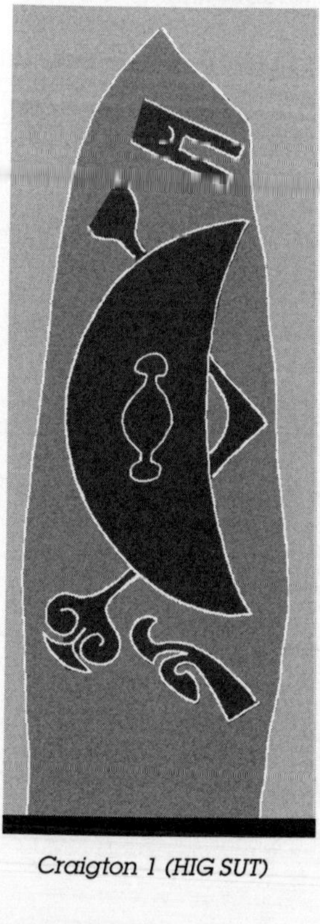

Craigton 1 (HIG SUT)

DUNROBIN CASTLE MUSEUM			
Dunrobin Castle, Nr Golspie KW10 6SF			D
Tel: 01408 633177			
May	Mon–Sat 1030–1600	Sun 1200–1600	
Jun/Sep	Mon–Sat 1030–1700	Sun 1200–1700	
Jul/Aug	Mon–Sat 1030–1700	Sun 1030–1700	
Oct	Mon–Sat 1030–1600	Sun 1200–1600	
	Entrance to Castle		
	£4.50; conc £2.80; child £2.50		
	group ea £4.20; conc £2.50; child £2.10		

1600 or 1700 is the final entry time to the Castle; the Museum remains open for entry half an hour after this. There is an excellent illustrated catalogue to the collection– 'Pictish Stones in Dunrobin Castle Museum' by Joanna Close-Brooks.

Clynekirkton 1 — 130 x 58 x 11cm O

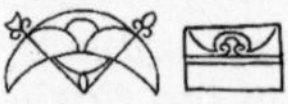

ECMS III, 38–39

The stone was found in Clyne Churchyard (NC 895 060), which was north-west of Brora.

On this intact but flaked slab is a **crescent and V-rod** over a **rectangle**. The crescent, decorated with erratic dome-and-wing pattern, has an arrow-like V-rod. The faint right end is arrow-headed and curlicued, the left arrow-flighted and also curlicued. In the upper part of the rectangle, which is horizontal and laterally divided by a double line, is a dome over a pelta between two spirals. From the dome an arc rises to the right. Another once rose to the left.

Clynekirkton 2 — 120 x 43 x 6cm O

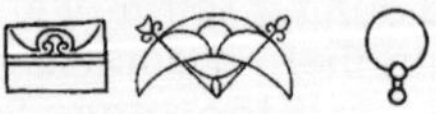

ECMS III, 39

Also from Clyne Churchyard this trimmed stone is said to have been found on Clyne Milton Farm (NC 914 069) two miles north of Brora.

Incised on it are the remains of a **rectangle**, a **crescent and V-rod** and a **mirror**. Only the left half of the huge rectangle survives. Incised at a slight angle and laterally divided with a double line it is decorated in both halves. In the upper part are low and wide domes or arcs filled with hatching and in the lower are parts of tall domes. Below is the crescent, with some of its right wing missing. Its centre is a slender pelta, and on either side are scrolls and wings with some hatching above them. The left rod end may be a arrow-flight. Only the left half of the mirror, which is below the crescent and V-rod, remains on the stone. It is plain-headed with a twin-bossed and twisted bar handle. The remains of the first two symbols are damaged by flaking.

Clynemilton 1 106 x 106 x 11cm **O**

ECMS III, 39–40

This irregularly-shaped slab was found on Clyne Milton Farm (NC 914 069) not far from the sea.

In two pieces, it has an arc-decorated **horseshoe** above a **crescent and V-rod** with scroll and wing pattern. As the break runs through the right side of the crescent some of the pattern is lost. The rod-ends are an arrowhead and flights, both complex and curliced. To the left is a plain-headed mirror with a pelta-shaped handle that ends in a boss.

Clynemilton 2 97 x 88 x 20cm **O**

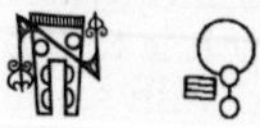

ECMS III, 40–41

This was found on Clyne Milton Farm also.

On the stone, the top of which is trimmed or broken, is a **mirror-and-comb** and only one other symbol, a magnificent **divided rectangle and Z-rod** with necked circular re-entrants in its upper part and a pair of semicircular re-entrants in each projection with a smaller arc between each pair. At each rod end is a pair of long curlicues, the right-hand ending in a ball. The mirror, which is to the right, has a unique handle, a figure of eight with a boss end, but is plain-headed. The comb, which is below the mirror, is single-sided and open-toothed, with a spiralled handle. There may once have been a symbol above the divided rectangle and Z-rod.

CRAIGTON 2 (*The Golspie Stone*)

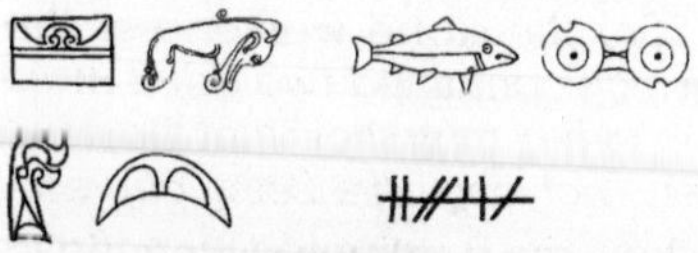

180 x 80 x 15cm **E**

ECMS III, 48–50

Although this cross-slab was moved to the museum from Golspie Churchyard (NC 837 002) in 1868 (where it was in 1780 and perhaps much earlier) there was a tradition that the stone had originally come from Craigton (NH 78 98). It may have had an intermediate resting-place at Kirkton (NH 799 986) where once St Carden's Chapel stood and been used as a tombstone there long after Pictish times. As Kirkton is the only known contemporary ecclesiastical site in the vicinity the stone may even have originated there. Craigton was not far from the chapel.

The cross-face bears a long-shafted cross surrounded by panels of interlace, whorls and key-pattern. It is badly damaged, and defaced by a later inscription. This reads, 'Heir is the bural plaec to Robert Gordon eldest son to Alex Gordon of Suthe[rland]'.

The much clearer carvings on the reverse are incised or in low relief. At the top is a large **rectangle** with corner spirals, which contains spirals and domes separated by a complex dividing bar. Next comes an equally large **elephant**, and below this major pair are four other symbols and various figures. Two of the latter are under the elephant. A man with a long queue of hair and a fringed and belted tunic walks to the right holding an axe in his outstretched right hand and a knife in the other. Facing him is a dog with a long tail curling up its back and scrolls in its body. Despite the scrolls the dog appears to be a figure rather than a symbol. Under it is a symbol, a **salmon** swimming from right to left. Under the salmon, which is smaller than the rectangle and elephant, are two even smaller symbols, a **flower** and a **crescent**. The flower, its two heads to the right, has a regularly-shaped and decorated triangular base with short 'legs'. The crescent, which is to the flower's right, is rimmed, and decorated with scroll shapes. Below the two is a **double-disc** slightly longer than the salmon. In each disc are two concentric rings, and the bar between the discs is concave-sided with an internal bar. Below the double-disc is a pair of intertwined fish-tailed serpents.

Running up the right-hand roll-moulding and across the top of the stone is an Ogam, which may read: ALLHHALLORREDDMQQNUUVVHRREIRF. The 'MQQ' may be, like the Formaston (ABE) fragment's 'MAQQ', 'son of' or 'descendant of', an Ogam element borrowed from Ireland.

Dunrobin 1 112 x 58 x 12cm **O**

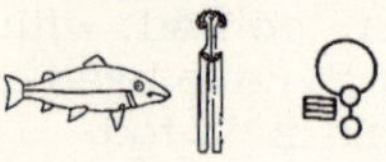

ECMS III, 42

Found three hundred metres south-west of Dunrobin Castle (at NC 849 006) the stone was one of the capstones of a cist which contained two adult male skeletons. The symbols' clarity may show that the stone was used as a capstone not long after being carved.

The symbols on this stone are a **salmon** swimming to the right, a horizontal **tuning-fork** with the prongs pointing left, and a **mirror-and-comb**. The tuning-fork handle is a decorated pelta-shape, and the plain-headed mirror has a 'double-disc' handle with a line running down the centre of the bar and into the disc rims. The comb, to the mirror's right, is double-sided, toothed and with a unique feature – a diamond pattern on the bar between the teeth.

Figure 37

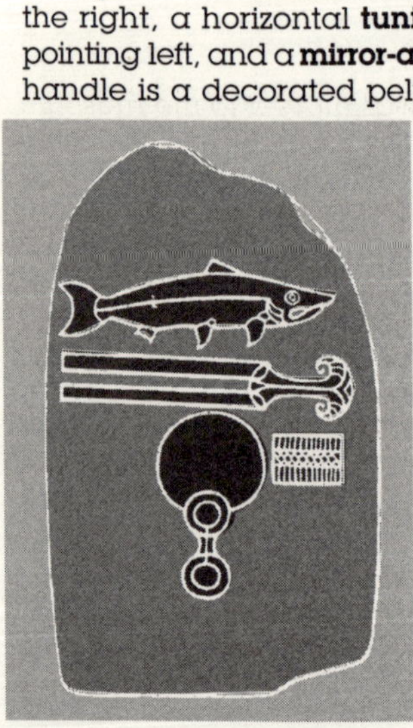

Dunrobin 1
(after ECMS fig.39)

Dunrobin 2 (*The Dairy Park Stone*)

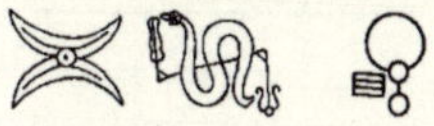

120 x 105 x 15cm **O**

Close-Brooks 1980

The stone was found in 1977 at NC 847 004, during ploughing in the Dairy Park below Dunrobin Castle.

It is almost intact and the symbol set complete – a **double-crescent**, a **serpent and Z-rod** and a **mirror-and-comb**. The double-crescent is the most ornate of this rare symbol. The wings are rimmed, and between them is decoration of dotted discs and arcs and hatching. The serpent, looping from right to left, is one of the three with scales. These are represented by a zigzag line with a line of dots on each side. The Z-rod has almost similar ball-ends and curlicues. Below is the mirror, plain-headed and with a twin-bossed bar handle. Both bosses are dotted. The comb, double-sided and clearly toothed, is also dotted along the central bar, and is a faithful representation of the type of bone comb found at Buiston Crannog in south-west Scotland.

This stone was almost certainly erected for a woman. It was found just below ground over a low cairn, in which was a long cist containing a female skeleton.

The carving is almost certainly contemporary with the skeleton, which was radiocarbon-dated to between the mid-sixth and mid-eighth centuries. The find provides compelling evidence that stones with a mirror-and-comb were carved for females – and that symbol stones were gravestones.

Golspie 130 x 60 x 6cm **O**

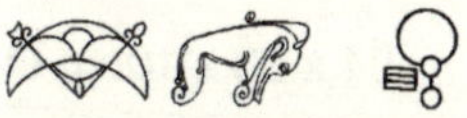

Davidson 1943

The stone was found in 1942 at NC 834 002 over an empty cist in a field on the north side of Golspie High Street. It is likely that the stone was placed over the grave after this had been despoiled.

The symbols are a **crescent and V-rod**, an **elephant** and a **mirror-and-comb**. The crescent is complexly-decorated with an inverted pelta and spirals, and the left rod-end is flighted, the right arrow-headed, and both curlicued. The elephant has the usual long scroll within the body and what may be a second 'rear paw' and a similar 'pellet' above the front foot. The front foot and the leading edge of the foreleg are 'rimmed' as far as the top of the snout. Such a rim is unique among Class I elephants. Isabel Henderson cites this elephant as a correct form for the symbol (1967, fig.18j, 113), but the rimmed foot and leg suggest a slightly later version. The Golspie crescent and V-rod, is also seen by Henderson as a correct form (ibid., fig.18a), but its complexity points again to lateness. Under the elephant is the mirror, plain-headed and with a twin-bossed bar handle. The comb beside it is single-sided and toothed, with small circles at its upper corners.

Kintradwell	NC 932 084

ECMS III, 43–45

All four stones were found three miles north-north-east of Brora, No.1 at NC 928 081 and the others at NC 932 084.

Kintradwell 1 — 96 x 33 x 9cm **O**

This irregular slab is incised with an **ogee** over a divided **mirror-case**. The ogee is similar to that at Drimmies (ABE). It has a central 'collar' and an arc in each wing. The mirror-case head, which rests on a plain concave-sided base, is wide-rimmed.

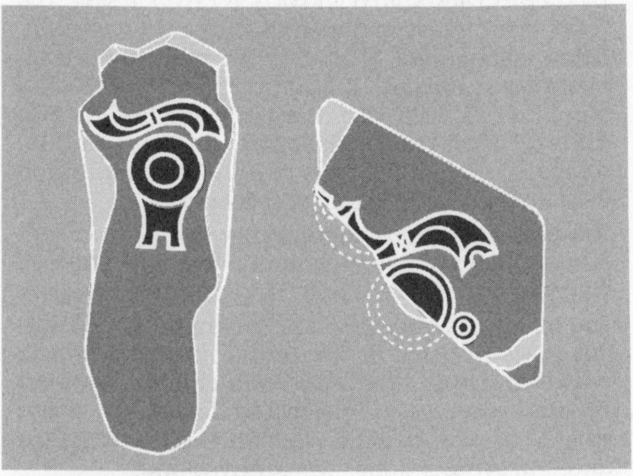

Figure 38

Ogee symbols compared: Kintradwell 1 (left) and 2 (HIG SUT) (after ECMS figs 40 & 41)

Kintradwell 2 — 84 x 38 x 10cm **O**

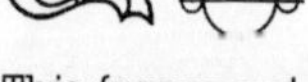

This fragment is incised with an **ogee** and part of a **triple-disc.** The ogee is not unlike that on No.1 but with an 'x' in the collar, an additional short arc at each end and a U-shaped re-entrant in each end. Below is what is left of the triple-disc – its right-hand ring and the upper part of the main disc. Both are rimmed.

Kintradwell 3 — 112 x 66 x 9cm **O**

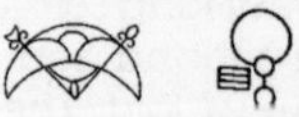

The stone appears to be almost intact, and is incised with a **mirror-and-comb** and only one other symbol, a **crescent and V-rod**. This is decorated with comma-like scrolls and has curliced rod ends, one arrow-headed and the other open-flighted. The mirror is plain, with a twin-bossed bar handle, and the comb is single-sided and toothed, its top three-pointed.

Kintradwell 4 — 45 x 30 x 5cm **O**

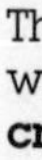

On this fragment are the prongs of a **tuning-fork**.

Little Ferry Links	NH 814 966

ECMS III, 45–48

The four, all fragments, were found at or not far from NH 814 966 on the links south-west of Golspie.

Little Ferry Links 1 — 19 x 19 x 11cm **O**

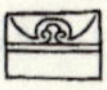

This is incised with two parallel lines, perhaps the dividing bar of a **rectangle**, below which are two spirals.

Little Ferry Links 2 — 43 x 28 x 7cm **O**

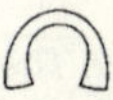

On this is a small, faint **horseshoe** and also a simple arrow-headed and curlicued rod-end.

Little Ferry Links 3 — 15 x 15 x 6cm **O**

? 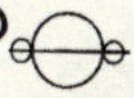

On No.3 are parts of two concentric circles with a smaller depression in their centre, part of another circle projecting to the left from these and less of another projecting downwards. This looks like some of the central decoration of a **triple-disc**, as on Keiss (HIG CAI), or may be the centre of a mirror-case like that on Inveraven 1 (MOR). (The style of the incising on No.3 is similar to that on No.1 and it is possible that the two may be fragments of the same stone.)

Little Ferry Links 4 — 30 x 20 x 9cm **O**

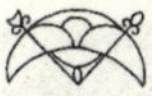 

This is one of two surviving fragments of one stone, and it bears part of a **crescent and V-rod**, the flighted end of the rod and a short length of the crescent's arch. The other part, in Inverness Museum (see p.110), has not only more of this symbol but also part of what may be a rimmed **mirror** below it.

Navidale — 96 x 45 x 10cm **O**

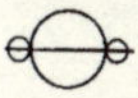 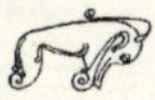

Macdonald and Laing 1970, 135–136, 143

On this slab is a faint **triple-disc** over a fainter **elephant**. The triple-disc has a wide-rimmed central disc with the small discs joined to it by three short lines, which may represent the attaching links of a cauldron's suspending rings. Only the line of the elephant's back, a part of its tail, both feet and some of its foreleg can be seen. It faces right.

This stone was found in 1968 at ND 042 162 in a burial-ground, close to Navidale Farm (east of Helmsdale), which was the site of a chapel dedicated to St Ninian. The name 'Navidale' (Sanctuary Dale) may show that the site was already regarded as sacred when the first Norse settlers came to Sutherland. A prehistoric burial was also found there.

Latheron 2 ΔΔ **B**

*c*30 x 70cm **E** ND 199 334
Stevenson 1959, 40

Latheron is at the junction of the A9 with the A99. The road to Latheron Mains is on the east side of the A9 fifty metres south of the junction. Permission should be asked at the whitewashed farmhouse which is less than 100 metres from the main road.

Part of a symbol stone on which is most of a **crescent and V-rod** is set into the south gable of the house four metres above ground-level. The crescent is decorated with a simple pelta in its centre and a wing on either side, and the rod is arrow-like. At the left end are what appear to be flights, and the right is a very indistinct arrowhead. Both are curlicued. Unfortunately the stone has been whitewashed too.

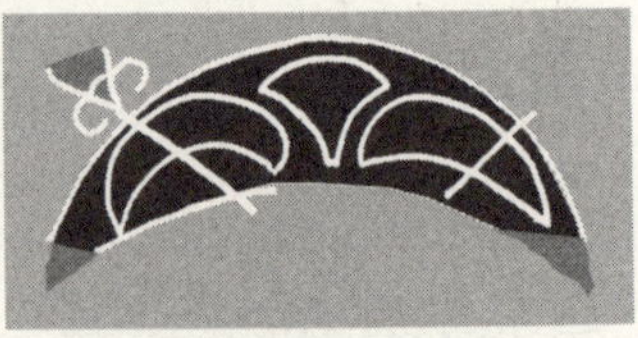

Crescent and V-rod: Latheron 2 (HIG CAI)

Figure 39

NORTHLANDS VIKING CENTRE

Old School, Auckengill, By Wick KW1 4XP **B**
Tel: 01955 603761 (Caithness Museums Service)

Jun–Sep	Daily	1000–1600
	£1.10; conc/child/group ea 60p	

Watenan 98 x 98 x 6cm **O**

Gourlay 1984, 131–132

These two fragments were discovered in 1977 on top of and beside a small kerbed cairn (ND 312 408) to the west of Watenan, which is south of Ulbster.

On the pieces are the wings and some of the rod of a **crescent and V-rod**. The upper part of the rod-ends and crescent are missing, and little decoration within the crescent is visible.

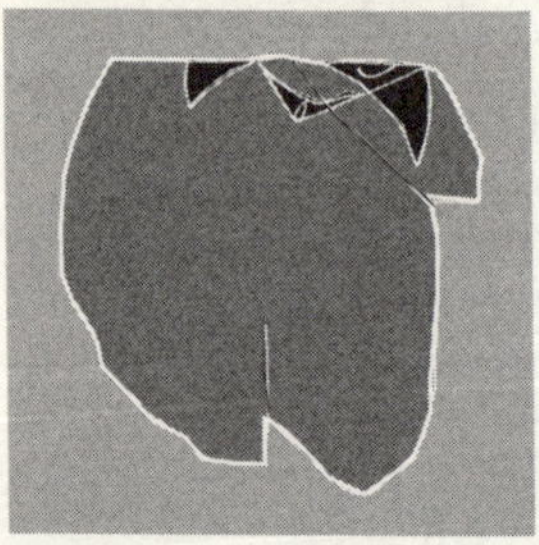

Figure 40

Crescent and V-rod: the Watenan (HIG CAI) fragment

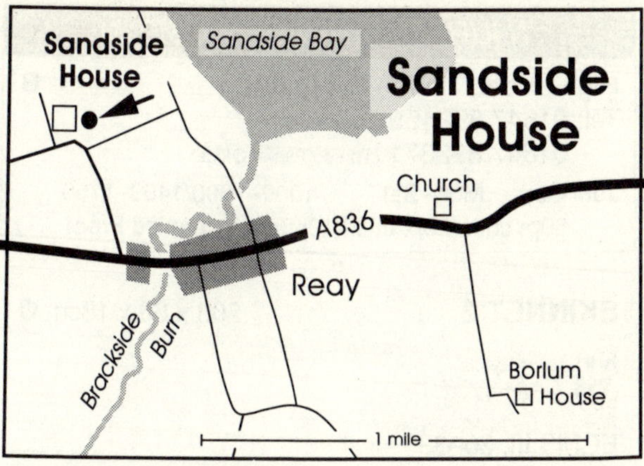

Sandside House

MAP above ΔΔΔ **B**

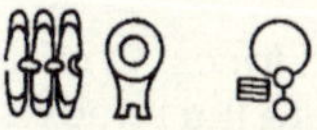

143 x 60 x 9cm **O** NC 952 652
ECMS III, 29–30

Sandside House is half a mile north-west of Reay. Its main entrance is on the north side of the A836 not far beyond the bridge over the Brackside Burn, which is at the west end of the village. The stone, in two pieces which have been fitted together, is fixed upside down to a wall at the foot of steps at the east side of the house. It faces west. Permission should be asked at the house. The stone was found in about 1850 on the links close to Reay.

On the stone are a **triple-oval**, a divided **mirror-case**, and a **mirror-and-comb**. The triple-oval, the finest of the five examples, is composed of three vertical cigar shapes, each with a top and bottom rim and linked by pairs of small circles. The head of the mirror-case is narrow-rimmed, with a small rimmed disc below the centre, and the base has sides like slender crescents. The mirror is also narrow-rimmed and has a twin-bossed handle, its 'bar' a single line. The comb is double-sided and toothed.

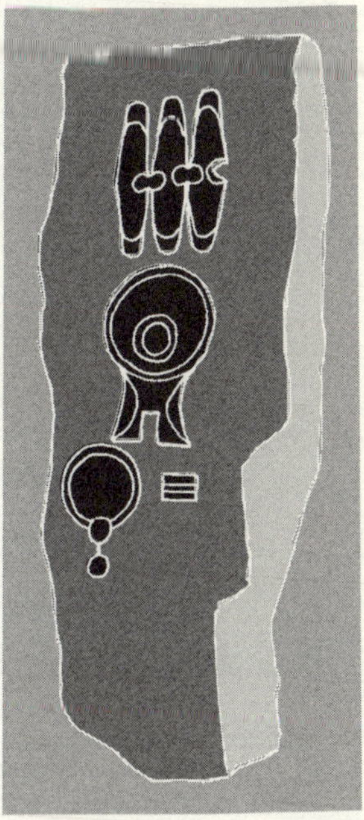

Sandside House (HIG CAI)

Figure 41

THURSO HERITAGE MUSEUM

High Street, Thurso KW14 8AZ **B**
Tel: 01847 892459 (Coordinator)
01847 892371 (Thurso Tourist Office)
Jun–Sep Mon–Sat 1000–1300/1400–1700
50p; conc 25p; child 10p (accompanied Free)

SKINNET 2 208 x 66 x 18cm O

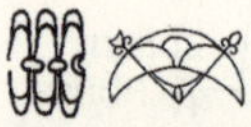

ECMS III, 30–33

This cross-slab was found in the ruins of an old chapel (ND 131 621). It was later moved to Thurso Museum, by which time it was in six or more pieces and the base missing.

The reassembled stone has two cross-faces. On the front, which is well lit by a window, are the remains of an equal-armed cross on a long shaft and square base. The cross-centre is a quadruple pelta, and the arms and shaft and base contain some interlace. The left arm is badly damaged. In each quadrant is a rimmed boss, a fish-monster-like creature is on either side of the shaft, and below the cross-base are the remains of a yoked pair of horses stepping out to the right. The horses are now headless and their hooves hidden by the concrete into which the slab is set.

On the reverse, which is against the light, is another equal-armed cross with a long shaft and square base. Below its base are the symbols, a **triple-oval** over a **crescent and V-rod**. Little is left of either. A band of cement covers most of what was the symbol-carved area. Only some of the upper points of the ovals, some of the left wing of the crescent, its right-hand rod end and the V-end of the rod can be seen. The rod end is curlicued and arrow-headed and the V-end twin-lined and hatched.

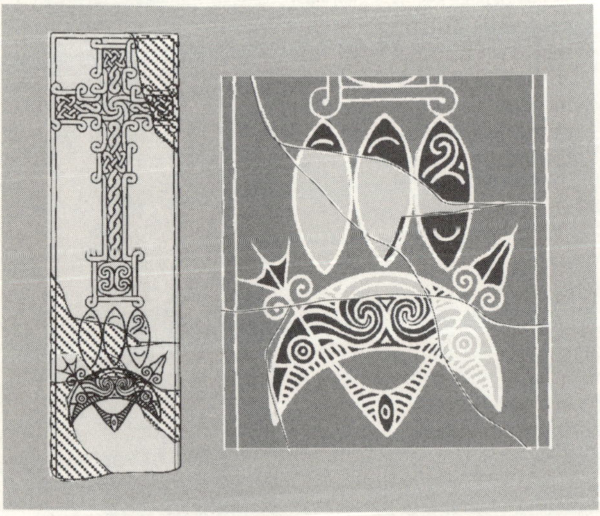

Figure 42

Skinnet 2 (HIG CAI): cross-slab showing missing (hatched) areas with detail of symbols below the cross (after ECMS fig.29A)

ULBSTER (*The Ulbster Stone*) 150 x 90 x 19cm **O**

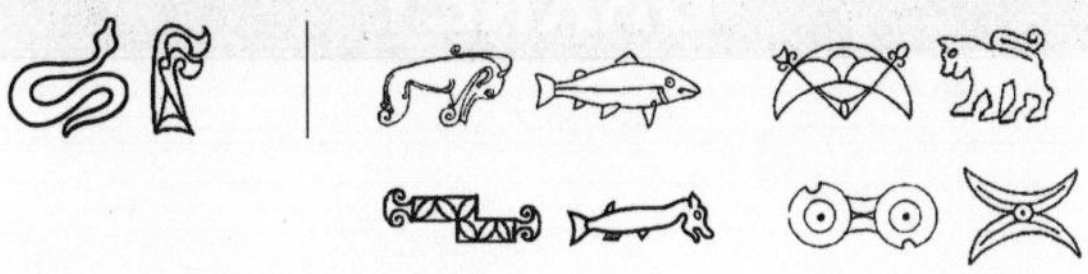

ECMS III, 33–35

This cross-slab, which is in the entrance hall, once stood in the old burial-ground at Ulbster, the site of St Martin's Chapel (ND 335 419), and later lay over a grave there.

The stone has not only two cross-faces but symbols on both. As one face is carved in low relief and the other little more than incised it may be a reused Class II stone.

On the low-relief face, which is worn and damaged, are the remains of an equal-armed cross with a square centre, a slender shaft and a rectangular base. The cross's parts were decorated with interlace and key pattern, and about it are or were figures and two of the stone's symbols. In the top right quadrant is what was a cow, and above the cross and in the top left quadrant may have been other animals. These areas are not only damaged but also defaced by initials and by an inscription 'THE ULBSTER STONE'. In each of the lower quadrants is a large-pawed beast, and below the left-hand beast are the remains of two kneeling Picts with between them a small cauldron. Below them is one of the symbols, a small **serpent** looping left. To the right of the cross's lower arm is the other symbol, a **flower**, its three heads thrusting to the left. Flaking has removed its base. Below is a now-headless horse and below that one with folded legs, perhaps a colt.

In the centre of the reverse face is an equal-armed Latin cross, its square arms and centre each incised with a saltire and filled with thick interlace. Around the cross are eight symbols, all in pairs. The upper left pair is an **elephant** over a **salmon**, the salmon swimming towards the cross, and the elephant, which has a long snout and a forwards-curling forefoot, facing away from it. To the right is a **crescent and V-rod** over a **beast** which faces the cross. The crescent and V-rod is whorl-decorated, and the rod, the lower part of which is twin-lined and hatched, has a flighted left end, and the right arrow-headed and curlicued. The beast is a dog-like creature with a long doubled-over tail curling up its back. In the bottom right quadrant is a **double-disc**, its discs rimmed and whorl-decorated and joined by two parallel bars, and below it is a **double-crescent** with a small dotted disc in the centre and arcs in each crescent. On the left side and near the base is a dog-headed **fish-monster** which is carved vertically and looks to the right. Almost balanced on its forehead is a vertical and rimmed **step**.

Birsay * (Reconstruction) ΔΔΔ **A**

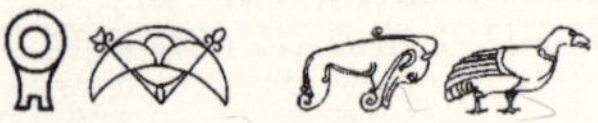

182 x 84 x 9cm **O** HY 240 285
Simpson 1959, 17

The Brough of Birsay is a tidal islet on the north-west corner of Orkney Mainland, twenty miles north-west of Kirkwall by the A965, the A986, the A967 and the A966. Birsay village is at the west end of the A966, less than half a mile from its junction with the A967. From the village a track goes north-west round the bay and towards the Point of Buckquoy to a carpark. From here at low tide one can walk along a causeway to the islet.

NB *Crossing this is not possible for about three hours before and after High Water (an hour before High Water at Kirkwall, the times of which are shown at the Harbourmaster's office there).*

On the islet is an Early Christian and Norse site, which includes a burial-ground. The fragments of the Birsay stone in the Museum of Scotland were dug up here, and a complete reconstruction of the stone now stands where they were found.

On it are the symbols as they may once have appeared. Near the top right corner is the **mirror-case**, its head rimmed and containing a small central rimmed disc about which are five whorls. The base is concave-sided with a double bottom line. To its left is the **crescent and V-rod**, which is remarkably like the Ulbster crescent and V-rod. Below the crescent is the **elephant**, its antenna and tail twin-lined and with linked scrolls within its body. Immediately below this is the **eagle**, which has a whorl behind the left leg.

The Birsay stone is, if it is Class I, one of only three Class I stones with figures as well as symbols. Below the symbols three relief-carved long-gowned warriors march from left to right carrying long spears behind square shields decorated with discs and central squares. The leader's shield is more ornate, with spiral decorations not unlike those in the crescent and V-rod, his spear is longer, and even his gown and hairstyle are grander. The three also wear waist-belts and short swords.

The other Class I stones with figures are the Collessie stone (FIF) and Rhynie 3 (ABE), one at least of which is early, perhaps pagan; for all its symbols' accuracy the Birsay stone is late. It is possible that its fragments, which are only 25mm. thick, were split from the back of a cross-slab.

* The surviving fragments of this stone are in the Museum of Scotland (see p.30)

GURNESS BROCH MUSEUM

Apr–Sep	Mon–Sat	0930–1830
	Sunday	1400–1830
	£2.00; conc £1.25; child 75p; group 10% disc	

This small site museum is beside the Broch of Gurness which is on the north edge of Aiker Ness on the north-east coast of Orkney Mainland. It is about sixteen miles from Kirkwall and can be reached by the A965 and the A966 (or by the A966 from Birsay). The site is signposted. From Georth on the A966 a minor road runs north-east to a car park, and the broch is beyond this by track and footpath.

Gurness ΔΔ B

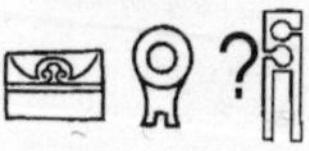

19 x 27 x 29cm **O** HY 382 269

Ritchie, JNG 1969, 130–132

The stone on display in the museum is an irregular block incised with three symbols side by side. It was found during the excavation of the broch in 1935. From left to right the symbols are a slender and rimmed vertical **rectangle**, a divided **mirror-case** and what may be a **divided rectangle**. The mirror-case is rather like that on the stone at Strathmiglo (FIF), except that above the base re-entrant is a downward pointing triangle. The 'divided rectangle' has long re-entrants in top and bottom. The stone may be a 'trial piece'.

TANKERNESS HOUSE MUSEUM

Broad Street, Kirkwall KW15 1DH **B**

Tel: 01856 873191

	Mon–Sat	1030–1230/1330–1700
May–Sep	Sunday	1400–1700
	£1.50; conc/child/archaeol Free	

Burrian 114 x 56 x 9cm O

RCAHMS 1946, vol.II, 17–18

The stone was found over a well during the excavation in 1936 of a probable broch at HY 308 168.

This rectangular slab, which is broken in two, has incised on it an **eagle** over a **crescent and V-rod** and below that a **mirror**. The eagle has a scroll behind the left leg and a neck-scroll, and the crescent is decorated with small discs, whorls between the rod-arms, and an arc in each wing. The left rod end is one of open arrow-flights and the right an arrowhead. Both are curlicued. The mirror is plain-headed and has a twin-bossed handle.

Ness

59 x 31 x 8cm **O**

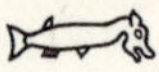

Burt 1991, 5

The fragment was found at Ness (HY 545 093) eight miles east of Kirkwall by Mr D. Harcus while he was lifting potatoes.

On it is most of a **fish-monster**, which faces left. It is beaked or long-snouted, and its curling body is divided into a plain front and a wider back part incised with parallel arcs.

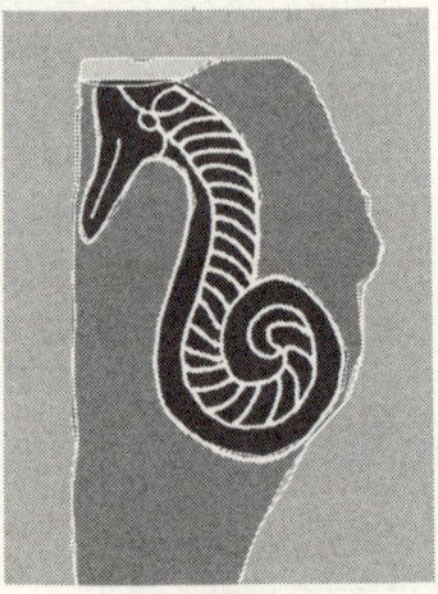

Ness (ORK): fragment with symbol

Figure 43

Pool

77 x 43 x 9cm **O**

? 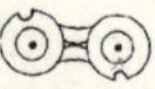

Hunter 1985

This undressed flagstone slab, one face of which is pecked with crude symbol-like motifs, was found in 1985 in use as a floor stone in the remains of fifth or sixth-century buildings at HY 619 379 on Sanday. (A fragment with a 'Pictish Ogam' inscription was found elsewhere in the same buildings.)

Its discovery as part of a structure of this period may indicate that Class I symbol stones were in use somewhat earlier than is commonly believed, but it is not at all certain that it is a symbol stone. The one recognisable 'symbol' is a small **double-disc**-like design with a straight-sided joining bar rather wider than the discs. It may be a 'trial piece'.

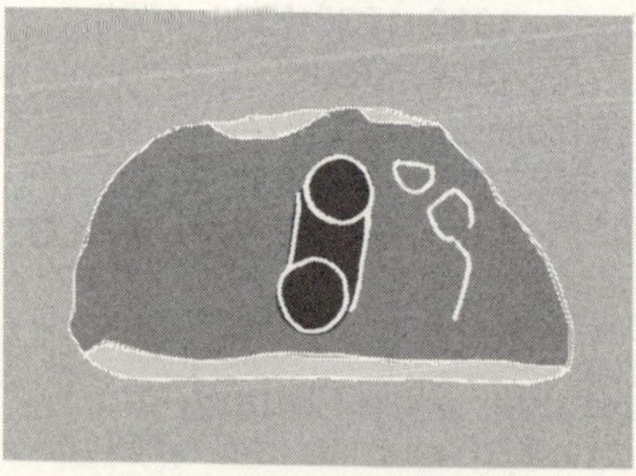

Figure 44

Double-disc: Pool (ORK)

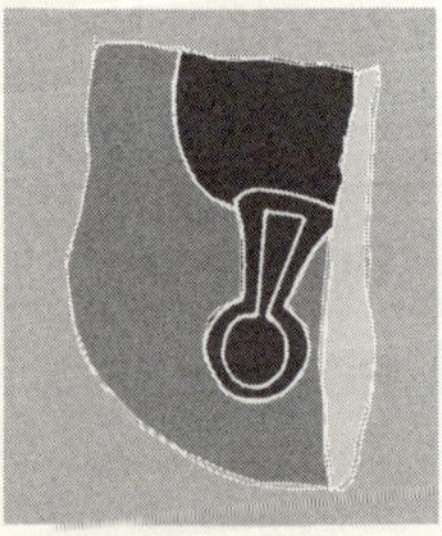

Figure 45

Mirror: Sands of Evie (ORK)

Sands of Evie

28 x 23 x 9cm **O**

Ritchie, JNG 1969, 130, 133

This fragment was found at HY 372 264 on the Sands of Evie, the beach west of Aiker Ness.

On it is part of a plain-headed **mirror** with a twin-lined handle shaped like an inverted keyhole.

Pabbay

Δ **D**

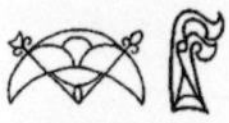

124 x 37 x 15cm **O** NL 607 875
ECMS III, 111–113

Pabbay is a small uninhabited island south of Barra and visitors must make their own arrangements to get there.

About one hundred and twenty metres inland from Bagh Ban on Pabbay's south-west coast is a small steep-sided mound to the east of a ruined cottage. This mound was the site of a chapel and the stone lies near the foot of the south-west face. It was first noticed lying in the graveyard some years before 1889. It is now proposed to re-erect the stone on site.

The stone is heavily lichened and lies close to others, but a deeply-incised cross near its top distinguishes it. Below the cross is a **crescent and V-rod** and below that a **flower**. Within the crescent are two small circles inside even fainter wing shapes, and at the end of the left rod are two arcs like the sides of a very broad arrowhead or spearhead. The other may be ball-ended. The flower, two-headed with the heads hanging to the right, is now only an outline. As the cross is off-centre in relation to the symbols and more deeply incised it is probably a later addition.

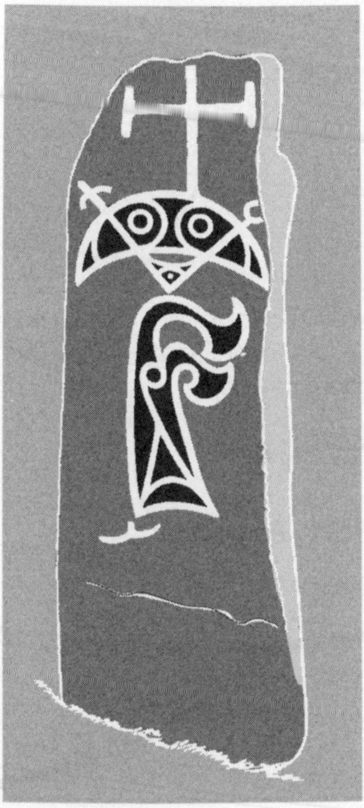

Figure 46

Pabbay (WLS) (after ECMS fig.116)

Dunadd HS ∆ D

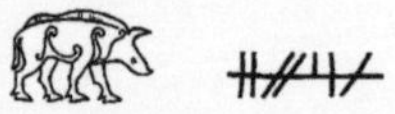

Christison 1905, 298; Jackson 1965 NR 837 936

Dunadd is a hill-fort close to the A816 a mile north of Kilmichael Glassary. Incised on a rock-face in this fortress of the Scots are two lines of 'Pictish Ogam' and a Pictish symbol. As Dunadd was captured by the Picts in 736AD these carvings may have been a consequence of the Pictish victory. Just below the summit is the carved face, now covered and protected by a stone-like glass-fibre replica.

Near the south end is the symbol, a **boar** facing right. The line of its back is barely obvious, but its legs and hooves and some of its head are fairly clear and something can be seen of scrolls within its body. These are clear in a ninety-year-old photograph, (Christison 1905, fig.22). A little more than a metre to the right of the boar is a depression like a human footprint, and at four o'clock from this is the Ogam.

Both the boar and the Ogam were probably carved soon after the capture of Dunadd, but it is unlikely that they were simply a sign of victory. The footprint and a deep basin near it may have have been to do with the proclaiming of kings of Dalriada, and although Dunadd was re-occupied by the Scots the Pictish carvings were not defaced.

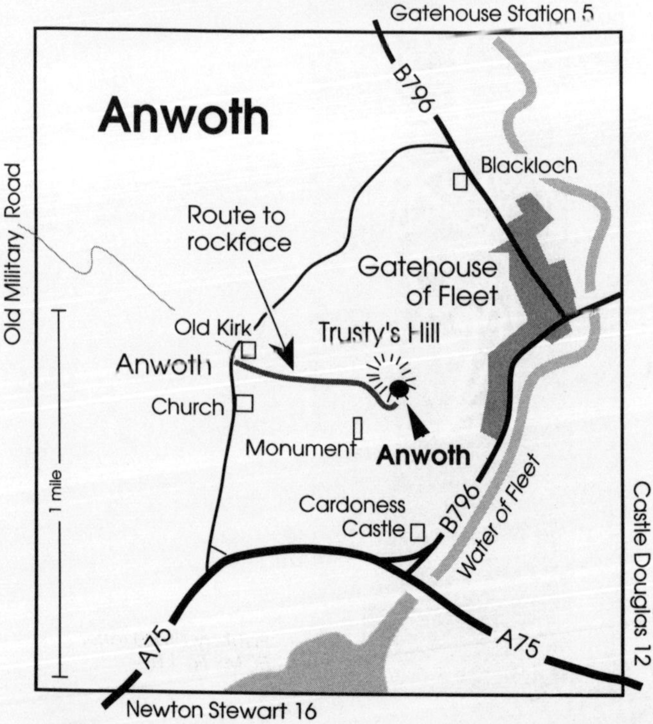

DUMFRIES and GALLOWAY 14

Anwoth MAP below opp ΔΔΔ **D**

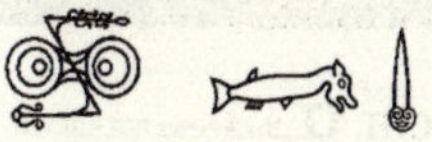

ECMS III, 477–479 NX 589 560

Half a mile up the B796 from Gatehouse of Fleet a minor road turns left to Anwoth. Three-quarters of a mile along it are the ruins of Anwoth Old Kirk, and beside the kirkyard is a gate into a field. On the far side is another gate from which a track climbs the tree-covered slope above it. At the top, where the trees and track end, is a gate through a dry-stone dyke and beyond this a plateau of rough grassy ground. At each side of it is a grass and gorse-covered ridge stretching south-eastwards, and about three hundred metres along the left-hand ridge is a gorse-clad mound called Trusty's Hill. On it are the remains of a small vitrified fort, the entrance on the south-east side and flanked by two rock outcrops. On one is a cage of iron railings enclosing a rock-face incised with symbols.

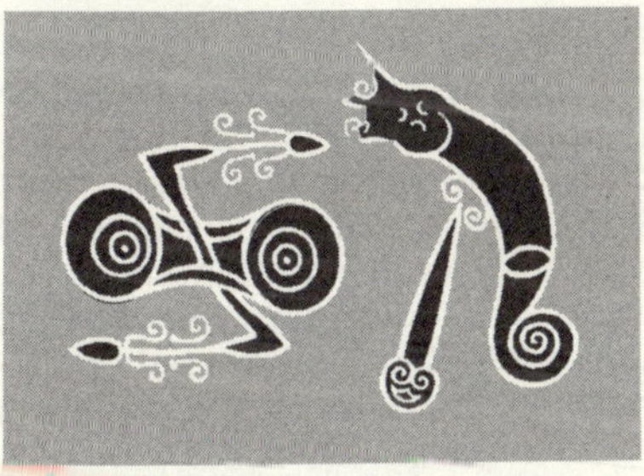

Figure 47

Anwoth (DUM): symbols (after ECMS fig.508)

The face, which looks east-north-east, is divided by a vertical fissure. On the right is a vertically-carved **fish-monster** beneath which a unique **sword** thrusts upwards, and on the left a **double-disc and Z-rod**. In each disc is a rimmed eccentric disc, the joining bar is composed of two crescents, and running over one and under the other is a Z-rod. The central arm and some of the upper and lower arm are double-lined, and the single lines that end them are identical, each spearheaded and adorned with two pairs of long curlicues. This is a late symbol and because the rod runs through the joining bar may be of Class II times. The sword's handle is like a tuning-fork's, but the blade is pointed and has no linear division.

The fort was in use in the seventh century, and the symbols may show that it was captured by Picts, perhaps late in that century.

A circular head with two long spiral-ended antennae is probably a later addition – as are the many initials and dates.

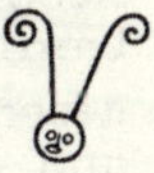

15 LOST STONES

ABERDEENSHIRE

Clatt 2 38 x 25cm **O** (thickness not known)

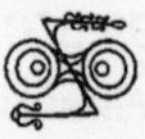

ECMS III, 158

On this Class I fragment, which was found in Clatt Kirkyard (at NJ 538 260) not long before 1903 (and photographed *c*1905 beside Clatt 3), were the remains of a **double-disc and Z-rod**. The one complete remaining disc was wide-rimmed with a unique joining-bar which was plain and, despite Allen's drawing (ECMS fig.165), straight.

Old Deer 182 x 76cm **O** (thickness not known)

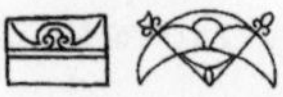

ECMS III, 162

This Class I stone stood outside the Abbey of Deer (NJ 969 481) until about 1850. On one face was an incised cross; on the other were two incised symbols, both upside-down in relation to the cross – which was presumably therefore a later addition. The symbol pair comprised a **rectangle** with whorl and dome decoration, and below it a **crescent and V-rod** with dome and wing decoration and a lateral oval 'flight'.

Rhynie 4 (?) 157 x 69cm **O** (thickness not known)

Logan 1829, 55; Stuart 1856, 5; ECMS III, 183

Rhynie 4 is first reported in 1797 (*Statistical Account* (1982 edn vol.15, 489)), as 'A large stone, about five feet in diameter, on which there are some hieroglyphic characters, and standing on the Moor of Rhynie ... Part ... has been lately broken:'. According to the Ordnance Survey of 1866 the stone's original site had been at NJ 4982 2699, but by then the remains were in a barn wall at NJ 4998 2715. Logan had reported them as in a stable wall and that they had been 'taken from the materials of a former School-house'. Stuart echoed Logan but also quoted the 1797 report. Allen stated that the stone originally stood at the Mains of Rhynie but was afterwards broken up and part built into a barn wall.

It seems that Rhynie 4 once stood south of the village and, although broken, was still upright in 1797.

The remains may have then been built into a schoolhouse but if so were later built into a barn or stable wall. They disappeared after the building was taken down, sometime before 1903.

On the fragment was most of the head of an **elephant**, half of a plain **crescent and V-rod**, its surviving (right-hand) rod-end leaf-shaped but not curlicued, and half of a large rimmed and broad-handled **mirror**.

ANGUS

Strathmartine Kirkyard	NO 378 353

STRATHMARTINE 3 40 x 51cm O (thickness not known)

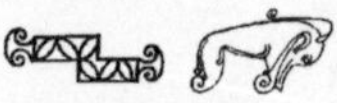

ECMS III, 231–232; Laing & Laing 1984, 267

A **step** and an **elephant** were incised on the reverse of this small cross-slab. The L-shaped step is thought by Lloyd and Jennifer Laing to perhaps represent a type of Roman helmet. The elephant faces right but only its upper part remains, showing a shoulder scroll, a 'chin' scroll-line and a twin-lined antenna.

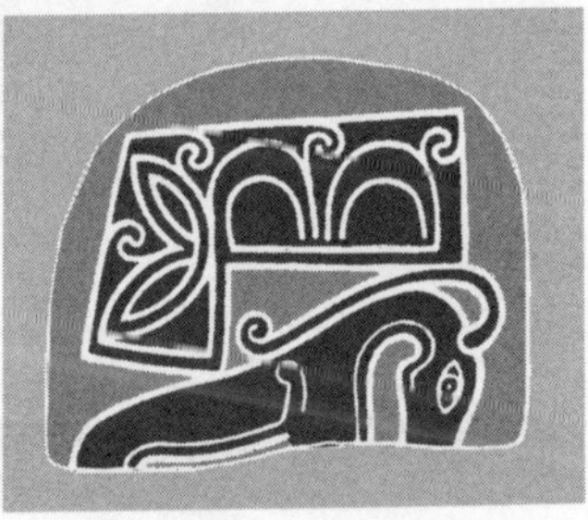

Strathmartine 3 (ANG) (after ECMS fig.245B)

Figure 48

STRATHMARTINE 5 38 x 38 x 5cm O

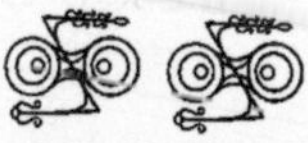

ECMS III, 233

On the relief-carved reverse of this cross-slab fragment was the spiral-filled left-hand disc of a **double-disc and Z-rod**. The rod, which had a spear-pointed and floriated upper arm, was a true Z. Below it was the upper angle of a more conventional backward Z-rod, part of another **double-disc and Z-rod** which had been parallel to the first.

STRATHMARTINE 6 33 x 27cm O (thickness not known)

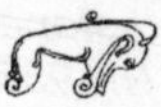

ECMS III, 233–234

Another cross-slab fragment, it bore on its reverse most of a well-shaped **elephant** in relief and facing right, but in one respect unique. In addition to a high shoulder spiral, a scroll or lobe above the hind leg and twin-lined antenna and tail, it had four legs, not just the 'additional paws' which many have.

CITY OF DUNDEE

Linlathen 66 x 51cm **O** (thickness not known)

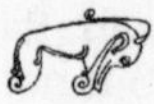

ECMS III, 208

This Class I fragment is said to have been found in 1834 between the double capstones of a Bronze Age cist in a tumulus called Cairn Greg (at NO 466 338) two miles north of Broughty Ferry.

Incised on it was most of a fine **elephant** with shoulder scroll and additional 'forepaw'.

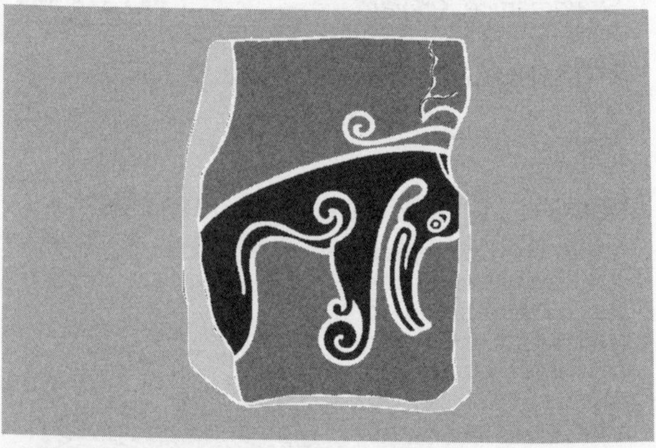

Figure 49

Linlathen (DUN) (after ECMS fig.225)

HIGHLAND

BADENOCH AND STRATHSPEY

Lynchurn 178 x 46 x 25cm **O**

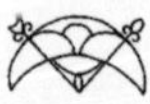

Mitchell 1874, 688–689; ECMS III, 105

This Class I stone was found before 1870, in a field at Lynchurn Farm at NH c953 206. 'Mr Grant [the farmer] was breaking it up for a lintel when he observed some sculpturing on it and desisted... Unfortunately it had sustained considerable injury before the sculpturing was noticed' (Mitchell, 688). It was then erected near its findspot but later removed to be used as a grave stone. Trimmed square and with its symbol replaced by an inscription – 'H.C. Stuart, Vicar of Wragby, d.1884' – this much-abused stone was then erected in Kincardine Kirkyard, at NH 938 155. Recent searches have failed to locate it.

On it had been most of an incised **crescent and V-rod** containing spiral and dome decoration. The surviving (right) rod-end was a curlicued flight. The pattern of right-hand flight and left-hand arrowhead also occurs in the other Badenoch and Strathspey examples (Inverallan, Advie and Finlarig), but is otherwise extremely rare.

CAITHNESS

Crosskirk (size of replica) 69 x 66cm **O**

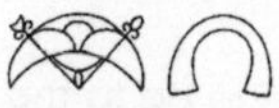

ECMS III, 30 (Thurso Castle); Henry forthcoming

This Class I stone, although said to have been found in a broch (at ND 025 701), may instead have been discovered in a cairn between the broch and the burial-ground nearby. This was in 1846. Incised on it were a dome-decorated **crescent and V-rod**, its rod arms flighted, arrow-headed and curlicued, and a **horseshoe**, which had a spiralled 'hinge' and contained arcs. The stone was reportedly presented to the King of Denmark.

SUTHERLAND

Kintradwell 5 Size not known

? ?

RCAHMS 1994, 19

A 'Stone with Incised Pictish Symbols was unearthed by a strong gale of wind about A.D. 1852' in the immediate vicinity of where several stone coffins, some containing human bones, were found. This was at NC 930 079, close to the seashore three miles north of Brora and not very far from the findspots of the other Kintradwell stones. Although No.5 is said to have been deposited in Dunrobin Castle Museum, it has not been identified there.

Langdale 112 x 68 x 8cm **O**

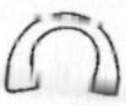

Mackay 1906, 128–129

This Class I fragment, found in 1905 below ground on farmland (at NC 69 44), was incised with a shallow arch or **horseshoe**.

MORAY

Balneilan 71 x 35cm **E**

ECMS III, 152; Stuart 1867, 61

Reported as built into a wall of the Balneilan farm buildings (NJ 149 259) and said to have come from a nearby stone circle, this Class I fragment was incised with a **disc** containing three small discs within a twin-lined rim. The one complete small disc was also rimmed.

Drainie 1 76 x 63 x 10cm **O**

ECMS III, 124

This Class I trimmed fragment was said to be in the Elgin Museum, but there is no recent record of it there. The fragment, which was found in 1855 while pulling down Kineddar manse (at NJ 223 696, beside the old kirk), was incised with the right-hand upper part of a **crescent and V-rod**, a spiralled and complexly-decorated version with a curlicued arrowhead.

Tom na Heron Size not known

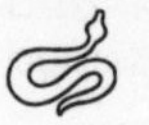 (?)

RCAHMS 1994, 13

This stone, once at NJ 208 310, went missing before being fully recorded. In the *Ordnance Name Book for the County of Banff* (1869, 136), the surveyor, Sapper James Gray of The Royal Engineers, wrote '...there was formerly a Sculptured Stone with the figure of a **serpent** and other symbols incised thereon the meaning of which was unknown at the time of the removal of the said Stone', and that he could not discover when the stone had been removed.

(RCAHMS card NJ 2 SW 1 describes the vicinity as having '...about 250 stone clearance heaps...'. As this is a great number, some could be burial cairns. Many are concentrated into a strip about half a mile long (from north to south) and 150 metres wide. The stone stood within the south end of this strip.)

ORKNEY

Orphir 1 Size not known

RCAHMS 1994, 19

'...found in the present [1939] excavations [Orphir, at HY 33 04 on Orkney Mainland] is part of a Pictish Symbol stone engraved with **crescent and V-rod**'. (Minute of 24 Mar 39, J S Richardson)

Orphir 2 Size not known

RCAHMS 1994, 19

'There is a symbol stone built into the north west corner of the pend tower [HY 33 04 on Orkney Mainland]. On it are crescent and V-shaped rod symbol and a rectangular object.' (Minute of 12 Jul 39, J S Richardson)

A photograph of this stone built laterally into a wall is held by RCAHMS. The **rectangle** is small and plain; the **crescent** is also plain and the **V-rod** ends are a circular flight and a leaf-shaped head, both bisected by the rod.

Oxtro Size not known

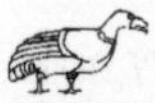

RCAHMS 1946, 11–12

When the Oxtro broch (HY 254 268) on Orkney Mainland was excavated in the early 1870s a large number of short cists was found in its upper level. 'The figure of an **eagle** was boldly cut on the covering stone of one of the cists... but... this relic [was]... built into the wall of one of the farm offices' (at Boardhouse, HY 249 275).

SHETLAND

Sandness 117 x 41 cm* **O** (thickness not known)

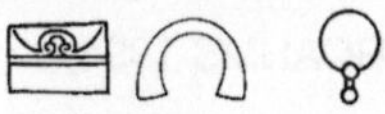

ECMS III, 4

This perhaps intact stone was seen in the wall of Sandness Church (HU 191 577) in 1774 and sketched.

On it was a **rectangle** containing a horizontal dividing line with a circular whorl in its centre, a very plain **horseshoe** and a plain-headed **mirror**, its handle a single line between circular bosses. This mirror is similar to the one on Tillytarmont 1 (ABE) and the horseshoe is not unlike that on Newton of Collessie (FIF).

** Allen's dimensions (1'3" x 9" [38 x 23cm]) appear to be too small and also out of proportion.*

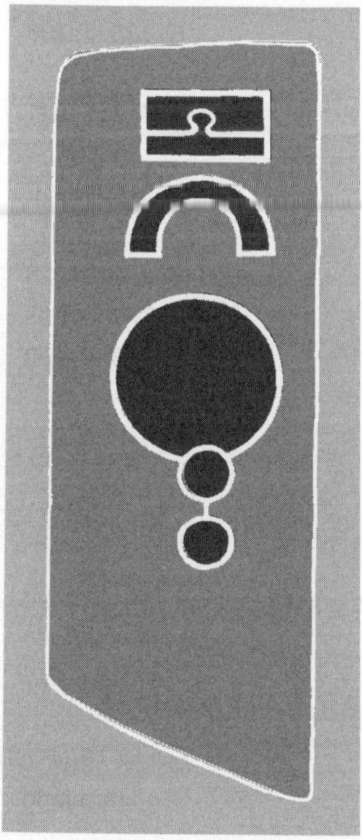

Figure 50

Sandness (SHE) (after ECMS fig.2)

16 ? SYMBOL STONES

This is a list of stones and fragments that may have been classed elsewhere as symbol stones but which are not regarded as such by this compiler. A rough indication of the reason for excluding a stone from this guide is expressed by the use of asterisks after its name:

*	no symbols
**	insufficient evidence
***	not Pictish

ABERDEENSHIRE

Corrachree * — ECMS III, 159
NJ 462 047 — field

Dunnicaer 6 * — ECMS III, 201
?Lost or ?at NJ 913 023 — garden

Redstone Hill * — RCAHMS 1994, 12
Lost NO 655 794

Rhynie 7 * — RCAHMS 1994, 10
Woodhill House, Aberdeen

ANGUS

Arbirlot * — ECMS III, 205–206
NO 602 404 — Manse garden

Baggerton ** — ECMS III, 206
Lost NO *c*469 537

Farnell * — ECMS III, 219–221
Montrose Museum

Inchbrayock * — ECMS III, 223–224
Montrose Museum

Kinnell * — ECMS III, 225–226
NO 609 503 — Manse garden wall

Monifieth 3 * — ECMS III, 230
Museum of Scotland

Strathmartine 2 * — ECMS III, 231
McManus Galleries, Dundee

BORDERS

Borthwick *** — Lines and Robertson 1991, 19–20
NT 437 140 — outside farmhouse

DUMFRIES and GALLOWAY

Eggerness */*** — RCAHMS 1994, 6
NX 486 473 — farmland

FIFE

Walton * * * ECMS III, 344–345
NO 347 113 Crawford Priory

HIGHLAND

Craig of Hattel (CAI) * RCAHMS 1994, 14
Lost ND 188 690

Sandside 2 (CAI) * RCAHMS 1994, 14
NC 952 652 at house

Balblair (INV) * ECMS III, 95–96
NH 552 436 rockery

Essich House (INV) * * * RCAHMS 1994, 15
NH 690 456 Stonifield House

Kirtomy (SUT) * * ECMS III, 45
Lost NC 74 63

ORKNEY

Papa Westray * RCAHMS 1994, 20
Tankerness House

PERTHSHIRE AND KINROSS

Bullion * RCAHMS 1994, 22
Museum of Scotland

Dunkeld * ECMS III, 284–285
Dunkeld Cathedral

Kettins * ECMS III, 224–225
NO 238 391 kirkyard

Meigle 2 * ECMS III, 297–298
Meigle Museum

Meigle 8 * ECMS III, 303
Meigle Museum

Meigle 26 * ECMS III, 303–305
Meigle Museum

Moonshade * * RCAHMS 1994, 24
Lost NO 162 358

Murthly * ECMS III, 305–306
Museum of Scotland

SHETLAND

Cunningsburgh 2 * ECMS III, 16–17
Museum of Scotland

Lerwick * ECMS III, 3–4
Museum of Scotland

Mail * RCAHMS 1994, 20
The Shetland Museum, Lerwick

Uyea * ECMS III, 4–5
Museum of Scotland

17 REFERENCES

The titles listed here are restricted to those quoted as references within the text. For a comprehensive bibliography of Pictish studies arranged by author and subject see:

Burt, JRF
A Pictish Bibliography
In Nicoll, EH (ed) *A Pictish Panorama: The Story of the Picts and a Pictish Bibliography*, 33–184. Balgavies, Angus, 1995

A

Anderson, J 1904
Notices of a sculptured stone with ogham inscription, from Latheron...
PSAS, 38 (1903–04), 534–541

Ashmore, PJ 1980
Low cairns, long cists and symbol stones
PSAS, 110 (1978–80), 346–355

Atkinson, N 1994
Wester Denoon (Glamis parish) Pictish cross-slab
DES (1994), 82

B

Burt, JRF 1991
An illustrated catalogue of the Pictish stones of Orkney
PASN, 9 (Winter 1991), 1–8

C

Calder, CST

1947
Notice of two standing stones (one with Pictish symbols) on the lands of Peterhead Farm...
PSAS, 81 (1946–47), 1–7

1951
Note on a Pictish cross-slab from Gellyburn, Perthshire
PSAS, 85 (1950–51), 175–177

Callander, JG 1927
A symbol stone from Fiscavaig, Skye...
PSAS, 61 (1926–27), 241–243

Cameron, AD 1969
Pictish symbol stone at West Balblair, Beauly, Inverness-shire
PSAS, 101 (1968–69), 288–289

Christison, D 1905
Report on the Society's excavation of forts on the Poltalloch Estate, Argyll, in 1904–5
PSAS, 39 (1904–05), 259–322

Close-Brooks, J

1980
Excavations in the Dairy Park, Dunrobin...
PSAS, 110 (1978–80), 328–345

1989
Pictish Stones in Dunrobin Castle Museum
Derby

C

Corrie, JM 1926
Notice of... (2) a symbol stone from East Lomond Hill, Fife...
PSAS, 60 (1925–26), 32–34

D

Davidson, JM 1943
A Pictish symbol stone from Golspie, Sutherland
PSAS, 77 (1942–43), 26–30

DES
Discovery and Excavation in Scotland. Dundee

E

ECMS
Allen, JR and Anderson, J 1903
The Early Christian Monuments of Scotland, 3 parts. Edinburgh. (Rep with an Introduction by Isabel Henderson, 2 vols. Balgavies, Angus, 1993)

Edwards, AJH 1926
Excavation of a number of graves in a mound at Ackergill, Caithness
PSAS, 60 (1925–26), 160–179

F

Ferguson, W 1956
Two Pictish symbol stones recently found at Tillytarmont, Rothiemay, Aberdeenshire
PSAS, 88 (1954–56), 223–224

Friell, JGP and **Watson, WG** (eds) 1984
Pictish Studies: Settlement, Burial and Art in Dark Age Northern Britain. (BAR, *Brit Ser*, 125) Oxford

G

Gourlay, R 1984
A symbol stone and cairn at Watenan, Caithness
In Friell and Watson (eds), 131–133

Gray, TE 1992
New symbol stone identified in Forres
PASJ, 2 (Autumn 1992), 25–26

Greig, M and **Addy, J** 1995
Birse Manse (Birse Parish) symbol stone
DES (1995), 34

H

Henderson, I

1962
Two Pictish symbol stones, (i) Flemington farm, Aberlemno, Angus...
PSAS 95 (1961–62), 219–221

1967
The Picts. London

Henry, D forthcoming
The Pictish symbol stone from Crosskirk, Caithness
PASJ

Hunter, JR 1985
Sanday – Pool (Cross & Burness p): broch, symbol stone...
DES (1985), 66

Hutcheson, A 1911
Notice of fragments of sculptured stones at the Church of Tealing, near Dundee
PSAS, 45 (1910–11), 420–427

I

Inglis, J

1983
Dead Man's Hole, Wantonwells
DES (1983), 11

1987
Patterns in stone...
In Small, A (ed) *The Picts: a new look at old problems*, 73–79. Dundee

J

Jackson, KH 1965
The Ogam inscription at Dunadd
Antiquity, 39 (1965), 300–302

Jervise, A 1857
Notices descriptive of the localities of certain sculptured stone monuments in Forfarshire, etc.
PSAS, 2 (1854–57), part I: 187–99, part II: 242–51

Joass, JM

1868
Note of five kists... on... the Parish of Edderton and of a kist... in the same neighbourhood
PSAS, 7 (1866–68), 268–269

1906
Donation of rubbing
PSAS, 40 (1905–06), 346–347

L

Laing, LR and **Laing, J** 1984
The date and origin of the Pictish symbols
PSAS, 114 (1984), 261–276

Lines, M 1989
Halhill Farm (Collessie Parish) sculptured stone
DES (1989), 17

Lines, M and **Robertson, N** 1991
Borthwick Stone
PASN, 8 (1991), 19–20

Logan, J 1829
Observations on several monumental stones in the North of Scotland
Archaeologia, 22 (1829), 55–58

M

Macdonald, ADS and **Laing, LR**

1968
Early ecclesiastical sites in Scotland: a field survey, Part I
PSAS, 100 (1967–68), 123–134

1970
Early ecclesiastical sites in Scotland: a field survey, Part II
PSAS, 102 (1969–70), 129–145

Mackay, A 1906
Notes on a slab with incised crescentic design...
PSAS, 40 (1905–06), 128–133

MacLeod, FT 1910
Notes on sculptured monumental slabs, an undescribed symbol stone... in Skye
PSAS, 44 (1909–10), 373–389

Marwick, H 1924
Symbol stone from Greens, St Andrew's, Orkney
PSAS, 58 (1923–24), 297–299

Mitchell, A 1874
Vacation notes in Cromar, Burghead, and Strathspey
PSAS, 10 (1872–74), 603–689

P
PASJ
Pictish Arts Society Journal. Edinburgh

PASN
Pictish Arts Society Newsletter. Edinburgh

PSAS
Proceedings of the Society of Antiquaries of Scotland. Edinburgh

R
Radford, CAR 1959
The Early Christian and Norse Settlements at Birsay, Orkney. Edinburgh

RCAHMS
The Royal Commission on the Ancient and Historical Monuments of Scotland:

1928
– *Ninth Report with Inventories of Monuments and Constructions in the Outer Hebrides, Skye and the Small Isles*. Edinburgh

1946
– *Twelfth Report with an Inventory of the Ancient Monuments of Orkney and Shetland*, 3 vols. Edinburgh

1994
– *Pictish Symbol Stones: A handlist 1994*. Edinburgh

Richardson, JS 1907
Note of an undescribed sculptured stone with symbols in the Island of Raasay
PSAS, 41 (1906–07), 435–436

Ritchie, J

1910
The sculptured stones of Clatt, Aberdeenshire
PSAS, 44 (1909–10), 203–215

1915
Notes on some Aberdeenshire sculptured stones and crosses
PSAS, 49 (1914–15), 33–49

1916
Description of sculptured symbol stone at Rayne... Aberdeenshire
PSAS, 50 (1915–16), 279–287

Ritchie, JNG 1969
Two new Pictish symbol stones from Orkney
PSAS 101 (1968–69), 130–133

Robertson, NM 1989
PAS North Perthshire field trip
PASN (Winter 1989), 2–5

S
Shepherd, IAG and **Shepherd, AN** 1978
An incised Pictish figure and a new symbol stone from Barflat, Rhynie, Gordon district
PSAS, 109 (1977–78), 211–222

Simpson, WD

1926
Notes on ... a symbol stone recently found in Mortlach Churchyard, Banffshire...
PSAS, 60 (1925–26), 273–280

S

Small, A

1962
Fairygreen Collace
DES (1962), 36

1964
Inveravon
DES (1964), 23

Stevenson, RBK

1952
Long cist burials, particularly those at Galson (Lewis) and Gairloch (Wester Ross), with a symbol stone at Gairloch
PSAS, 86 (1951–52), 106–111

1955
Pictish art
In Wainwright, FT (ed) *The Problem of the Picts*, 97–128. Edinburgh

1959
The Inchyra Stone and some other unpublished Early Christian Monuments
PSAS, 92 (1958–59), 33–55

1969
Strathmiglo: Pictish stone
DES (1969), 25

1971
Falkland: Pictish stones
DES (1971), 21

Stuart, J

1856
Sculptured Stones of Scotland. Aberdeen

1867
Sculptured Stones of Scotland, Volume Second. Edinburgh

T

Taylor, DB 1966
Longforgan: symbol stone fragment
DES (1966), 38

Thomas, C 1963
The interpretation of the Pictish symbols
Archaeological Journal, 120 (1963), 31–97

Trewin, NH

1972
North Tillytarmont Farm: Pictish stone
DES (1972), 1

1974
North Tillytarmont: Pictish stone
DES (1974), 5

W

Wainwright, FT

1951
A symbol stone at Kinblethmont, Angus
PSAS, 85 (1950–51), 180–182

1961
The Inchyra Ogham. Dundee

Wedderburn, LMM and **Grime, DM** 1984
The cairn cemetery at Garbeg, Drumnadrochit
In Friell and Watson (eds), 151–67

Woodham, AA 1974
Kintore: symbol stone and quern
DES (1974), 5

MAPS

18

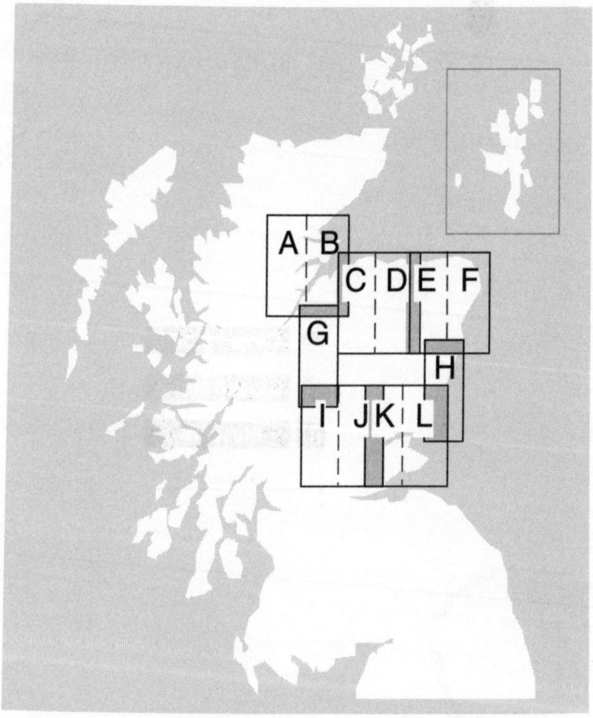

The area covered by the general location maps A–L which are on the following pages (152–163).

An Index to the maps can be found on page 164.

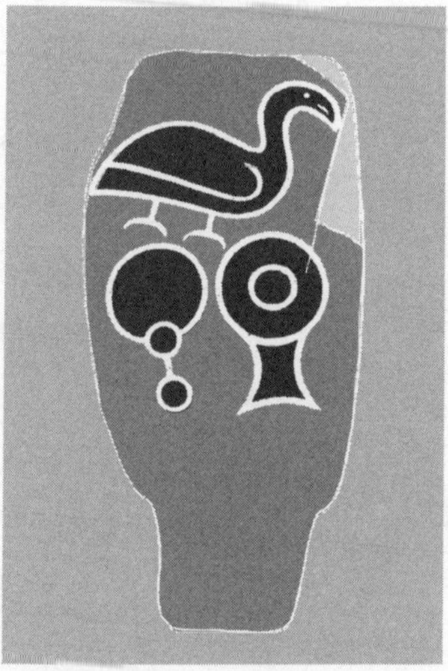

Figure 51

Tillytarmont 1 (ABE), see p.94 (after ECMS fig.201)

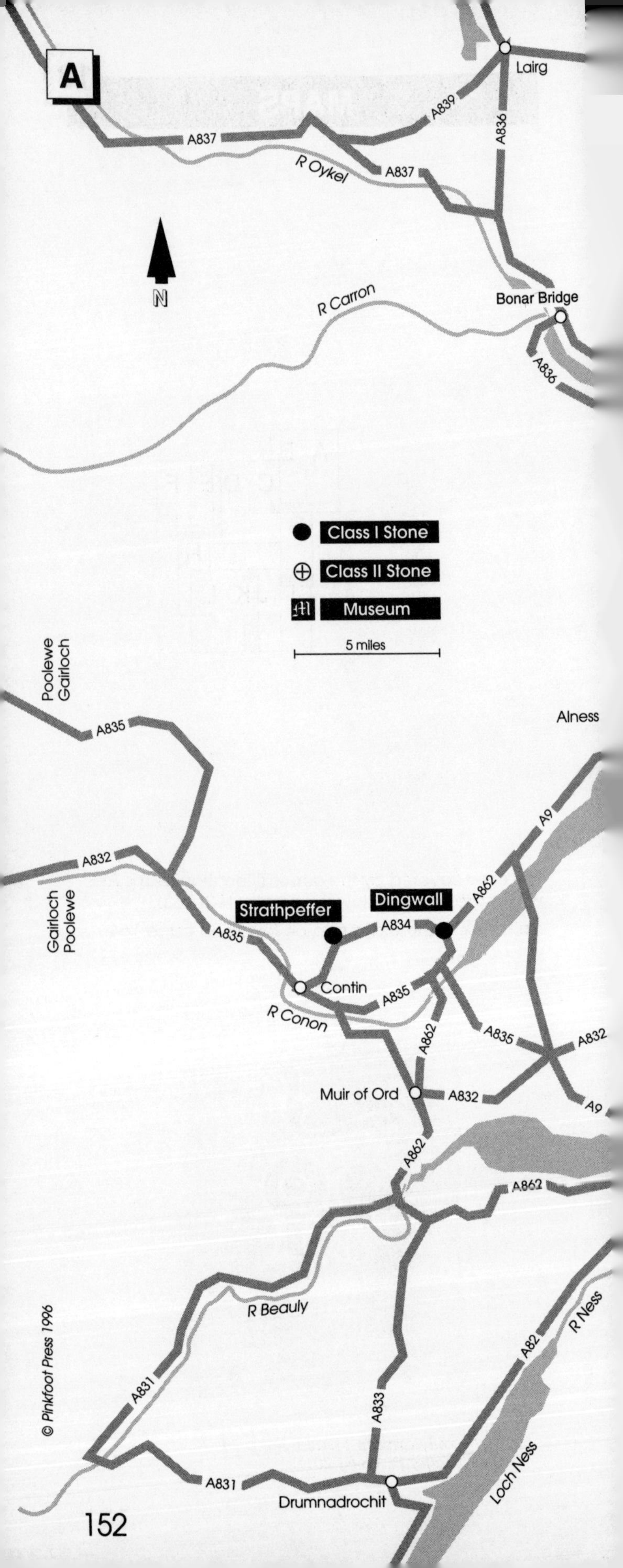
A
Lairg
A839
A836
A837
R Oykel
A837
N
Bonar Bridge
R Carron
A836
Class I Stone
Class II Stone
Museum
5 miles
Poolewe
Gairloch
A835
Alness
A9
A832
Gairloch
Poolewe
Strathpeffer
Dingwall
A862
A834
A835
Contin
A835
R Conon
A862
A835
A832
Muir of Ord
A832
A9
A862
A862
R Beauly
R Ness
A82
A831
A833
Loch Ness
A831
Drumnadrochit
© Pinkfoot Press 1996

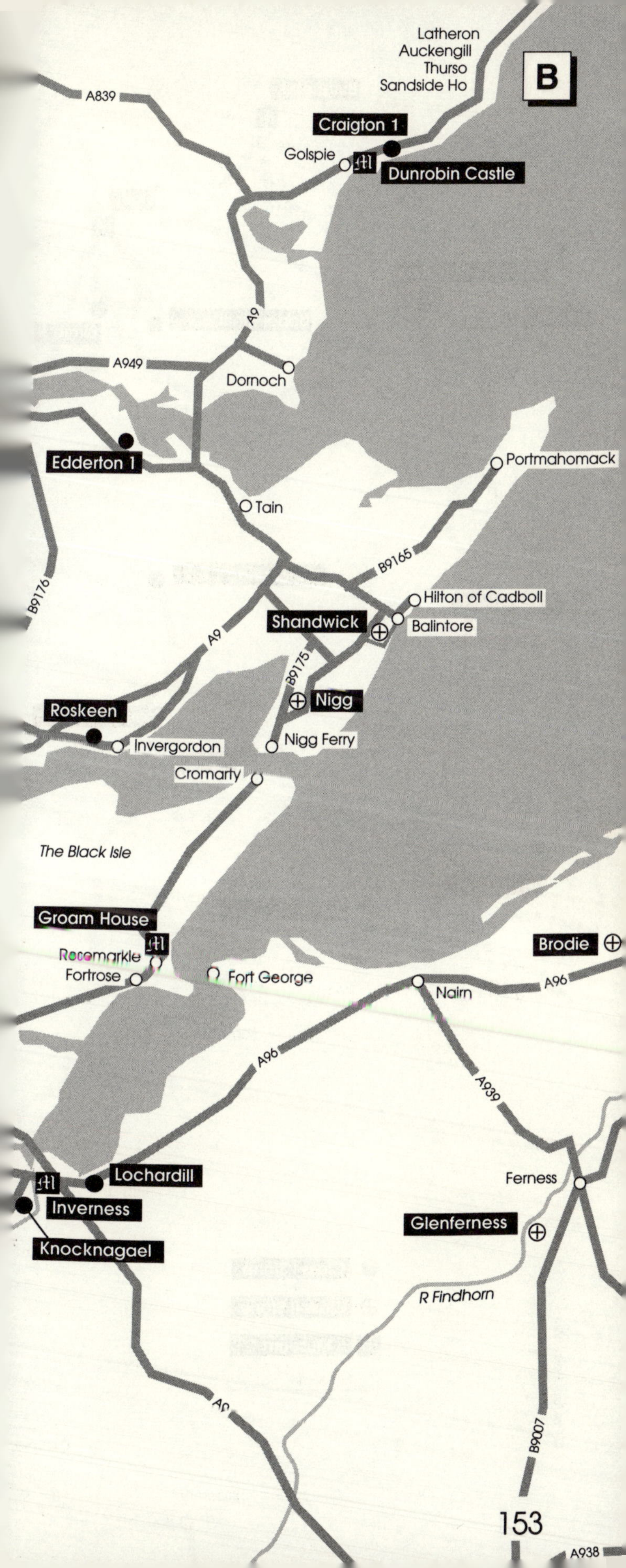

B
Latheron
Auckengill
Thurso
Sandside Ho
A839
Craigton 1
Golspie
Dunrobin Castle
A9
A949
Dornoch
Edderton 1
Portmahomack
Tain
B9165
B9176
Hilton of Cadboll
Shandwick
Balintore
A9
B9175
Nigg
Roskeen
Invergordon
Nigg Ferry
Cromarty
The Black Isle
Groam House
Rosemarkie
Fortrose
Fort George
Brodie
Nairn
A96
A96
A939
Lochardill
Inverness
Knocknagael
Ferness
Glenferness
R Findhorn
B9007
A938

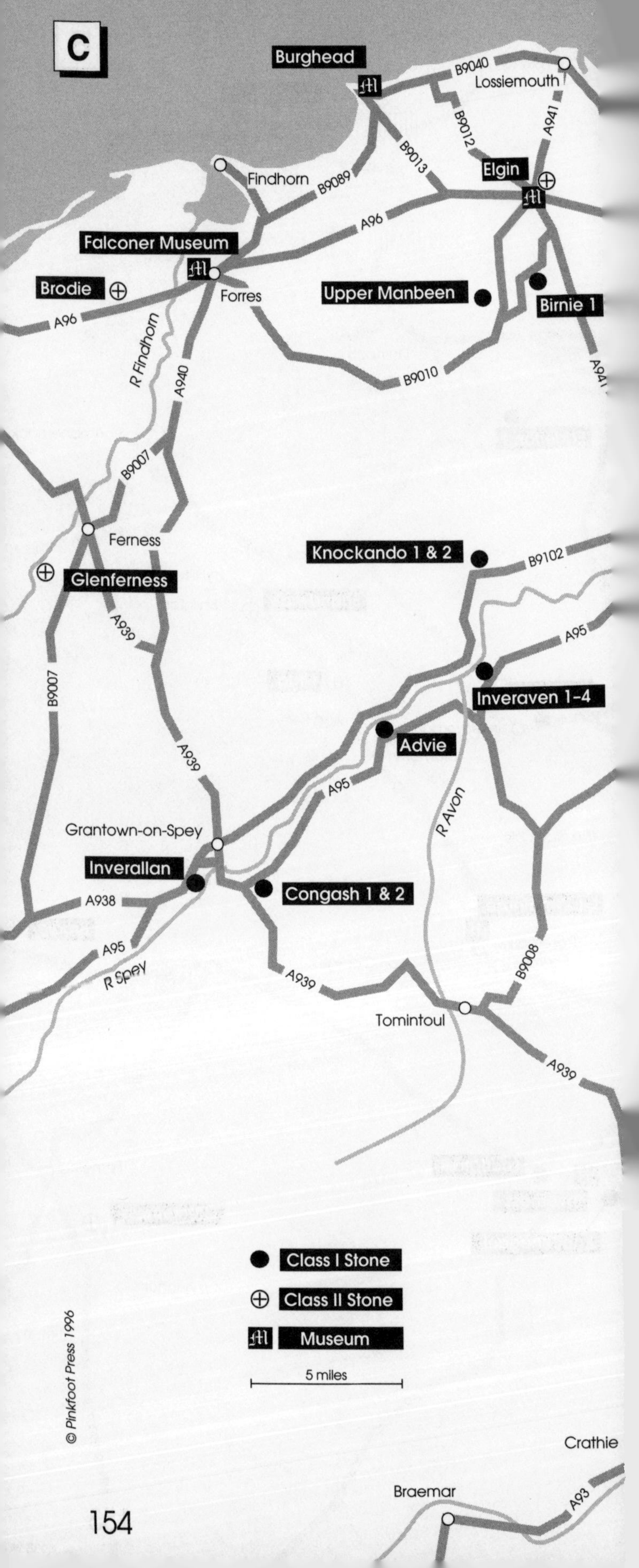

C
Burghead
B9040
Lossiemouth
B9012
A941
B9013
Findhorn
B9089
Elgin
A96
Falconer Museum
Brodie
Forres
Upper Manbeen
Birnie 1
A96
R Findhorn
A940
B9010
A941
B9007
Ferness
Knockando 1 & 2
B9102
Glenferness
A939
A95
Inveraven 1-4
B9007
Advie
A939
A95
R Avon
Grantown-on-Spey
Inverallan
Congash 1 & 2
A938
A95
R Spey
A939
B9008
Tomintoul
A939
Class I Stone
Class II Stone
Museum
5 miles
Crathie
Braemar
A93

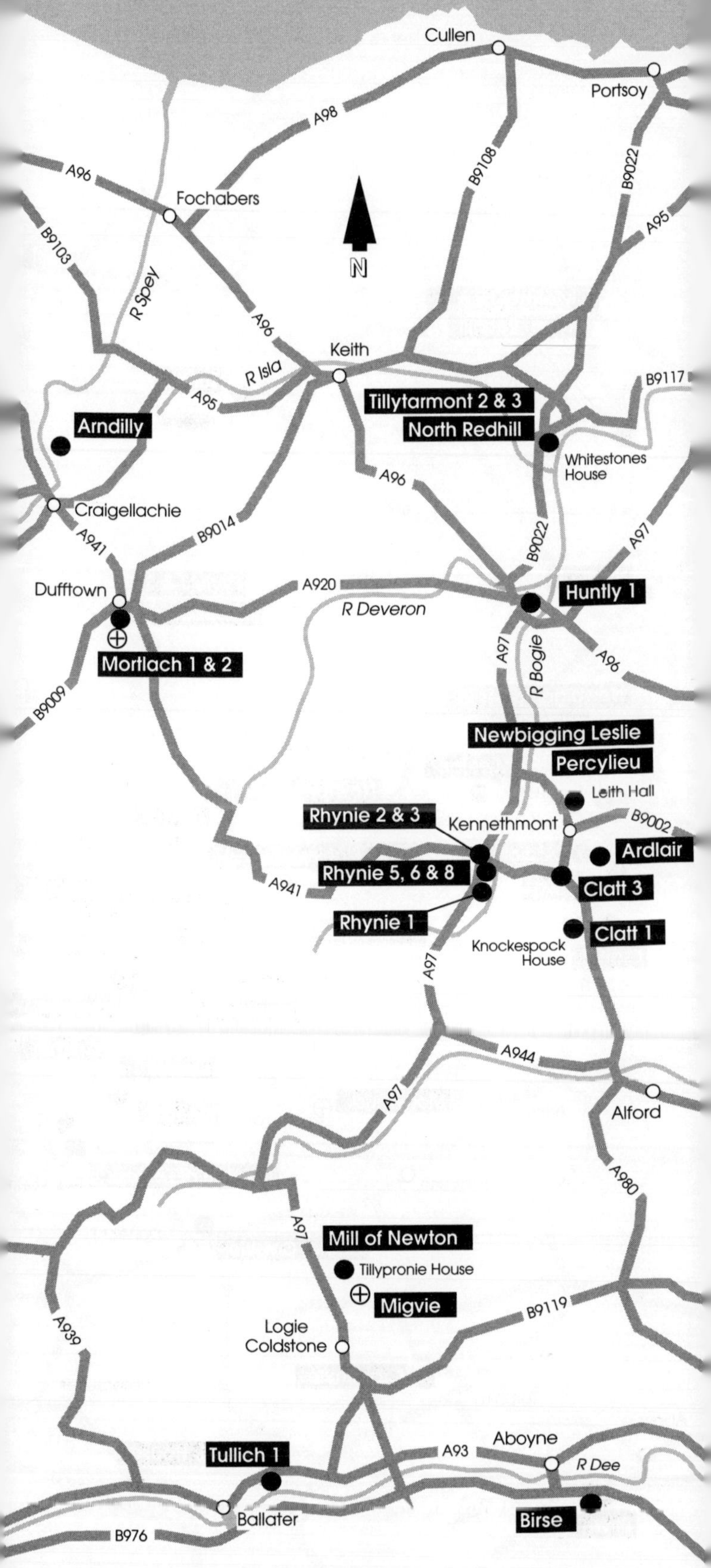
Cullen
Portsoy
A98
B9108
B9022
A96
Fochabers
N
A95
B9103
R Spey
A96
Keith
R Isla
A95
B9117
Tillytarmont 2 & 3
North Redhill
Arndilly
Whitestones House
A96
Craigellachie
B9014
A941
B9022
A97
Dufftown
A920
R Deveron
Huntly 1
Mortlach 1 & 2
A97
R Bogie
A96
B9009
Newbigging Leslie
Percylieu
Leith Hall
Rhynie 2 & 3
Kennethmont
B9002
Ardlair
Rhynie 5, 6 & 8
Clatt 3
A941
Rhynie 1
Clatt 1
Knockespock House
A97
A944
Alford
A97
A980
A97
Mill of Newton
Tillypronie House
Migvie
A939
B9119
Logie Coldstone
Aboyne
A93
R Dee
Tullich 1
Ballater
Birse
B976

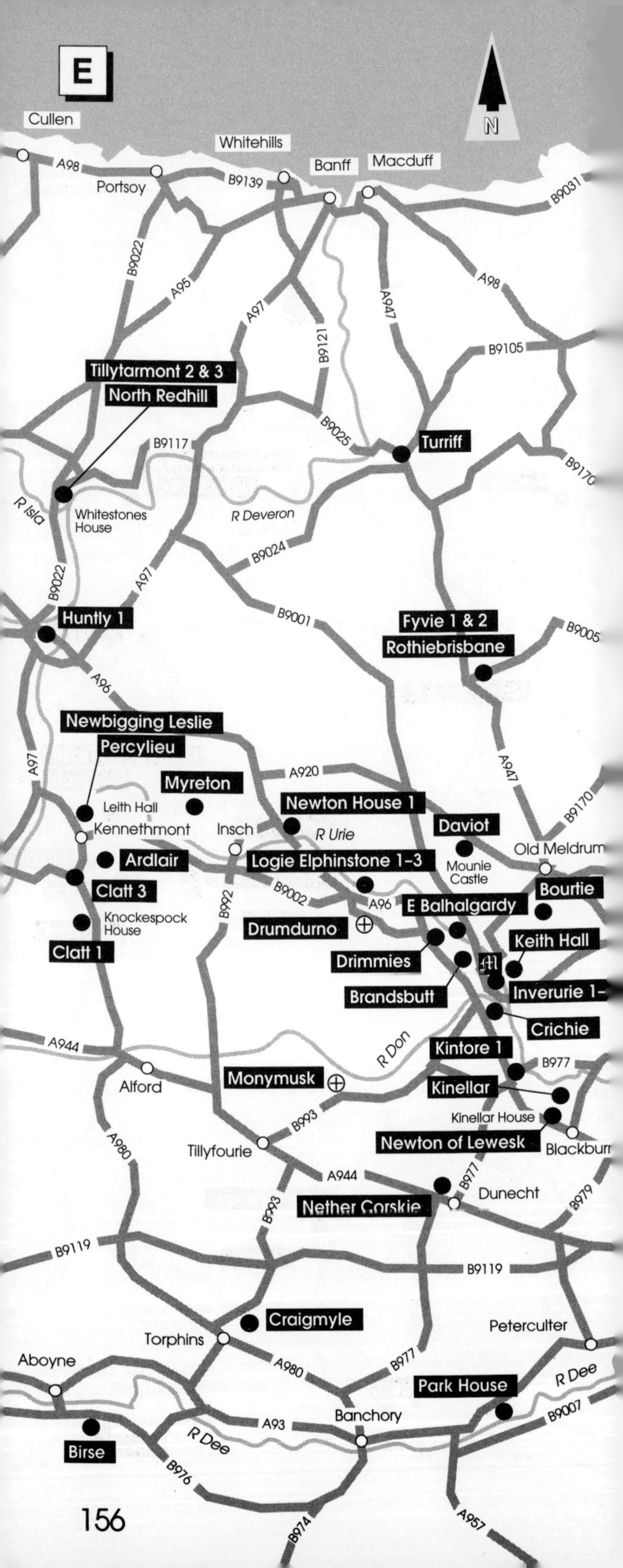
E
N
Cullen
Whitehills
Banff
Macduff
Portsoy
A98
B9139
B9031
B9022
A95
A97
B9121
A947
A98
B9105
Tillytarmont 2 & 3
North Redhill
B9025
Turriff
B9117
B9170
R Isla
Whitestones House
R Deveron
B9024
B9022
A97
Huntly 1
B9001
Fyvie 1 & 2
Rothiebrisbane
B9005
A96
Newbigging Leslie
Percylieu
A97
A920
Myreton
A947
Newton House 1
B9170
Leith Hall
Daviot
Kennethmont
Insch
R Urie
Old Meldrum
Ardlair
Logie Elphinstone 1-3
Mounie Castle
Clatt 3
B9002
A96
Bourtie
B992
E Balhalgardy
Knockespock House
Drumdurno
Keith Hall
Clatt 1
Drimmies
Brandsbutt
Inverurie 1-
Crichie
A944
R Don
Kintore 1
B977
Alford
Monymusk
Kinellar
B993
Kinellar House
A980
Tillyfourie
Newton of Lewesk
Blackburn
A944
B977
Dunecht
Nether Corskie
B993
B979
B9119
B9119
Craigmyle
Peterculter
Torphins
Aboyne
A980
B977
R Dee
Park House
A93
Banchory
B9007
R Dee
Birse
B976
B974
A957

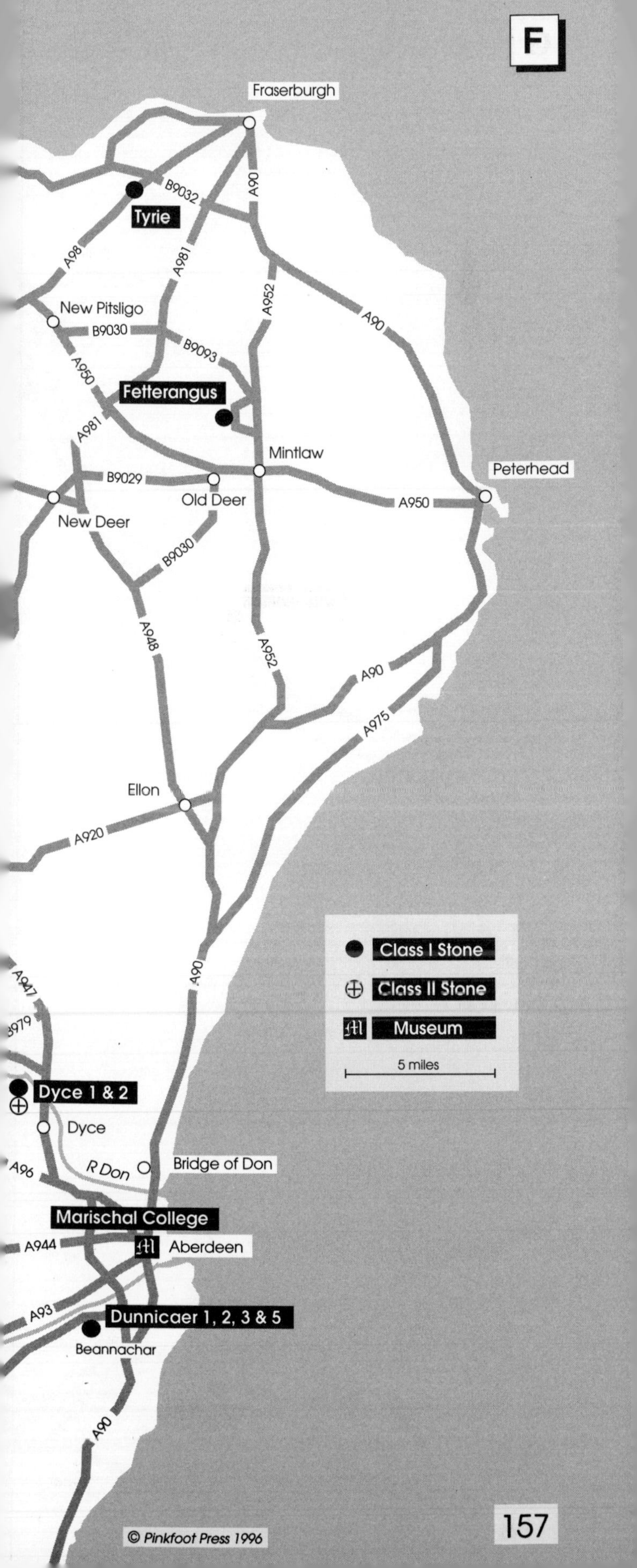
F
Fraserburgh
Tyrie
B9032
A90
A98
A981
A952
New Pitsligo
B9030
B9093
A950
Fetterangus
A981
Mintlaw
Peterhead
B9029
Old Deer
New Deer
A950
B9030
A948
A952
A90
A975
Ellon
A920
A947
B979
A90
Class I Stone
Class II Stone
Museum
5 miles
Dyce 1 & 2
Dyce
R Don
Bridge of Don
A96
Marischal College
A944
Aberdeen
A93
Dunnicaer 1, 2, 3 & 5
Beannachar
A90
© Pinkfoot Press 1996

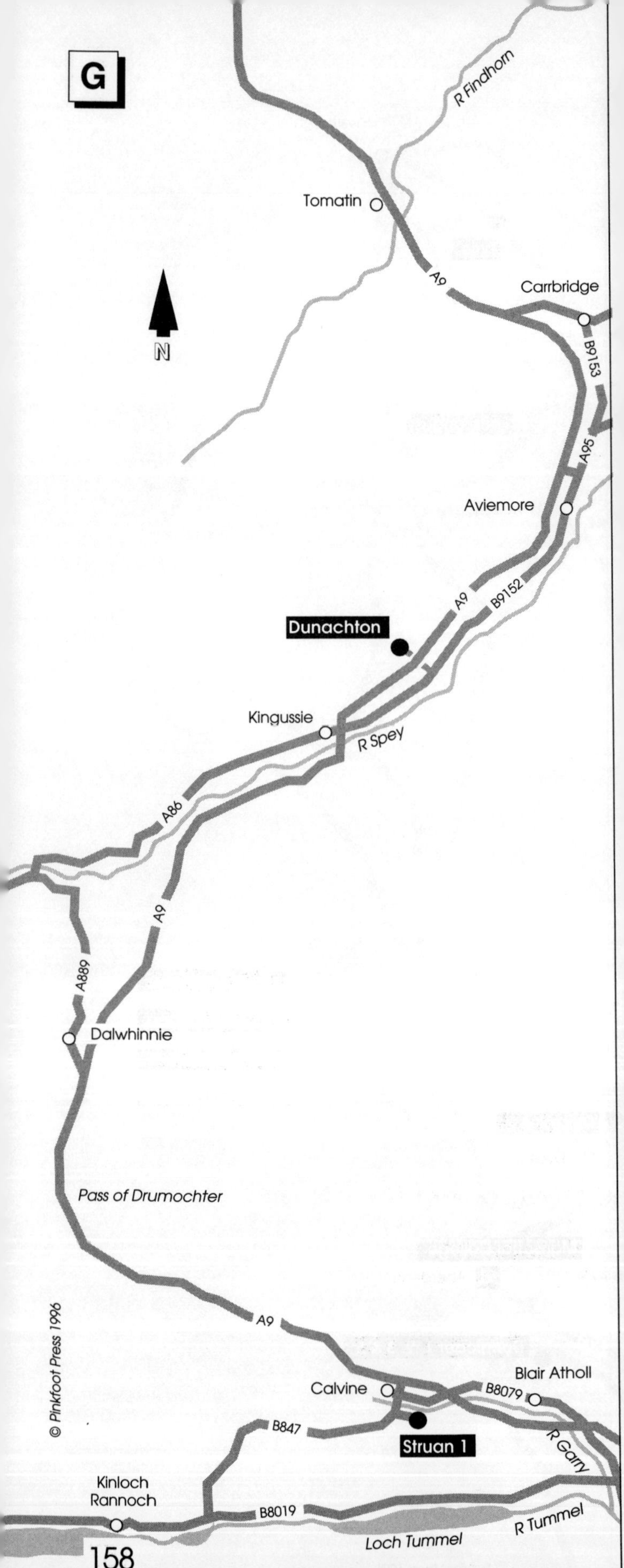
G
R Findhorn
Tomatin
N
A9
Carrbridge
B9153
A95
Aviemore
B9152
A9
Dunachton
Kingussie
R Spey
A86
A9
A889
Dalwhinnie
Pass of Drumochter
A9
Blair Atholl
Calvine
B8079
B847
Struan 1
R Garry
Kinloch
Rannoch
B8019
R Tummel
Loch Tummel
© Pinkfoot Press 1996

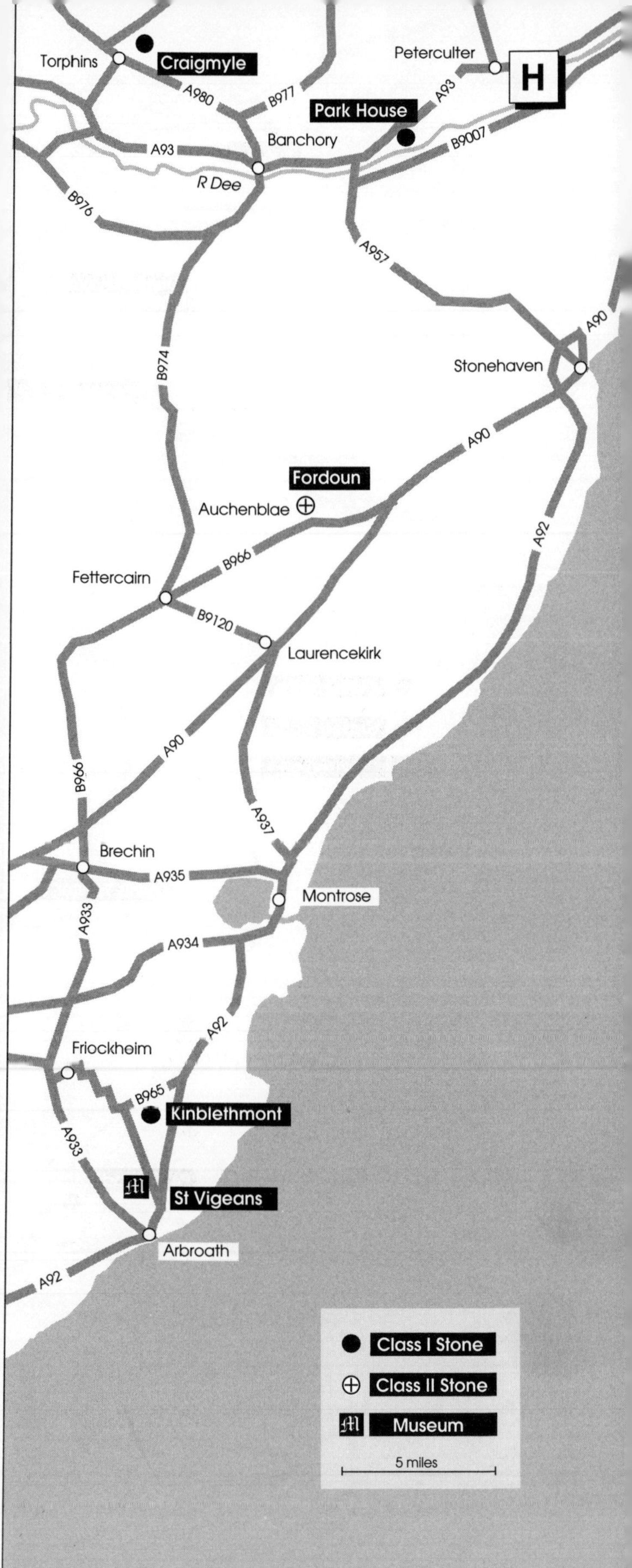

Torphins
Craigmyle
Peterculter
H
A980
B977
Park House
A93
Banchory
B9007
A93
R Dee
B976
A957
A90
Stonehaven
B974
A90
Fordoun
Auchenblae
A92
B966
Fettercairn
B9120
Laurencekirk
A90
B966
A937
Brechin
A935
Montrose
A933
A934
A92
Friockheim
B965
Kinblethmont
A933
St Vigeans
Arbroath
A92
Class I Stone
Class II Stone
Museum
5 miles

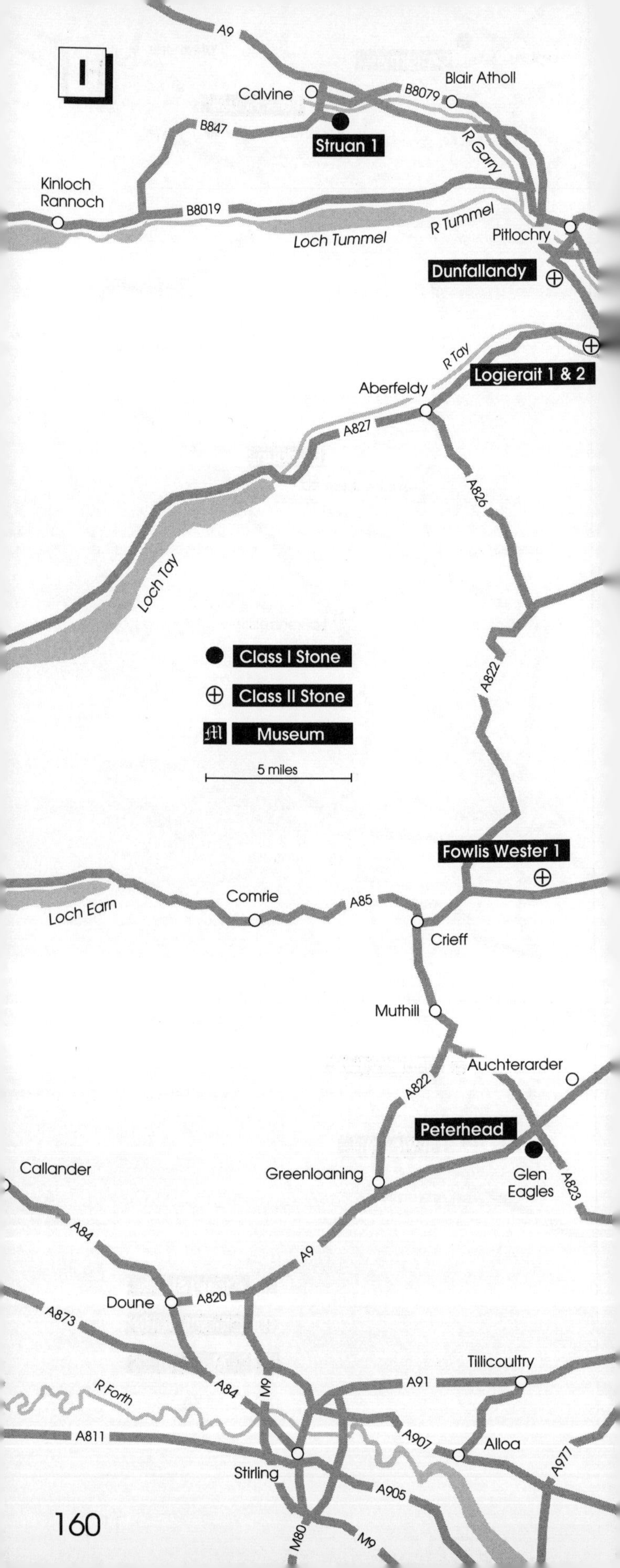
I
A9
Calvine
Blair Atholl
B8079
B847
Struan 1
R Garry
Kinloch
Rannoch
B8019
R Tummel
Loch Tummel
Pitlochry
Dunfallandy
R Tay
Logierait 1 & 2
Aberfeldy
A827
A826
Loch Tay
Class I Stone
Class II Stone
Museum
5 miles
A822
Fowlis Wester 1
Comrie
A85
Loch Earn
Crieff
Muthill
Auchterarder
A822
Peterhead
Glen
Eagles
A823
Callander
Greenloaning
A84
A9
Doune
A820
A873
Tillicoultry
R Forth
A84
M9
A91
A811
A907
Alloa
Stirling
A977
A905
M80
M9

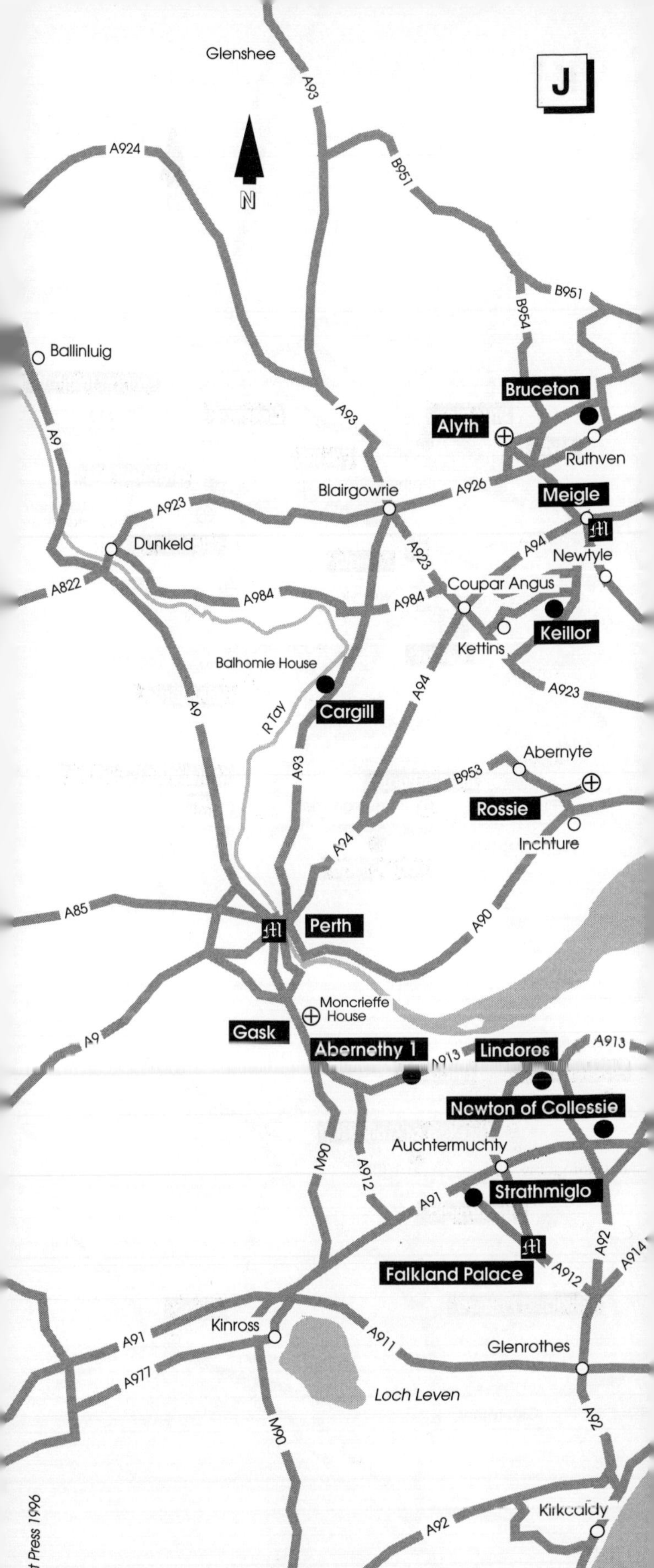
J
N
Glenshee
A93
A924
B951
B951
B954
Ballinluig
Bruceton
Alyth
Ruthven
A9
A93
Blairgowrie
A926
Meigle
A923
Dunkeld
A94
Newtyle
A923
A822
A984
A984
Coupar Angus
Kettins
Keillor
Balhomie House
Cargill
A94
A923
A9
R Tay
A93
Abernyte
B953
Rossie
Inchture
A94
A85
Perth
A90
Moncrieffe House
A9
Gask
Abernethy 1
A913
Lindores
A913
Newton of Collessie
Auchtermuchty
M90
A912
A91
Strathmiglo
A92
Falkland Palace
A912
A914
Kinross
A91
A911
Glenrothes
A977
Loch Leven
M90
A92
Kirkcaldy
A92

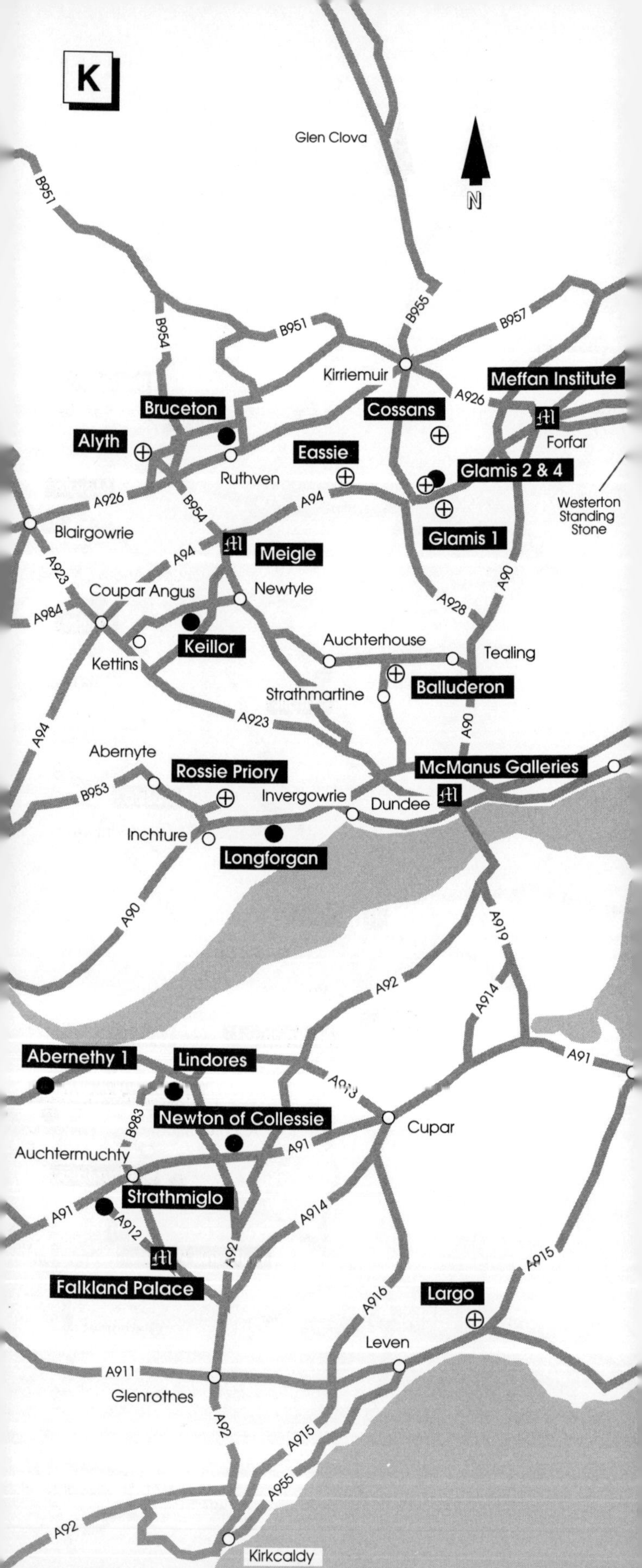
K
Glen Clova
N
B951
B955
B957
B954
Kirriemuir
Meffan Institute
A926
Cossans
Forfar
Bruceton
Alyth
Ruthven
Eassie
Glamis 2 & 4
Westerton
Standing
Stone
A926
B954
A94
Glamis 1
Blairgowrie
Meigle
A94
A90
A923
Coupar Angus
Newtyle
A928
A984
Keillor
Auchterhouse
Tealing
Kettins
Balluderon
Strathmartine
A923
A90
A94
Abernyte
Rossie Priory
McManus Galleries
B953
Invergowrie
Dundee
Inchture
Longforgan
A90
A919
A92
A914
A91
Abernethy 1
Lindores
A913
B983
Newton of Collessie
Cupar
Auchtermuchty
A91
A91
Strathmiglo
A912
A914
A92
Falkland Palace
A915
A916
Largo
Leven
A911
Glenrothes
A92
A915
A955
A92
Kirkcaldy

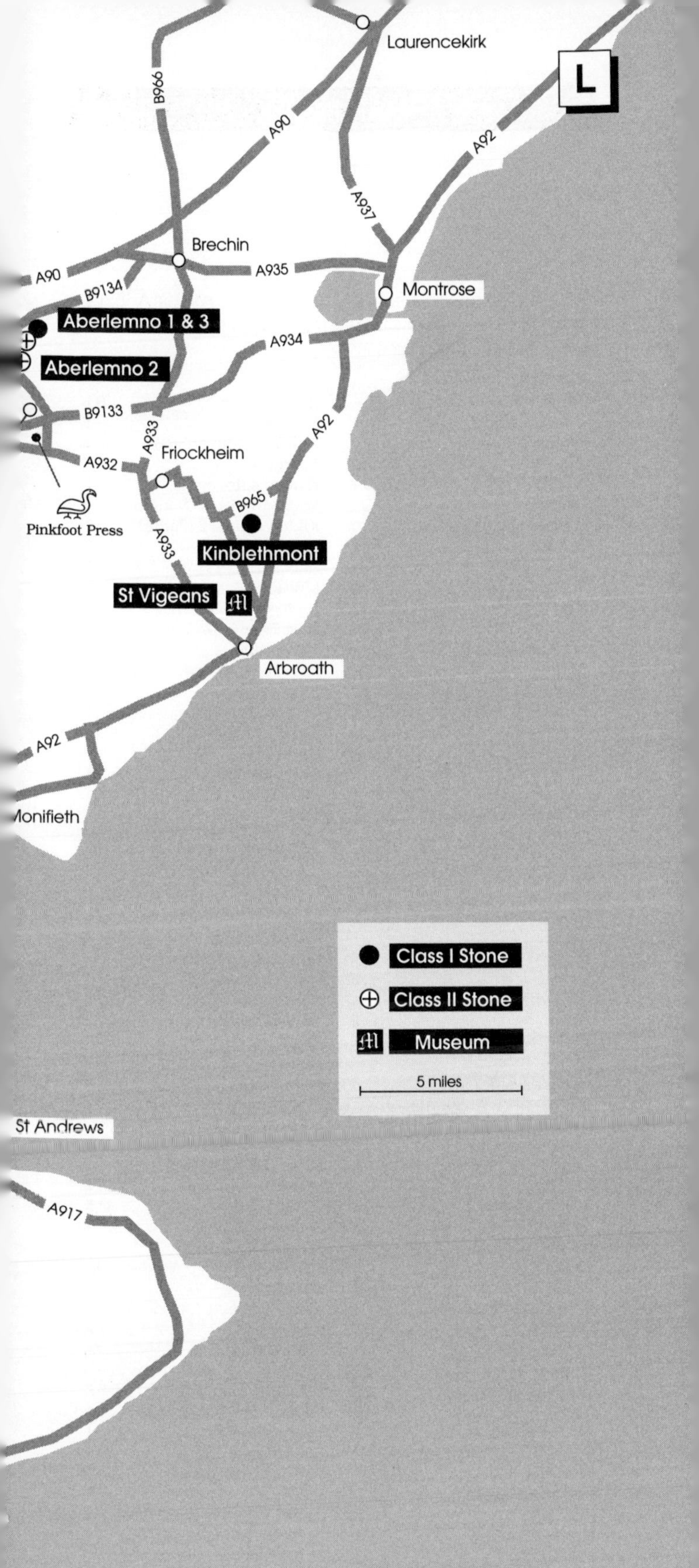
L
Laurencekirk
B966
A90
A92
A937
Brechin
A90
A935
B9134
Montrose
Aberlemno 1 & 3
A934
Aberlemno 2
B9133
A933
A92
Friockheim
A932
B965
Pinkfoot Press
Kinblethmont
A933
St Vigeans
Arbroath
A92
Monifieth
Class I Stone
Class II Stone
Museum
5 miles
St Andrews
A917

MAP INDEX

Index of stones which are located on maps A–L, or which are in museums situated within the area covered by the maps.

INDEX

The stones are arranged alphabetically and numbered accordingly.

KEY

*	No complete symbol set
HS	Historic Scotland
I	Inscription (other than Ogam)
NTS	National Trust for Scotland
M	Re-location proposed
O	Ogam inscription
P	Private house or grounds
S	Found standing
SS	Former standing stone

COUNCIL AREAS

ABE	Aberdeenshire	
ABN	City of Aberdeen	
ANG	Angus	
ARG	Argyll and Bute	
DUM	Dumfries and Galloway	
DUN	City of Dundee	
EDI	City of Edinburgh	
FIF	Fife	
HIG	Highland	
BAD	Badenoch and Strathspey	Administrative Areas
CAI	Caithness	Administrative Areas
INV	Inverness	Administrative Areas
NAI	Nairn	Administrative Areas
ROS	Ross and Cromarty	Administrative Areas
SKY	Skye and Lochalsh	Administrative Areas
SUT	Sutherland	Administrative Areas
MOR	Moray	
PER	Perthshire and Kinross	
ORK	Orkney	
SHE	Shetland	
WES	Western Isles	

No.	Name	Area	Present Location (October 1996)	Findspot	Page
1	**Aberlemno 1**	ANG	NO 523 559 Roadside HS M	Same S SS Cists in field Cup-marks	**60**
2	**ABERLEMNO 2**	ANG	NO 522 556 Kirkyard HS M	Same S	**61**
3	**ABERLEMNO 3**	ANG	NO 523 559 Roadside HS M	Same S Beside cairn	**60**
4	**Aberlemno 5**	ANG	DUN McManus Galleries	NO 524 556 Field near kirk	**58**
5	**Abernethy 1**	PER	NO 190 164 Foot of round tower HS	House foundations	**44**
6	**Ackergill 1**	HIG CAI	EDI Museum of Scotland	ND 348 550 Burial mound S O	**29**
*7	**Ackergill 2**	HIG CAI	EDI Museum of Scotland	ND 349 550 Near cist	**29**
8	**Advie**	HIG BAD	NJ 127 343 Kirk wall	NJ 142 353 Cemetery	**105**
9	**ALYTH**	PER	NO 243 488 In kirk	Near manse (by old kirk ruins)	**44**

A

10	**Anwoth**	DUM	NX 589 560 Beside fort	Rockface	**137**
11	**Ardlair**	ABE	NJ 555 278 Field P	Same S SS	**71**
*12	**Ardross 1**	HIG ROS	HIG INV Inverness Museum	NH 65 74 Wall	**109**
*13	**Ardross 2**	HIG ROS	HIG INV Inverness Museum	NH 65 74 Wall	**109**
14	**Arndilly**	MOR	NJ 291 471 Wall of Arndilly House P	Kirk wall (House on same site)	**96**
15	**BALLUDERON**	ANG	NO 375 376 Field P	Same S *St Martin's Stone*	**62**
*16	**Balneilan**	MOR	LOST	NJ 149 259 Farm wall (ex stone circle)	**141**
17	**Benbecula**	WES	EDI Museum of Scotland	NF *c*803 566 Shore	**30**
18	**Birnie 1**	MOR	NJ 206 587 Kirkyard	Kirkyard wall	**97**
19	**Birsay**	ORK	EDI Museum of Scotland	HY 240 285 Cemetery Replica on site HS	**30**

B

No.	Name	Area	Fresent Location (October 1996)	Findspot	Page
*20	**Birse**	ABE	NO 555 973 P	Manse garden wall (beside kirk)	**71**
21	**Bourtie**	ABE	NJ 805 249 Kirk wall	Same	**71**
22	**Brandsbutt**	ABE	NJ 760 224 Roadside HS	Near stone circle O	**72**
23	**BRODIE**	MOR	NH 984 577 Beside drive, Brodie Cas P	NH 990 584 Kirkyard O *Rodney Stone*	**97**
24	**Bruceton**	PER	NO 290 504 Field P	Same S Near coffins	**44**
25	**Burghead 1**	MOR	EDI Museum of Scotland	NJ 109 691 Fort	**30**
26	**Burghead 2**	MOR	Burghead Museum	NJ 109 691 Harbour below fort	**98**
27	**Burghead 3**	MOR	Elgin Museum	NJ 109 691 Fort	**99**
28	**Burghead 4**	MOR	Burghead Museum	NJ 109 691 House below fort	**98**

29	**Burghead 5**	MOR	ENG British Museum	NJ 109 691 Fort	(98)
30	**Burghead 6**	MOR	Elgin Museum	NJ 109 961 Harbour below fort	**100**
31	**Burrian**	ORK	Tankerness House Museum	HY 308 168 Broch	**133**
32	**Cargill**	PER	NO 148 362 Outside house P	NO 160 345 Wall	**45**
33	**Clatt 1**	ABE	NJ 544 241 Outside house P	NJ 539 260 Kirkyard wall	**72**
*34	**Clatt 2**	ABE	LOST	NJ 538 260 Kirkyard	**138**
35	**Clatt 3**	ABE	NJ 538 260 Kirkyard wall	Same	**72**
*36	**Clune Dores**	HIG INV	EDI Museum of Scotland	NH *c*605 354 Wasteland	**31**
37	**Clynekirkton 1**	HIG SUT	Dunrobin Castle Museum	NC 895 060 Kirkyard	**122**
38	**Clynekirkton 2**	HIG SUT	Dunrobin Castle Museum	NC 91 06 Field	**122**

No.	Name	Area	Present Location (October 1996)	Findspot	Page
39	**Clynemilton 1**	HIG SUT	Dunrobin Castle Museum	NC 91 06 Field	**123**
*40	**Clynemilton 2**	HIG SUT	Dunrobin Castle Museum	NC 91 06 Field	**123**
41	**Collace**	PER	ABN Marischal Museum	NO 207 332 Field	**93**
42	**Congash 1**	HIG BAD	NJ 058 262 ?Kirkyard wall P	Same S Site called *Parc-an-Caipel*	**106**
43	**Congash 2**	HIG BAD	NJ 058 262 ?Kirkyard wall P	Same S Site called *Parc-an-Caipel*	**106**
44	**COSSANS**	ANG	NO 401 500 Mound HS M	Same S Near cists *St Orland's Stone*	**63**
45	**Craigmyle**	ABE	NJ 640 024 Field P	Same S SS	**73**
46	**Craigton 1**	HIG SUT	NC 851 009 Wood P	NH 79 98	**121**
47	**CRAIGTON 2**	HIG SUT	Dunrobin Castle Museum	NH 79 98 or NH 799 986 Kirkyard O	**123**

48	**Crichie**	ABE	NJ 779 197 In henge P	NJ 780 197 East of henge S ?SS	**73**
49	**Crosskirk**	HIG CAI	LOST (?In Denmark)	ND 025 701 Cairn near burial-ground	**141**
50	**Cullaird**	HIG INV	Inverness Museum	NH 634 404 Field	**109**
51	**Daviot**	ABE	NJ 767 286 Outside castle P	NJ 760 288 Roadside	**74**
52	**Dingwall**	HIG ROS	NH 549 589 Kirkyard	Kirk lintel SS Cup-marks Reused	**115**
*53	**Drainie 1**	MOR	LOST	NJ 223 696 Manse (beside kirk ruins)	**142**
54	**Drimmies**	ABE	NJ 743 235 Farm entrance P	Garden wall	**74**
55	**Drumbuie 1**	HIG INV	EDI Museum of Scotland	NH 51 31 Over cist	**31**
56	**Drumbuie 2**	HIG INV	EDI Museum of Scotland	NH 51 31 Over cist	**31**
57	**DRUMDURNO**	ABE	NJ 704 247 Roadside HS M	Roadside S *The Maiden Stone*	**74**

No.	Name	Area	Present Location (October 1996)	Findspot	Page
58	**Dun Osdale**	HIG SKY	Dunvegan Castle Museum	NG 242 463 Near broch	**112**
59	**Dunachton**	HIG BAD	NH 821 046 Outside garden P	Steading door lintel	**106**
60	**Dunadd**	ARG	NR 837 936 Fort HS	Rockface O	**136**
61	**DUNFALLANDY**	PER	NN 946 565 Burial ground HS	Same (was chapel site) S	**46**
62	**Dunnicaer 1**	ABE	ABN NJ 913 023 Beannachar P	NO 884 847 Wall on top of stack	**91**
63	**Dunnicaer 2**	ABE	ABN NJ 913 023 Beannachar P	NO 884 847 Beach	**91**
64	**Dunnicaer 3**	ABE	ABN NJ 913 023 Beannachar P	NO 884 847 Beach	**91**
*65	**Dunnicaer 4**	ABE	ABN Marischal Museum	NO 884 847 Beach Reused Cup-marks	**93**
66	**Dunnicaer 5**	ABE	ABN NJ 913 023 Beannachar P	NO 884 847 Beach	**91**

67	**Dunnichen**	ANG	Meffan Institute, Forfar	NO *c*516 496 Over cist Replica near kirk	**58**
68	**Dunrobin 1**	HIG SUT	Dunrobin Castle Museum	NC 849 006 Over cist	**124**
69	**Dunrobin 2**	HIG SUT	Dunrobin Castle Museum	NC 847 004 Burial cairn	**125**
70	**Dyce 1**	ABN	NJ 875 154 In kirk ruins HS	Kirkyard wall	**92**
71	**DYCE 2**	ABN	NJ 875 154 In kirk ruins HS	In nearby glebe	**92**
72	**EASSIE**	ANG	NO 353 475 In kirk ruins HS	Near kirk ruins	**64**
*73	**E. Balhalgardy**	ABE	NJ 761 238 Farmhouse lintel P	Same	**75**
74	**E. Lomond Hill**	FIF	EDI Museum of Scotland	NO 244 062 Fort	**31**
75	**Easterton of Roseisle**	MOR	EDI Museum of Scotland	NJ *c*144 647 Cist Reused ?Cup-marks	**32**
76	**Edderton 1**	HIG ROS	NH 708 851 Field P	Same S SS Near stone circle and burial	**115**

No.	Name	Area	Present Location (October 1996)	Findspot	Page
77	**Edinburgh**	EDI	Museum of Scotland	NT *c*250 736 Princes Street Gardens	**32**
78	**ELGIN**	MOR	NJ 222 631 Elgin Cathedral HS	NJ 216 629 Near kirk	**99**
79	**Fetterangus**	ABE	NJ 981 506 Kirkyard	Same Illegible	**75**
80	**Finlarig**	HIG BAD	EDI Museum of Scotland	NH 991 254 Near kirk ruins	**32**
81	**Firth**	ORK	EDI Museum of Scotland	HY 378 171 House wall	**33**
82	**Fiscavaig**	HIG SKY	GLA St Mungo Museum	NG 33 34 Shore	**33**
83	**FORDOUN**	ABE	NO 726 784 In kirk	In old kirk *St Palladius Stone* I	**75**
*84	**FORMASTON**	ABE	Inverurie Museum	NJ 541 001 Kirkyard O	**78**
*85	**Forres 2**	MOR	Falconer Museum, Forres	NJ 034 587 Garden wall	**100**

86	**FOWLIS WESTER 1**	PER	NN 928 241 In kirk HS	NN 928 240 Near kirk S Replica on site	**47**
87	**Fyvie 1**	ABE	NJ 769 378 Kirk wall	Schoolhouse wall	**76**
88	**Fyvie 2**	ABE	NJ 769 378 Kirk wall	Same	**76**
89	**Gairloch**	HIG ROS	Gairloch Museum	NG 799 772 Glebe Near burials	**116**
*90	**Garbeg**	HIG INV	Inverness Museum	NH 511 323 Cairn cemetery	**110**
91	**GASK**	PER	NC 138 194 Grounds of Moncrieffe Ho P	NN *c*996 189 Field S	**48**
92	**GELLYBURN 2**	PER	Perth Museum	NO 094 392 House wall	**54**
93	**GLAMIS 1**	ANG	NO 394 465 Woodland P M	Same S Reused I/II	**64**
94	**GLAMIS 2**	ANG	NO 386 469 Manse garden P	Same S Cup-marks Reused I/II	**65**
*95	**Glamis 4**	ANG	NO 387 469 In kirk	NO 386 469 Manse rockery (nr kirkyard)	**66**

No.	Name	Area	Present Location (October 1996)	Findspot	Page
96	**GLENFERNESS**	HIG NAI	NH 937 426 Near river P	NH 936 425 S By cairn *Princess Stone*	**108**
97	**Golspie**	HIG SUT	Dunrobin Castle Museum	NC 834 002 Over cist	**125**
98	**Grantown**	HIG BAD	EDI Museum of Scotland	NJ 045 301 Mound	**33**
99	**Greens**	ORK	EDI Museum of Scotland	HY 542 032 Farmland	**33**
100	**Gurness**	ORK	Gurness Broch Museum HS	HY 382 269 Broch	**133**
101	**HILTON OF CADBOLL**	HIG ROS	EDI Museum of Scotland	NH 873 769 Near chapel ruins S	**34**
102	**Huntly 1**	ABE	NJ 529 400 Huntly Market Place	?NJ 518 360 ?Stone circle S SS Illegible	**77**
*103	**Huntly 2**	ABE	EDI Museum of Scotland	NJ 558 376 Field	**35**
104	**Inchyra**	PER	Perth Museum	NO 190 212 Over grave O Reused	**54**

105	**Inverallan**	HIG BAD	NJ 027 260 Kirkyard	Kirk fabric Indistinct	**107**
106	**Inveraven 1**	MOR	NJ 183 376 Kirk wall	Kirk foundations	**100**
107	**Inveraven 2**	MOR	NJ 183 376 Kirk wall	Kirk foundations	**101**
*108	**Inveraven 3**	MOR	NJ 183 376 Kirk wall	Kirk foundations	**101**
109	**Inveraven 4**	MOR	NJ 183 376 Kirk wall	Kirkyard	**101**
110	**Invereen**	HIG INV	EDI Museum of Scotland	NH 797 311 Field	**35**
111	**Inverurie 1**	ABE	NJ 780 206 Cemetery	Kirk or kirkyard wall Reused	**77**
*112	**Inverurie 2**	ABE	NJ 780 206 Cemetery	Kirk or kirkyard wall	**77**
*113	**Inverurie 3**	ABE	NJ 780 206 Cemetery	Kirk or kirkyard wall	**78**
114	**Inverurie 4**	ABE	NJ 780 206 Cemetery	Kirk or kirkyard wall	**78**

No.	Name	Area	Present Location (October 1996)	Findspot	Page
115	**Keillor**	PER	NO 273 398 Roadside mound	Same (Burial mound) S	**48**
116	**Keiss**	HIG CAI	EDI Museum of Scotland	ND 339 585 Building floor	**35**
117	**Keith Hall**	ABE	NJ 788 214 Moat P	NJ 780 202 River	**79**
118	**Kinblethmont**	ANG	NO 641 472 In house P	NO 638 473 Field ?Cup-and-ring-mark	**66**
119	**Kinellar**	ABE	NJ 821 144 In kirk	Kirk foundations	**79**
120	**KINGOLDRUM 1**	ANG	EDI Museum of Scotland	NO 334 550 Kirk fabric	**36**
121	**Kingsmills**	HIG INV	Inverness Museum	NH 67 44 Byre step	**110**
122	**Kintore 1**	ABE	NJ 793 163 Kirkyard	Same Reused	**80**
123	**Kintore 2**	ABE	EDI Museum of Scotland	NJ 794 163 Mound near kirk Reused	**36**

124	**Kintore 3**	ABE	EDI Museum of Scotland	NJ 794 163 Mound near kirk	**37**
125	**Kintore 4**	ABE	Inverurie Museum	NJ 790 162 Garden	**78**
126	**Kintradwell 1**	HIG SUT	Dunrobin Castle Museum	NC 928 081 Near broch	**126**
127	**Kintradwell 2**	HIG SUT	Dunrobin Castle Museum	NC 932 084 Beach	**126**
128	**Kintradwell 3**	HIG SUT	Dunrobin Castle Museum	NC 932 084 Beach	**126**
*129	**Kintradwell 4**	HIG SUT	Dunrobin Castle Museum	NC 932 084 Beach	**126**
130	**Kintradwell 5**	HIG SUT	LOST	NC 930 079 Near coffins	**141**
*131	**KIRRIEMUIR 1**	ANG	Meffan Institute, Forfar	NO 384 540 Kirk foundations	**67**
132	**KIRRIEMUIR 2**	ANG	Meffan Institute, Forfar	NO 384 540 Kirk foundations	**67**
133	**Knockando 1**	MOR	NJ 187 429 Kirkyard	NJ 203 422 Burial ground	**102**

No.	Name	Area	Present Location (October 1996)	Findspot	Page
*134	**Knockando 2**	MOR	NJ 187 429 Kirkyard	NJ 203 422 Burial ground	**102**
135	**Knocknagael**	HIG INV	NH 662 448 Highland Council HQ HS	NH 657 413 Field S ?SS ?Not on orig site	**111**
*136	**Langdale**	HIG SUT	LOST	NC 69 44 Field	**141**
137	**LARGO**	FIF	NO 423 035 Outside kirk M	Largo Estate One piece as drain cover	**41**
138	**LATHERON 1**	HIG CAI	EDI Museum of Scotland	ND 198 332 Byre wall O	**37**
*139	**Latheron 2**	HIG CAI	ND 199 334 House wall P	Same	**128**
140	**Lindores**	FIF	NO 260 163 In morthouse P	NO *c*263 172 Hilltop S	**41**
*141	**Linlathen**	DUN	LOST	NO 466 338 Cist	**140**
*142	**Little Ferry Links 1**	HIG SUT	Dunrobin Castle Museum	NH *c*814 966 Links	**127**

*143	**Little Ferry Links 2**	HIG SUT	Dunrobin Castle Museum	NH *c*814 966 Links	**127**
*144	**Little Ferry Links 3**	HIG SUT	Dunrobin Castle Museum	NH *c*814 966 Links	**127**
*145	**Little Ferry Links 4**	HIG SUT	Dunrobin Castle Museum	NH *c*814 966 Links 2 fragments (4 & 4a)	**127**
*145a	**Little Ferry Links 4a**	HIG SUT	HIG INV Inverness Museum	NH *c*814 966 Links (see 145 above)	**110**
146	**Lochardill**	HIG INV	NH 690 456 In house P	NH *c*665 438 Wall Not on display	**111**
147	**Logie Elphinstone 1**	ABE	NJ 703 259 House grounds P	NJ 69 26 Near stone circle ?S	**82**
148	**Logie Elphinstone 2**	ABE	NJ 703 259 House grounds P	NJ 69 26 Near stone circle ?S O Reused	**82**
149	**Logie Elphinstone 3**	ABE	NJ 703 259 House grounds P	NJ 69 26 Near stone circle ?S	**82**
150	**LOGIERAIT 1**	PER	NN 967 520 Kirkyard	Same S	**49**
151	**LOGIERAIT 2**	PER	NN 967 520 In kirk	Kirkyard	**50**

No.	Name	Area	Present Location (October 1996)	Findspot	Page
*152	**Longforgan**	PER	NO 310 300 In kirk	NO 306 299 Field	**50**
*153	**Lynchurn**	ABE	?LOST or still in kirkyard (NH 938 155)	NH *c*953 206 Field Completely defaced	**140**
154	**MEIGLE 1**	PER	Meigle Museum HS	NO 287 446 Kirkyard S Cup-marks	**51**
*155	**MEIGLE 3**	PER	Meigle Museum HS	NO 287 446 Kirk wall	**52**
156	**MEIGLE 4**	PER	Meigle Museum HS	NO 287 447 Kiln near kirk	**52**
157	**MEIGLE 5**	PER	Meigle Museum HS	NO 287 447 Kiln near kirk	**53**
158	**MEIGLE 6**	PER	Meigle Museum HS	NO 287 446 Kirk	**53**
*159	**MEIGLE 7**	PER	Meigle Museum HS	NO 287 446 Kirk	**53**
160	**MIGVIE**	ABE	NJ 437 068 Kirkyard	Same S	**83**

161	**Mill of Newton**	ABE	NJ 432 C80 Outside house P	NJ 432 046 Mound S	**83**
162	**MONIFIETH 1**	ANG	EDI Museum of Scotland	NO 495 324 Kirk foundations	**37**
*163	**MONIFIETH 2**	ANG	EDI Museum of Scotland	NO 495 324 Kirk foundations	**37**
164	**MONYMUSK**	ABE	NJ 685 152 In kirk	NJ *c*703 151 Field S	**84**
165	**MORTLACH 1**	MOR	NJ 324 392 Kirkyard	Same S	**103**
166	**Mortlach 2**	MOR	NJ 324 393 In kirk	NJ 324 392 Kirkyard	**103**
167	**Myreton**	ABE	NJ 610 303 Burial cairn HS	Same S *Picardy Stone*	**84**
168	**Navidale**	HIG SUT	Dunrobin Castle Museum	ND 042 162 Burial ground Chapel site	**127**
*169	**Ness**	ORK	Tankerness House Museum	HY 545 093 Field	**134**
170	**Nether Corskie**	ABE	NJ 748 096 Stone circle P	Same S SS	**85**

N

No.	Name	Area	Present Location (October 1996)	Findspot	Page
171	**Newbigging Leslie**	ABE	NJ 540 300 Leith Hall Gardens NTS	NJ 603 258 Field	**81**
172	**Newton House 1**	ABE	NJ 662 297 Outside house P	NJ 664 285 Near graves S	**85**
173	**Newton of Collessie**	FIF	NO 293 132 Field P	Same S SS	**42**
174	**Newton of Lewesk**	ABE	NJ 815 129 Outside house P	NJ *c*692 276 Field ?Over grave	**86**
175	**NIGG**	HIG ROS	NH 805 717 In kirk	Kirkyard S	**117**
*176	**North Redhill**	MOR	NJ 530 471 Garden, Whitestones Ho P	NJ 560 467 Wall	**104**
177	**Old Deer**	ABE	LOST	NJ 969 481 Abbey	**138**
*178	**Orphir 1**	ORK	LOST	HY 33 04 During excavations	**142**
179	**Orphir 2**	ORK	LOST	HY 33 04 Tower wall	**142**

O

*130	**Oxtro**	ORK	LOST	HY 254 268 Broch (Cist cover)	**143**	O
131	**Pabbay**	WES	NL 607 875 Face of chapel mound M	Graveyard	**135**	P
132	**Park House**	ABE	NC 730 977 House grounds P	NO *c*794 984 Moorland	**86**	
133	**Percylieu**	ABE	NJ 540 300 Leith Hall Gardens NTS	NJ 523 265 Near cairns and stone circle	**81**	
134	**Peterhead**	PER	NN 924 098 Field P	Same S SS ?Over low cairn	**56**	
135	**Pool**	ORK	Tankerness House Museum	HY 619 379 Building floor	**134**	
*136	**Poolewe**	HIG ROS	NG 861 809 Kirkyard	Same	**118**	
137	**Raasay**	HIG SKY	NG 547 368 Roadside	NG *c*54 36 Near shore	**113**	R
138	**Rhynie 1**	ABE	NJ 497 263 Field P	Same S In enclosure *The Craw Stane*	**87**	
139	**Rhynie 2**	ABE	NJ 498 272 Village Green	NJ 499 270 Field Illegible	**88**	

No.	Name	Area	Presen: Location (October 1996)	Findspot	Page
190	**Rhynie 3**	ABE	NJ 498 272 Village Green	NJ 499 270 Field Illegible	**88**
191	**Rhynie 4**	ABE	LOST	?NJ 498 270 Field S	**138**
192	**Rhynie 5**	ABE	NJ 500 265 Shelter near kirkyard	NJ 499 265 Kirk foundations Cup-marks	**88**
193	**Rhynie 6**	ABE	NJ 500 265 Shelter near kirkyard	NJ 499 265 Kirk foundations	**89**
194	**Rhynie 8**	ABE	NJ 500 265 Shelter near kirkyard	NJ *c*497 262 Field (near Rhynie 8)	**89**
195	**ROSEMARKIE 1**	HIG ROS	Groam House Museum	NH 737 576 Under kirk floor	**116**
196	**Roskeen**	HIG ROS	NH 681 690 Field P	Field S SS	**118**
197	**ROSSIE**	PER	NO 292 308 In old kirk P	Kirkyard	**56**
198	**Rothiebrisbane**	ABE	NJ 769 378 Fyvie kirk wall	NJ 746 378 Drain cover	**76**

199	**ST MADOES 1**	PER	Perth Museum	NO 197 212 Kirkyard	**55**
200	**ST VIGEANS 1**	ANG	St Vigeans Museum HS	NO 638 429 Kirk floor I	**69**
201	**ST VIGEANS 2**	ANG	St Vigeans Museum HS	NO 638 429 Kirk floor	**70**
*202	**ST VIGEANS 3**	ANG	St Vigeans Museum HS	NO 638 429 Kirkyard	**70**
*203	**ST VIGEANS 4**	ANG	St Vigeans Museum HS	NO 638 429 Kirk fabric	**70**
*204	**ST VIGEANS 5**	ANG	St Vigeans Museum HS	NO 638 429 Kirkyard	**70**
*205	**ST VIGEANS 6**	ANG	St Vigeans Museum HS	NO 638 429 Kirk foundations	**70**
206	**Sandness**	SHE	LOST	HU 191 577 Kirk wall	**143**
*207	**Sands of Evie**	ORK	Tankerness House Museum	HY 372 264 Shore	**134**
208	**Sandside House**	HIG CAI	NC 952 652 Outside house P	Links	**129**

No.	Name	Area	Present Location (October 1996)	Findspot	Page
*209	**SCOONIE**	FIF	EDI Museum of Scotland	NO 384 017 Kirk O	**38**
210	**SHANDWICK**	HIG ROS	NH 856 747 Field	Same S Burial field	**119**
211	**SKINNET 2**	HIG CAI	EDI Museum of Scotland	ND 131 621 Chapel ruins	**130**
212	**South Ronaldsay**	ORK	EDI Museum of Scotland	ND 471 908 Kirk window-sill Reused	**38**
213	**Strathmartine 1**	ANG	DUN McManus Galleries	NO 374 361 Field S	**59**
214	**STRATHMARTINE 3**	ANG	LOST	NO 378 353 Kirkyard	**139**
*215	**STRATHMARTINE 4**	ANG	EDI Museum of Scotland	NO 378 353 Kirkyard	**38**
216	**STRATHMARTINE 5**	ANG	LOST	NO 378 353 Kirkyard	**139**
*217	**STRATHMARTINE 6**	ANG	LOST	NO 378 353 Kirkyard	**139**

218	**Strathmiglo**	FIF	NO 217 102 Outside kirkyard	NO 209 101 Fallen gatepost	**43**
219	**Strathpeffer**	HIG ROS	NH 485 585 Field	?NH 513 593 ?Near kirkyard	**120**
*220	**Struan 1**	PER	NN 809 653 In kirk	Kirkyard	**57**
221	**TARBAT 1**	HIG ROS	EDI Museum of Scotland	NH 915 840 Kirkyard	**39**
*222	**TEALING**	ANG	DUN McManus Galleries	NO 403 379 Kirk wall	**59**
223	**Tillytarmont 1**	ABE	ABN Marischal Museum	NJ 533 473 Field ?Burial field	**94**
224	**Tillytarmont 2**	ABE	MOR NJ 530 471 Whitestones House P	NJ 533 472 Field ?Burial field	**104**
225	**Tillytarmont 3**	ABE	MOR NJ 530 471 Whitestones House P	NJ 533 473 Field ?Burial field	**104**
226	**Tillytarmont 4**	ABE	ABN Marischal Museum	NJ 533 472 Field ?Burial field	**95**
227	**Tillytarmont 5**	ABE	ABN Marischal Museum	NJ 533 472 Field ?Burial field	**95**

No.	Name	Area	Present Location (October 1996)	Findspot	Page	
228	**Tom na Heron**	MOR	LOST	NJ 208 310 By cairns S	**142**	T
229	**Torgorm**	HIG ROS	HIG INV Inverness Museum	NH *c*559 549 Field	**110**	
230	**Tote**	HIG SKY	NG 421 491 Roadside	NG 418 492 Door-jamb	**114**	
231	**Tullich 1**	ABE	NO 391 975 Kirk ruins	Kirk lintel	**90**	
*232	**Turriff**	ABE	NJ 723 499 Manse garden wall P	Same	**90**	
233	**Tyrie**	ABE	NJ 930 631 In kirk	In kirk foundations	**90**	
234	**ULBSTER**	HIG CAI	Thurso Heritage Museum	ND 335 419 Burial ground S Reused	**131**	U
*235	**Upper Manbeen**	MOR	NJ 187 576 Field P	Same S	**103**	
*236	**Wantonwells**	ABE	ABN Marischal Museum	NJ 614 274 Field	**95**	W

*237	**Watenan**	HIG CAI	Northlands Viking Centre	ND 312 408	Cairn	**128**
238	**Wester Balblair**	HIG INV	Inverness Museum	NH 510 453	Road bottoming	**111**
*239	**WESTER DENOON**	ANG	Meffan Institute, Forfar	NO 350 434	?From field dyke nr chapel site	**68**
240	**Westfield 1**	FIF	Falkland Palace Museum NTS	NO 238 073	Farm building	**40**
*241	**Westfield 2**	FIF	Falkland Palace Museum NTS	NO 238 073	Farm building	**40**
242	**WOODRAE**	ANG	EDI Museum of Scotland	NO 519 566	Castle kitchen floor	**39**

* No complete symbol set : HS Historic Scotland : I Inscription (other than Ogam) : M Re-location proposed

NTS National Trust for Scotland : O Ogam inscription : P Private house or grounds : S Found standing : SS Former standing stone

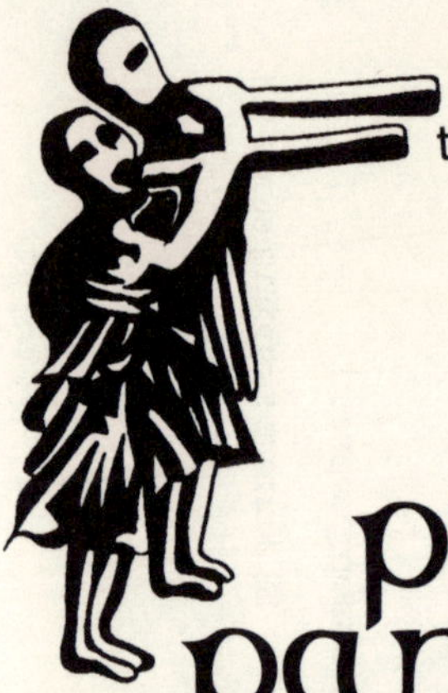

The essential companion to Pictish studies

a Pictish Panorama

Edited by
Eric H. Nicoll

Introduction by
Magnus Magnusson

ISBN 1 874012 10 5 CASEBOUND £30
200PP. 290 x 214MM; 36 B/W ILLUSS

Comprising:

A Pictish Bibliography

Compiled by
J.R.F. Burt

(A select annotated bibliography of works relating to the Picts arranged by author and subject; containing over 800 items – this valuable research tool will become the essential companion for every student of the Picts)

and

The Story of the Picts

(Six introductory essays covering history, art, language, place-names, and religious and secular archaeology)

Contributors:

Dauvit Broun, Katherine Forsyth
W.F.H. Nicolaisen, Isabel Henderson
Anna Ritchie, Edwina Proudfoot

Published on behalf of The Pictish Arts Society
Sponsored by Historic Scotland and Inveresk plc

'The book will be of tremendous interest to both the specialist and the interested amateur – like myself – alike.' *Magnus Magnusson*

'A book which should find a place on the shelves of any reference collection concerned with early Scottish history.' *Reference Reviews*

'The Pinkfoot Press is fast establishing itself as one of Scotland's most courageous small publishers... with *A Pictish Panorama*, we have another gift to scholarship but one with a strong appeal to anyone intrigued by this colourful episode in Scotland's past.' *Welcome*

THE EARLY CHRISTIAN MONUMENTS OF SCOTLAND

J Romilly Allen and Joseph Anderson

Introduction by

Isabel Henderson

Foreword by

Anna Ritchie

ISBN 1 874012 05 9 SET OF TWO VOLUMES PBK £49

1200 pp. 215 x 148 mm, 2500+ b/w illuss

This classic survey, first published in 1903 by the Society of Antiquaries of Scotland, is still, after more than ninety years, the essential reference book on Scotland's amazingly rich heritage of Pictish and Early Christian carved stones. The complete three-part original is now presented in a practical easy-to-handle two-volume format.

Volume 1 contains Joseph Anderson's art historical appraisal of the monuments and Romilly Allen's masterly and profusely illustrated analysis of their ornament and symbols.

Volume 2 comprises a classified, descriptive catalogue of the stones with photographs and detailed line drawings.

This edition has a Foreword by Anna Ritchie and a new Introduction by Isabel Henderson. In her well-researched, absorbing essay, 'The making of *The Early Christian Monuments of Scotland*', Dr Henderson explores the historical background of the publication; the character and achievement of the two authors; their working methods; and the tremendous impact of ECMS since its first appearance right up to the present day.

£10 OFF

SPECIAL PRICE OFFER FOR PURCHASERS OF THE *FIELD GUIDE*...

TO TAKE ADVANTAGE OF THIS HUGE SAVING – ORDER ON THE FORM PRINTED OVERLEAF